Ian McEwan

Twayne's English Authors Series

Kinley Roby, Editor
Northeastern University

TEAS 518

IAN MCEWAN
Jane Bown

Ian McEwan

Jack Slay, Jr.

LaGrange College

Twayne Publishers
An Imprint of Simon & Schuster Macmillan
New York

Prentice Hall International
London • Mexico City • New Delhi • Singapore • Sydney • Toronto

Twayne's English Author Series No. 518

Ian McEwan
Jack Slay, Jr.

Twayne Publishers
An Imprint of Simon & Schuster Macmillan
1633 Broadway
New York, NY 10019

Library of Congress Cataloging-in-Publication Data

Slay, Jack.
  Ian McEwan / by Jack Slay, Jr.
     p. cm. — (English authors series ; 518)
  Includes bibliographical references and index.
  ISBN 0-8057-4578-5
  1. McEwan, Ian—Criticism and interpretation. I. Title. II. Series: Twayne's English
authors series ; 518.
PR6063.C4Z87 1996
823'.914—dc20   95-25615
                                                                                CIP

10 9 8 7 6 5 4

Printed in the United States of America

For Lori and Kirk and Justin

Contents

Preface

Reviewing an early work by Ian McEwan, John Leonard remarked that the writer's "mind is an interesting place to visit, but I wouldn't want to live there. It is dark, and smells of ether. Freud hangs from the rafters on a meat hook. The footlocker is full of human skulls. Scorpions and bats abound. Every sexual transaction is a failure. We are somewhere between Samuel Beckett and the Rolling Stones."[1] Ten years, four novels, and a handful of film scripts later, reviewer Laurie Muchnick echoed similar sentiments: "Ian McEwan's an ordinary-looking bloke, really. Especially for someone who writes the way he does."[2] Conventional wisdom has tended to view McEwan as a fine writer tainted by his too frequent ventures into the horrors that reside in the darkest of psyches and ids. The indistinguishability between the mundane and the horrible, the perversions of the ordinary, the visceral twistings of everyday life: these are the fascinations of McEwan, the distinctive subjects of his novels, stories, and drama.

During the past 20 years there has been a fecundity of British fiction that has been both critically praised and commercially successful; British writers such as Martin Amis, Julian Barnes, Angela Carter, Salman Rushdie, Fay Weldon, and Will Self have written powerful, intense works that have called attention to the foibles and blunders of contemporary society. In their writings they have challenged the precepts and determinations of their societies, questioning and then defying the restraints predetermined by sex and class, by the politics of wealth, culture, and gender. McEwan is certainly one of the most noteworthy of contemporary authors; writing with a fearlessness combined with a viciously lean prose, he confronts boldly the weaknesses and shames of our selves and our societies. He focuses a particular interest on the machinations of relationships—and the resultant codes of sexual behavior. Concentrating on the ways in which these interpersonal alliances serve as microcosms of their societies, these relationships are often characterized by violence and confusion, tainted by a world of chaos, desolation, and destructive hierarchies.

McEwan's earlier writing is characterized by a literature of shock, a conscious desire to repel and to discomfit the reader. It is a fiction inundated with incest, regression, brutality, perversion, and murder.

Beginning with his second story collection and continuing through his most recent novels, however, this literature of shock metamorphoses into a more socially conscious literature. This evolution in his writing allows McEwan to illustrate more precisely how the chaotic and turmoiled state of the modern world, especially as it appears in the forms of degenerated cities and corrupted governments, acts as a deterrent for viable, life-affirming relationships, how it, in turn, destroys the individual. McEwan is especially adamant in his castigation of the patriarchal ideologies that are created and encouraged by contemporary society. Remarkably, in the midst of this chaos and turmoil, McEwan manages to maintain a sense of the ordinary, distressing though it may be. These disturbances, he insists, are simply the disquieting venues of our everyday lives.

Acknowledgments

Permission to quote from the following works by Ian McEwan has been kindly granted by the author: *Soursweet* © 1980 by Ian McEwan; *The Imitation Game and Other Plays* © 1982 by Ian McEwan; *The Ploughman's Lunch* © 1985 by Ian McEwan; *The Cement Garden* © 1988 by Ian McEwan; *The Comfort of Strangers* © 1989 by Ian McEwan; *First Love, Last Rites* © 1989 by Ian McEwan; and *In Between the Sheets* © 1990 by Ian McEwan.

Permission to quote from *The Innocent* and *Black Dogs* has been granted by Doubleday, a division of Bantam Doubleday Dell Publishing Group, Inc.

Excerpts from *The Child in Time* copyright © 1987 by Ian McEwan. Reprinted by permission of Houghton Mifflin Co. All rights reserved.

An early version of Chapter Seven appeared in *Critique* 35, no. 4 (Summer 1994): 205–18 as "Vandalizing Time: Ian McEwan's Child in Time." Part of Chapter Four was published in *Notes on Contemporary Fiction* 25, no. 2 (March 1995) as "The Absurdity of Love: Parodic Relationships in Ian McEwan's 'Reflections of a Kept Ape' and 'Dead as They Come.'"

I would like to thank Ian McEwan for his generous assistance and continued interest in this project. I would like to thank Professor Dick Penner; his guidance and encouragement were integral in molding not only this book but the author as a better scholar as well. I am also appreciative of Professor Mary E. Papke; her genuine interest, scholarly advice, and generous friendship were each an enlightenment and a pleasure. This work, quite literally, could not have been done without them. I would like to thank, too, my friends and colleagues at LaGrange College; their interest and encouragement have been invaluable. Finally, I would like to thank my families: my mother and father, my brother and sister, for their lifelong encouragement, their constant faith; and Lori, Kirk, and Justin, for their enduring patience and love. To all these people—all, in part, collaborators—I am indebted.

Chronology

1948   Ian Russell McEwan born 21 June in Aldershot, England, the only child of David and Rose McEwan. Spends early life in military outposts such as Singapore and Libya.

1959   Attends Woolverstone, a boarding school in Suffolk.

1966   Enters the University of Sussex. Begins writing fiction.

1970   Graduates from Sussex with an honors B.A. in English literature. Enters creative writing program at University of East Anglia. Studies under Malcolm Bradbury and Angus Wilson.

1971   Obtains M.A. in creative writing.

1972   Travels to Afghanistan. Sells first short story, "Homemade," to *New American Review.*

1975   Publishes first collection of stories, *First Love, Last Rites.*

1976   Receives Somerset Maugham Award for *First Love, Last Rites.* "Jack Flea's Birthday Celebration" airs on the BBC on 10 April.

1978   Publishes second collection of stories, *In Between the Sheets,* and first novel, *The Cement Garden.*

1979   BBC halts production on filming of television adaptation of "Solid Geometry."

1980   "The Imitation Game" airs on the BBC on 24 April.

1981   Publishes *The Imitation Game* and *The Comfort of Strangers,* which is shortlisted for the Booker Prize.

1982   Marries Penny Allen.

1983   Is named by *Granta* as one of the 20 Best Young British Novelists. London Symphony Orchestra performs *Or Shall We Die? The Ploughman's Lunch* is released and receives the *Evening Standard* Award for best film, best director (Richard Eyre), and best screenplay.

1985   Publishes *Rose Blanche.*

1987   Publishes *The Child in Time*, which wins Whitbread Book of the Year award.

1988   *Soursweet* is released.

1989   Publishes *The Innocent*. Travels with wife to Berlin to watch the fall of the Berlin Wall. Awarded an honorary doctorate of literature from University of Sussex.

1992   Publishes *Black Dogs*, which is shortlisted for the Booker Prize.

1993   *The Good Son* is released.

1994   Publishes *The Daydreamer*.

We live in Gothic times.

—Angela Carter, *Fireworks*

The thing called society is, I believe, insane.

—Martin Amis, *Time's Arrow*

Chapter One
Meeting Ian McEwan

Ian McEwan creates dark portraits of contemporary society, writing to expose the haunting desires and libidinal politics that lurk beneath the facade of an everyday world. His characters—incestuous siblings, heartbroken gorillas, sadomasochistic lovers, infatuated prime ministers, corpse dismemberers—play the depraved lovers' games of a modern wasteland, hoping that the procurement of any sustaining relationship can provide refuge from the chaos and turmoil of their very lives and worlds.

Ian Russell McEwan was born on 21 June 1948 to David McEwan and Rose Lilian (Moore) McEwan in the military garrison town of Aldershot, England. Rose McEwan had a son and a daughter from a previous marriage (her first husband died during World War II); the youngest of his half-siblings was 10 years older than McEwan and he, therefore, considered himself "psychologically, an only child."[1] David McEwan had joined the army—because of unemployment in Glasgow—at the age of 17 (having lied about his age) as a regular enlisted soldier in 1934 (he was eventually promoted to the rank of major). McEwan, consequently, spent his childhood—one he has described as secure and content if a bit overprotected—in such outposts of the empire as Singapore and Libya. In 1959, at age 11, McEwan was sent back to England to attend a state-run boarding school called Woolverstone Hall in Suffolk—a period he remembers "as just *empty time.*"[2] McEwan recalls Woolverstone as "quite a tough school and yet academically good and socially probably a lot livelier, more interesting, less arrogant than most English public schools";[3] still, he found himself only "a mediocre pupil" (Hamilton, 12). Completing public school, he attended the University of Sussex in Brighton, concentrating in French and English literature and earning a B.A. honor degree in English in 1970 (in 1989 he was awarded an honorary doctorate from the University). During his third year at Sussex, he began writing fiction. Discovering that "the University of East Anglia were offering an M.A. for which one could submit a little bit of fiction instead of the written thesis" (Hamilton, 15), McEwan entered the program (which was under the supervision of novelists Malcolm Bradbury and Angus Wilson) and obtained his master's degree in creative writing in 1971. In 1972 he dipped briefly into the counterculture, making the requisite pilgrimage along the hippie trail to Afghanistan—a period he remembers as "long, long weeks of waiting. Boredom and smoking hash in huge quantities without any real point" (Hamilton, 17).

After selling his first story in 1972—"Homemade" to *New American Review*—McEwan began to write earnestly, at first concentrating on stories and then chiefly on novels; however, McEwan—saying that he occasionally feels confined by fiction—frequently forays into other forms: drama for television and film, children's books, radio plays, even an oratorio.

In 1974 Jonathan Cape accepted *First Love, Last Rites* (which originated from his thesis) for publication and released it the following year. The collection received the Somerset Maugham Award in 1976. This was followed by a second collection of stories, *In Between the Sheets,* and his first novel, *The Cement Garden,* both published in 1978. During this period McEwan also began writing television plays, three of which were collected in 1981 as *The Imitation Game. The Comfort of Strangers* was also published in 1981 and was McEwan's first nomination for the Booker Prize. McEwan's oratorio, entitled *Or Shall We Die?* (with a score by Michael Berkeley), a deeply moving piece concerning the threat of nuclear annihilation, was performed at the Royal Festival Hall in London in February of 1983 by the London Symphony Orchestra and Chorus; it was later performed in 1985 at Carnegie Hall in New York City.

Motivated by the political accessibility of his drama, McEwan returned to screenwriting and produced *The Ploughman's Lunch,* which was filmed and released in 1983. The film garnered much critical praise and was the winner of the 1983 *Evening Standard* Award for best film, best screenplay, and best director. It was also during 1983 that McEwan was named by *Granta* as one of the 20 Best Young British Novelists (along with such writers as Martin Amis, Kazuo Ishiguro, Julian Barnes, and Salman Rushdie). Ever fascinated by film, McEwan adapted Timothy Mo's novel *Sour Sweet* for film in 1988.

In recent years McEwan has devoted himself to the novel, publishing *The Child in Time* in 1987 (which won the Whitbread Book of the Year prize), *The Innocent* in 1989, and *Black Dogs,* a second nomination for the Booker Prize, in 1992. McEwan has also penned two children's books, *Rose Blanche*[4] in 1985 and *The Daydreamer* in 1994.

In December 1982 McEwan married Penny Allen, an alternative healer and astrologer, who had two daughters from a previous marriage; they have had two sons. Currently, McEwan lives with his family in Oxford, England.

In assessing McEwan's work, John Fletcher finds that he is "very much a product of the new British univeisities, those popularly known as 'plate-glass universities' to distinguish them from the older 'red-brick universities' . . . [that] set out to revolutionize curricula and the general structure of academic life in Great Britain."[5] Likewise, McEwan can also be seen as a descendant of the Angry Young Man generation of the late 1950s, who were in large part products of the red-brick universities. In this, he is similar to other contemporary British writers (such as Martin Amis, Will Self, J. G. Ballard, Angela Carter, Fay Weldon, and Salman Rushdie) as well as American writers (especially the contemporary Southern Gothics like Barry Hannah, Harry Crews, Cormac McCarthy, and Joy Williams), who present mordant, even vicious, views of modern society. The Angry Young Men repudiated and ridiculed tradition and, simultaneously, also questioned, in usually angry terms, the new society that emerged in postwar England, producing such works as Kingsley Amis's *Lucky Jim* (1954), John Braine's *Room at the Top* (1957), John Osborne's *Look Back in Anger* (1957), and Alan Sillitoe's *Loneliness of the Long Distance Runner* (1960). Cynical, rude, boisterous, these novelists and their antiheroes demonstrated a particular bitterness against outmoded political values.

Similarly, writers of the 1970s, 1980s, and 1990s depict the tensions—and necessities—of rebelling against restrictive, destructive societies. And just as the Angry Young Men adopted a neorealism for their works—countering the high experimentalism of the modern period—so, too, have a majority of these contemporaries chosen realism, countering the experimentalism of postmodernism. This choice emphasizes the importance they feel about the social messages inherent in their works. Frequently, these writers use their fiction to convey the anger they feel toward the weaknesses, blunders, and injustices of society. McEwan often protests the disgrace that is innate to a patriarchy; in later works, he objects to the oppressive power of unchallenged governments. His contemporaries are every bit as vocal. J. G. Ballard, for instance, states that "the ultimate role of [his novel] *Crash* is cautionary," warning against the dangers of a technology-obsessed society.[6] In *Einstein's Monsters* (1987), a collection of nuclear parables, and *London Fields* (1989) Martin Amis rails against the insanity of nuclear weaponry, calling it the "worst thing that has ever happened to the planet."[7] In *The Cloning of Joanna May* (1989) Fay Weldon warns of the potential danger of nuclear power plants; in the background of her novel is the nuclear accident at Chernobyl, an incident that made "a large world into a small one, by reason of our common fear."[8]

Realism allows accessible reading to a tremendous audience; the message of these writers, therefore, *is* heard. In a large sense, British literature has come full circle, returning to the reformative literature of the Victorian Age, to the societal warnings, bemoanings, and railings of such writers as Dickens, Eliot, and Carlyle. The concerns have transmogrified from the horrors of slums and labor conditions to the terrors of nuclear armaments and unconscionable patriarchies; nonetheless, the novelists' concerns for their own cultures and societies—for *humanity*—are every bit as sound, true, and heartfelt. British literature has long been characterized by conscience; McEwan and his contemporaries simply continue the tradition.

Although frequently characterized by the blackest of dark humor (especially in their creation of bizarre and monstrous narrators), these contemporary writers make caustic and penetrating assessments of the brutality of human nature, often finding blame in the politics of the society itself. In classifying McEwan with other contemporary authors, Laurie Muchnick says,

> McEwan is part of a now-approaching-middle-aged generation of male British writers who have changed their country's literature from one of genteel domestic excavations to a muscular, wide-ranging examination of the (post) modern condition. The Brit Pack—Martin Amis, Julian Barnes, Salman Rushdie, Kazuo Ishiguro, Bruce Chatwin, McEwan—has produced some of the most exciting fiction and quasi-fiction of the last 10 years, and has evolved from a bunch of young upstarts to a still provocative yet highly commercial literary establishment. (Muchnick, 102)

McEwan, though, wishes to disassociate his writing from any fixed literary movement or pigeonhole: "I know lots of writers and I like them as people, and there are certain of their works, their novels, stories, that I like, but I certainly can't locate myself inside any shared, any sort of community taste, aesthetic ambition or critical position or anything else. I don't really feel part of anything at all."[9]

Critics and reviewers are also of the consensus that McEwan's works distinguish themselves and thereby separate him from the myriad contemporary writers. In themes and ideals, however, McEwan does share a close alliance with his fellow British novelist and close friend Martin Amis (b. 1949). In the direction and energy of their fiction, the two are similarly concerned, similarly ingenious. Like McEwan, Amis writes with a vicious dark humor, a keen insight into the modern world, and a mordant perception of our society. He often aims to shock and disgust, creating unappealing characters who partake heartily of violence and lust. His earliest works are similar to McEwan's in their portrayals of debased people living in a debased world. For instance, his first novel, *The Rachel Papers* (1973)—which earned him the Somerset Maugham Award—is a ribald account of adolescent sexual adventures; *Dead Babies* (1976), his second novel, details the events of a shocking, drug-filled weekend that explodes in violence and murder. Though he is more satirical, more playful (critics have often chastised him for his excesses in Nabokovian wordplay, literary allusions, overly ornate language, and metafictional proclivity), and more offensive (he frequently has to defend himself against accusations of sexism) than McEwan, Amis is obviously just as horrified and disgusted with the state of the world, and he uses the sharpness of his satire to expose the failings of society. For example, *Money: A Suicide Note* (1984)—which follows the exploits of John Self, a character who embodies the worst traits of an acquisitive, greedy society—is especially scathing in its portrait of the empty consumerism and vulgar excesses of contemporary society. After marriage and children, Amis, like McEwan, became even more socially conscious, forcefully using works like *Einstein's Monsters* and *London Fields* to call attention to what he sees as the greatest sin of his age: the creation of nuclear arms. Finally, just as McEwan has succeeded in doing, Amis has come to the forefront of this generation's writers, forging a fiction that is both rich and rewarding.

Despite similar concerns, McEwan manages to separate himself from the countless writers of today. Recognizing his importance as an author, critics have praised his sharp, poetic prose and his unflinching portrayals of modern society. Though some find his unsavory and often appalling subject matter repugnant, even repulsive, most contend that its shock value is reflective of the world itself. McEwan presents himself as a chronicler of the true nature of humankind and their frequently confused, often perverse societies. By presenting the debauchery beneath the civility, the grotesquerie beneath the banality, he writes to entertain as well as to warn. In one sense, McEwan composes cautionary letters to the people of a bewildered age.

Throughout the great variety of his writings, McEwan's principal concern is that of relationships. As McEwan himself explains, "I just have a habit of watchfulness. There are two areas where I look. One is how people are with their children, because that fascinates me a great deal. And the other thing is couples, married or otherwise."[10] He therefore incorporates an immense array of interpersonal alliances into his fiction, examining the attachments between lover and lover, husband and wife, parent and child, brother and sister. Relationships are, naturally, a concern of most writers, but McEwan's portrayal of human interaction is marked by the range of relationships he examines. The most intimate of these alliances reflect the social worlds in which they are enacted, becoming, in essence, microcosms of these worlds.

McEwan's primary interest in his presentation of relationships is the exploration of the codes of sexual behavior that exist between men and women. In *Short Stories and Short Fictions* Clare Hanson states that McEwan "stresses the disjunction between sex and gender identity, and through the games played by his 'characters' we perceive ways in which an enlightened understanding of the codes of sexual behavior can lead to some kind of rapprochement between the sexes."[11] Both men and women see viable relationships as the balm in life; however, because of the destructive hierarchies that exist within contemporary society, women are, more often than not, seen as the subservient and the submissive in both their societies and relationships. McEwan challenges these preconceptions, presenting through his fiction the ways in which men and women reexamine and reevaluate their stereotypical (socially predetermined) roles. McEwan's female characters frequently break through these societal barriers, becoming the strength within the alliance; for example, Julie in *The Cement Garden,* Lily in *Soursweet,* Julie in *The Child in Time,* and Maria in *The Innocent* are all portrayed as the dominant ones within their relationships, ascertaining for themselves and for their partners an alliance that is loving as well as life-affirming. In McEwan's fiction, then, relationships are recognized as the necessary refuge in a dehumanizing world.

McEwan's study of male-female relationships is also influential in shaping the direction of his fiction. His earliest fiction, for example, is characterized by repellant characters and their inhumane, brutal actions; there is a conscious desire to shock readers, forcing them to gaze directly into the horrors of contemporary society. Describing the characters of McEwan's early work, Jonathan Raban says,

McEwan's characters are adolescents; they bristle with the sudden violent consciousness of selfhood like a hatching pupae. Or they are children, prematurely burdened with egos that give them the wizened gravity of infants in Renaissance paintings. Or they are men whose bodies have grown but whose minds have never broken free of the appalling second womb of puberty. Cruelty comes easily to them: they can wound or kill with the offhand grace of animals for whom the self is the only reality. They are profoundly disturbed by their own capacity to love another, which creeps up on them from behind like a pad-footed intruder on their barred and bolted rooms. They are endlessly curious about the world, but their curiosity has the roving neutrality of creatures in a zoo, unsure of what to focus on. They belong to no society. They are alarmingly in touch with blood and slime.[12]

These repulsive, dangerous creatures are an integral part of McEwan's portrait of the everyday world, and his work, consequently, contains blunt, visceral images of society.

This is not to say, however, that McEwan offers a random collection of psychopaths, debauchers, and other aberrant individuals; rather, these characters—the incestuous siblings in *The Cement Garden* and "Homemade"; the regressors in *The Cement Garden, The Child in Time,* and "Jack Flea's Birthday Celebration"; the vicious murderers in "Butterflies," *The Comfort of Strangers,* and *The Innocent*; the monstrous narrators in "Conversation with a Cupboard Man" and "Dead as They Come"; the cross-dressers in "Disguises" and *The Cement Garden*—are the embodiments of our neighbors, our acquaintances, ourselves. Although this literature of shock is especially—even exceedingly—prevalent in his first novel and his short story collections, McEwan's desire to startle the reader is evident throughout his canon (even his two most recent novels, *The Innocent* and *Black Dogs,* contain scenes overwhelming in their vicious verisimilitude). McEwan, however, objects to being classified as a writer solely of shock horror, and rightly so. In the end, his fiction is a reflection not of an imaginary world but of the reality of ordinary life.

Much of McEwan's literature of shock portrays the brutalization and mistreatment of women by a patriarchal society; as he begins to mature as a writer, his approach to the relationships between men and women becomes increasingly more feminist; he becomes more and more a proponent of equality between the sexes. With the publication of works such as "The Imitation Game" and *The Comfort of Strangers,* McEwan found himself again typecast, this time as "that still-rare beast, a male feminist writer."[13] Though McEwan objects to the classification, saying that he "didn't want to be a man appropriating women's voices,"[14] he nonetheless strongly remonstrates against the subjugation of females within society, illustrating how "patriarchy corrupts our intimate relationships."[15] Rebelling against the foibles of a male-dominated culture, McEwan proclaims the necessity of creating a world in which the sexes are equal.

Finally, in much of his later fiction, McEwan becomes more politically conscious, creating portraits of Britain as it is today. For example, in *The Ploughman's Lunch* McEwan explores the duplicitous nature of British politics, examining the way in which governments purposely distort and reinvent their past histories in order to better serve their present needs. In *The Child in Time* he imagines a near-future England that is controlled by a conservative extremism. In *Black Dogs* he addresses the inherent evils of world politics. He continuously draws attention to the political chaos of contemporary society, showing how this turmoil affects entire countries as well as individuals.

Ironically, through all of McEwan's fiction, a sense of the ordinary also prevails, albeit a disquieting one. Relationships, then, which at first seem bizarre and inordinate, ghastly and perverted, often, upon closer examination, are revealed to be perfectly ordinary responses to the mitigating circumstances. In depicting this ordinary-within-the-extraordinary, this normality-within-the-abnormality, McEwan calls attention to the societies that mandate these disquieting elements, challenging the precepts as well as the societies themselves.

In a letter to the author, McEwan says, "I will say that to be taken seriously is all any writer can ask for."[16] McEwan's canon has certainly merited a serious, thoughtful examination. His dark portraits of the modern world are works that should be taken to heart. He has undoubtedly, irrevocably influenced contemporary fiction.

Chapter Two

A Shock into Literature: *First Love, Last Rites*

A young boy, determined to cleanse himself of the embarrassing stigma of his virginity, seduces and beds his 10-year-old sister. A husband, who treasures a nineteenth-century criminal's penis in a jar, "disappears" his wife into a surfaceless plane. A man revenges himself by pouring a pan of boiling oil into the lap of an antagonizing co-worker. An aunt forces her nephew to don dress and blonde wig before coming down to dinner. Welcome to the world of Ian McEwan. As obvious, McEwan's is a bizarre and inordinate world indeed.

First Love, Last Rites, McEwan's first published work, garnered much critical praise, but many readers were made uncomfortable by the harshness and savagery of many of the stories. McEwan's desire to shock, to stun, and sometimes even to repulse the reader is an integral component of his fiction and is evident in a great variety of jolting scenarios, including the incestuous union in *The Cement Garden,* the brutal sadomasochistic murder of *The Comfort of Strangers,* and the excruciatingly detailed dismemberment of *The Innocent.* McEwan's fiction implies that without squirming (and occasionally revelling) in the brutalities of everyday life, we become blind to them; by forcing us to witness the atrocities of contemporary society, McEwan also forces us to acknowledge them. And acknowledging them, he asserts, is only a step away from reforming them.

Still, many readers find the intensity of McEwan's style combined with the disturbing subjects of his stories a bit disconcerting. *First Love, Last Rites* prompted Julian Barnes to remark that McEwan seemed "addicted to the casual violences of life,"[1] an understandable reaction since any plot synopses of the stories make them appear lurid, absurd, even psychotic. For example, in describing the mixture with which McEwan "baits" his tales, Robert Towers finds "dirt, scum, pus, menstrual blood, pathetic obesity, total chinlessness, enforced transvestitism, early teenage incest, child abuse and child murder."[2]

McEwan obviously agrees with Angela Carter's assessment: "We live in Gothic times."[3] In fact, many of McEwan's contemporaries—Martin Amis, J. G. Ballard, Will Self, Kathy Acker, Angela Carter, Harry Crews, Cormac McCarthy, Barry Hannah—readily acknowledge this tenet of modern society: they know this age as a time of serial killers and capital punishment, of Jim Jones and Saddam Hussein, of AIDS and crack babies, of Chernobyl and Three Mile Island. Our societies, our cultures, these writers realize, are ones of cruelty and mindless violence (a world in which violence is, indeed, virtually celebrated), of the grotesque. This state of the world prompted Bradford Morrow and Patrick McGrath, in the introduction to their collection *The New Gothic,* to say,

> We stand at the end of a century whose history has been stained perhaps like no other by the blacker urges of human nature. The prospect of apocalypse—through human science rather than divine intervention—has redefined the contemporary psyche. The consolation that Western souls once found in religion has faded. . . . Now hell is decidedly on earth, located within the vaults and chambers of our own minds.[4]

Contemporary authors agree: in this hellish existence, violence and the grotesque have become the universal human condition. As a consequence, in contemporary fiction acts of seemingly gratuitous sexual abuse, mayhem, murder, and humiliation are ubiquitous: accompanied by a generous dose of the absurd, violent characters and perverse acts rule. J. G. Ballard's *Crash,* for instance, introduces a character who wishes to die (as a result of wounds to his genitalia) in a head-on collision with Elizabeth Taylor. Ballard's *High-Rise* (1975) depicts an apartment complex collapsing into savagery, its inhabitants becoming murderers and cannibals. Amis's *Dead Babies* concludes in carnage, with five characters being violently killed and two committing suicide. Carter's *The Passion of New Eve* (1977) relates the exploits of a man transformed into a woman by means of forced surgery. Kathy Acker's females are constantly raped (frequently by their fathers) and abused, which leads them into violent, disturbed lives. Bret Easton Ellis's *American Psycho* (1990) is a litany of misogynistic degradation and abuse. Harry Crews's *A Feast of Snakes* (1976) ends with the protagonist losing his mind, killing four people, and being thrown into a pit of rattlesnakes. Cormac McCarthy's *Blood Meridian* (1985) explores the settling of the American West, where all people—White, Mexican, Indian—match one another atrocity for atrocity, all taking willing part in such acts as massacres, necrophilia, scalping, and, of course, murder. Will Self's *My Idea of Fun* (1993) depicts a character who tortures, kills, and disembowels a pit bull, then fellates its detached penis; later the same character decapitates a tramp and then "address[es himself] sexually to his severed neck."[5] These writers, then, know this world as one in which "some days even a cup of coffee is violence,"[6] in which "the grotesque is the order of the day" (Carter, 25).

These writers have long had to defend the "excessiveness" of their work. They are, universally, unanimously, quick to point out that their works, and the shock inherent within, are revelations into the soul of society; the purpose of these violences and brutalities is to expose, to caution. In "Children of the Pied Piper," his pseudo-defense of Bret Easton Ellis's *American Psycho*, Norman Mailer argued that "art has now become our need to be terrified. We live in the fear that we are destroying the universe, even as we mine deeper into its secrets."[7] These contemporary writers, then, realize that we live in a virtually unshockable society, a world in which inflation is rampant, unspeakable acts are ubiquitous, and structures—social, religious, political—are crumbling. In a sense, then, *everything* goes.

Though most authors are quick to defend themselves by arguing that these works are simply mirrorings of society, however, there is a bold, obvious line between the shock that draws a curious audience and the shock that enlightens. Works such as Acker's *Blood and Guts in High School* (1984), Berkoff's *Gross Intrusion* (1977), Ellis's *American Psycho*, Amis's *Dead Babies*, and even McEwan's *First Love, Last Rites*—indeed, the titles themselves are meant to attract by means of sensationalism— obviously use shock to lure a readership. As sole works, Amis's and McEwan's books probably would have been quickly forgotten; however, both authors have succeeded in developing the darker themes of those early works, proving that these shocks into literature were, in fact, the origins of a more profound social consciousness. Like McEwan and Amis, other writers use the cruelties and violences of their work to forewarn the audience. For example, Acker's *Great Expectations* (1982), *Blood and Guts in High School*, and *Empire of the Senseless* (1988) and Carter's *The Passion of New Eve* all use visceral, barbaric cruelties to protest the violence of patriarchal societies. Ballard, in much the same way, uses his second disaster trilogy—*Crash*, *Concrete Island* (1974), and *High-Rise*—to warn of the brutal, violent seductions of a technology-dominated world. Will Self lets us know immediately that *My Idea of Fun* is more than a collection of atrocities and shocks: subtitling his novel "A Cautionary Tale," he warns the reader, much as Amis does in *Money*, against the conscienceless obsessions of greed and consumerism. This literature of shock, embraced by a great many contemporary writers, becomes both a means of attracting and entertaining, and, more importantly, in the most competent of hands, a voice of foreboding, a blaring and insistent foghorn along the murky shoals of contemporary society.

In defending the shock that supports his fiction, McEwan says that the subject which compels him to write is not "what is nice and easy and pleasant and somehow affirming, but somehow what is bad and difficult and unsettling. That's the kind of tension I need to start me writing" (Ricks, 526). Still, McEwan finds that he is "slightly shocked at all this shock. . . . I've yet to meet somebody who said: 'Your stories are so revolting I couldn't read them'" (Ricks, 527). In one sense, then, the stories in *First Love, Last Rites* are not extraordinary but ordinary, not artificial but authentic. McEwan admittedly writes toward powerful climaxes in these stories, and although it is quite clear that he is consciously writing in order to shock his readers, it is also just as obvious that he wants us to recognize the sordidness and filth of the outside, *real* world. He wants us, also, to realize that, more often than not, the seemingly bizarre characters and circumstances of his fiction are frequently ordinary, necessary responses of those existing in society gone mad. Commonplace and familiar though they may be, the acts of violence and barbarity of *First Love, Last Rites* are certainly symptomatic of a young writer; McEwan obviously wants to entice an audience. We witness not merely blood and repulsiveness but the origin of a social conscience, something that is nurtured and more completely developed in McEwan's works to come.

First Love, Last Rites is an appropriate introduction to McEwan's work, not only in its shock value but also because it ushers in many of his dominant themes—incest, regression, the cruelty of the city, isolation in crowded societies, the difficulty of love—as well as presents his primary concern with interpersonal relationships. Three of the stories—"Homemade," "Last Day of Summer," and "Disguises"—concern adolescents and their anguished initiations into the alien world of the adult.

McEwan further explores the theme of the outcast, the outsider, in another four stories: "Conversation with a Cupboard Man," "Butterflies," "Solid Geometry," and "Cocker at the Theatre." Finally, in the title story, "First Love, Last Rites," he presents a ray of optimism, displaying the hopes and strengths that are possible in a sustaining relationship.

In these eight stories and their diverse explorations of relationships, McEwan's literature of shock is ever prevalent; we encounter incest, murder, cross-dressing, and pedophilia. As prominent is the characters' indifference to shock. McEwan intimates that the modern world has immunized us against the shock that is predominant in our very lives.

Initiates: Crossing the Shadow Line

McEwan states that his interest in writing about adolescents stems from the fact that they are an "extraordinary, special case of people; they're close to childhood, and yet they are constantly baffled and irritated by the initiations into what's on the other side—the shadow line, as it were. They are perfect outsiders, in a sense, and fiction—especially short stories, and especially first-person narratives—can thrive on a point of view which is somehow dislocated, removed" (Ricks, 526). The protagonists of "Homemade," "Last Day of Summer," and "Disguises" are all initiates, each attempting in his own way to cross the shadowy division between naïveté and experience, between childhood and adulthood. In "Homemade," the first story of the collection, we are introduced to a young, cruel, unlikable narrator who relates, quite emotionlessly, the tale of his seduction of his 10-year-old sister. Surprisingly, he is not interested in committing incest with his sister Connie in order to gratify any perverted longing within himself, nor does he wish to satisfy any vicarious thrill that he secretly harbors. He seduces his sister because he sees his virginity as an embarrassment, the last step before crossing the shadow line into maturity. He uses intercourse, then, to propel himself into what he perceives as "that vast, gloomy and delectable mansion" of adulthood.[8] He is convinced by his society that this barrier must be traversed, that the real world of "Mommies and Daddies" must be attained at any cost.

The narrator at one point states that "my innocence was remarkable" (*FLLR,* 12). He views his innocence as a stigma, as a disgrace that must be erased as quickly as possible. He is guided through much of his innocence by Raymond, a friend who is a year older; although more knowledgeable in the vices of adulthood, Raymond is inept in experiencing the full pleasure of them: he "choke[s] and fumble[s]" over cigarettes (*FLLR,* 10), "[feels] nothing at all" with marijuana (*FLLR,* 10), gets sick while drinking whiskey, is apprehended while shoplifting. Still, the narrator respects him as his guide into experience, saying, "For all these acquired tastes Raymond was my Mephistopheles, he was Virgil to my Dante, showing me the way to a Paradiso where he himself could not tread" (*FLLR,* 12).

When Raymond eventually broaches the subject of their virginity, the narrator sees it as the last vestige of innocence: "I was made aware of and resented my virginity; I knew it to be the last room in the mansion, I knew it to be for certain the most luxurious, its furnishings more elaborate than any other room, its attractions more deadly, and the fact that I had never had it, made it, done it, was a total anathema, my malodorous albatross" (*FLLR*, 13). The ritual of intercourse and all its rudiments, however, are vague, enigmatic to the narrator. His sexual innocence is absolute: he admits, for example, that he has observed only two naked females, one his mother, "vast and grotesque, the skin hanging from her like flayed toad-hides," and his sister, who is an "ugly bat" (*FLLR*, 14). Later he thinks "about cunt . . . [but] still [not knowing] just exactly what a cunt was" (*FLLR*, 17–18). His most embarrassing moment, which fully exposes his sexual ignorance as well as his profound innocence, occurs as he is attempting to perform the incestuous act with Connie: he literally does not know how to accomplish the task. "I think," the narrator says, "perhaps I had in mind a warm fleshy chamber, but as I prodded and foraged, jabbed and wheedled, I found nothing other than tight, resisting skin" (*FLLR*, 22). In the end, it is the 10-year-old Connie who shows him the secret, who allows him to explore the last room in the mansion.

Despite his enormous desire to enter the adult world, the narrator's view of this world is patronizing. He laughs, for example, at his uncles' and his father's gifts of "hard-earned shillings . . . because I knew that a good afternoon's work in a bookshop [stealing and reselling books] earned more than they scraped together in a week" (*FLLR*, 15). In describing the game of "Mommies and Daddies" that leads to incest, the narrator says, "I was plunged into the microcosm of the dreary, everyday, ponderous banalities, the horrifying, niggling details of the life of our parents and their friends, the life that Connie so dearly wanted to ape" (*FLLR*, 20). This perfectly ordinary world, to the narrator, seems perfectly mundane, but however banal that adult world might appear, he aches to be initiated into it, whatever the sacrifice, whatever the ritual, simply because it *is* the adult world. The narrator finally earns his laurel of adulthood, then, in the incestuous act: "I felt proud, proud to be fucking, even if it were only Connie . . . , even if it had been a crippled mountain goat I would have been proud to be lying there in that manly position, proud in advance of being able to say 'I have fucked,' of belonging intimately and irrevocably to that superior half of humanity who had known coitus, and fertilized the world with it" (*FLLR*, 23–24).

The act, however is remarkably impotent; it is a gesture void of any significant emotion. Nonetheless, the narrator derives great satisfaction from it, recognizing neither the cruelty nor the meaninglessness.

Even the older, wiser narrator, in recounting this memory, makes no amends for the corruption of Connie's innocence; there is, ultimately, no voice of censure. This voice of blatant indifference further emphasizes McEwan's literature of shock. With no condemnation, we are forced to perceive the experience as the narrator does: as something ordinary, as something that must be accomplished in order to gain a more prominent position in the world. Essentially, the alliance between brother and sister is created by misguided necessity; the narrator attains this higher plateau, making his way into the adult world, smugly satisfied with both his achievement and its results. He never realizes the painful insignificance of his endeavor; he remains, then, as innocent as he began.

With "Last Day of Summer" McEwan introduces another adolescent, one much more sympathetic and likable than the narrator of "Homemade" but just as unsuccessful and as unfortunate in his relationships. In "The Unforgettable Momentum of Childhood Fantasy" McEwan confesses that for years he had "daydreamed of grown-ups conveniently and painlessly dissolved . . . , leaving me and a handful of competent friends to surmount dangers without ever being called in to tea."[9] This fantasy comes to fruition in both "Last Day of Summer" and his first novel, *The Cement Garden*. The short story, first published in February of 1975 in *American Review*, portrays a group of young people who form a small commune. Unlike the parentless family in *The Cement Garden*, however, this group of young adults does not discover the horror of monotony in their sudden freedom; rather, they thrive on this newfound independence. They work together preparing and cleaning up after meals, cultivating a garden and fruit trees, pitching in to move in a new tenant, sharing chores to keep the commune in working order; they are organized, responsible, and efficient. They create for themselves a peaceful and lovely world within the world. Nonetheless, in the midst of this community of uninhibited freedom, the central characters—the narrator and Jenny—remain isolated, separate from the family unit; ultimately, the two form an alliance, finding comfort in friendship. The narrator takes Jenny under his young wing and brings her into his confidence, showing her the secret wonders of his lonely world; Jenny, in turn, becomes a surrogate mother to both the narrator and the baby Alice, providing a love that has been painfully absent from the commune.

The 12-year-old narrator is a precursor to Jack of *The Cement Garden.*
Like Jack, he is suddenly cast into a parentless world and left to fend for
himself. Distancing himself, as does Jenny, he remains quietly detached.
Unlike Jack and the other characters in *The Cement Garden,* the narrator
of "Last Day" does not see his new liberty as a great adventure; rather,
he views it as a perfectly ordinary happenstance. Because of this, he
adapts to the lifestyle with apparent ease. He is responsible (as the story
opens, he has just finished mowing the lawn); he is intelligent (he is an
avid bird-watcher, able to recognize numerous birds by their song); he is
accepting. He accepts the situation, and, more important, he is the only
character who accepts Jenny, seeing her for the person she truly is
beneath all her excess weight. When he first takes her to the river, they
stop to listen for birdsong; in the silence Jenny is beset with nervous giggles. The narrator states that he wants "her to hear the blackbird so
much I put my hand on her arm, and when I do that she takes her hand
away from her nose and smiles" (*FLLR,* 46). This touch of humanity
reassures Jenny and seals their friendship. With the narrator, Jenny is
comfortable, relaxed; her nervous laughter becomes "easy and kind of
rhythmic, not hard and yelping like before" (*FLLR,* 47). The two characters, isolated in their respective worlds, bond, providing one another
with understanding and companionship.

   After Jenny has resided in the commune for awhile, the narrator
notices that "there's something in the way the others treat Jenny. Like
she's outside things, and not really a person like they are" (*FLLR,* 49).
Jenny is the perennial misfit of McEwan's fiction; she is the stereotypical
fat girl, ignored and cast out by her society because of her obesity. When
she enters the commune, the others welcome her, but she never becomes
one with the group, never becomes part of their family. The older characters are ill at ease with her; the narrator notes that they "are still both-
ered when she [laughs her nervous, yelping laughter], they sort of look
away as if it is something disgusting that would be rude to look at"
(*FLLR,* 48). Further, when the others smoke hashish, Jenny leaves the
room, obviously disapproving of the habit, and the others "sort of resent
it" (*FLLR,* 49). Neither does she dress as the others do in "jeans and
Indian shirts," preferring rather "dresses with flowers on and ordinary
things like my mother or the lady in the post office wears" (*FLLR,* 50).
Although she is rejected by people her own age, she is readily accepted
by the narrator and the baby Alice. In her initiation, she finally finds
solace and welcome in the relationships she forms with the youngest of
the commune.

When Jenny first arrives, the narrator several times describes her as "pink," at one point even commenting, "Everywhere she's pink" (*FLLR,* 42). As she is initiated into acceptance, Jenny loses her bashful, awkward innocence, her "pinkness"; likewise, the adjective momentarily disappears from the narrator's descriptions. As the two characters begin to forge their friendship, Jenny follows instinct, becoming the mother figure of the commune, quickly establishing a new order: "Somehow she makes more space in [the kitchen]. She scrapes paint off the north window to let in more light. . . . [S]he arranges the pots and plates so that you always know where they are and even I can reach them" (*FLLR,* 47). As the narrator has adopted her, so, too, does Jenny take special care of him, cleaning his room, changing his sheets, cooking the best meal he has had in two years. Jenny, too, is the one who forces him to prepare for school, taking charge of getting his hair cut and shopping for school uniforms. The narrator at first argues against this, but Jenny's metamorphosis into motherhood is so complete that his protestations are quickly and easily quelled. After all, she brings into the commune a love and a kindness that have long been absent, filling a void in the boy's life.

Besides caring for the narrator, Jenny also readily obeys other maternal instincts, accepting and mothering the baby Alice, who is the fatherless child of Kate, another member of the commune. The mother is obviously bewildered, even unhappy with her baby, resenting the time that it takes to be a mother. The narrator says that Kate "always looks sad when she speaks to Alice" and that she speaks to her "as if she doesn't really want to be speaking to Alice at all" (*FLLR,* 43). The baby instantly responds to Jenny, however, immediately developing a bond. During Alice's first encounter with Jenny, the narrator says, "It's the first time I've heard [Alice] laugh like that" (*FLLR,* 45). In time Jenny "becomes Alice's mother" (*FLLR,* 50); their relationship develops to the point that the baby refuses her biological mother, preferring instead the ministrations and attention of Jenny, a more ordinary mother.

As well as the relationships among Jenny, Alice, and the narrator progress, they are, unfortunately, not enough to guarantee either happiness or survival. On the last day of summer, the three take the narrator's boat for a final outing; in a fit of convulsive laughter, Jenny upsets the boat, and both she and Alice are drowned. Through the story and its catastrophic conclusion, McEwan indicates that their relationship will sustain neither Jenny nor the narrator; friendship is simply not enough. In the moment before Jenny's death, the narrator again uses "pink" to describe her: "her laugh is getting tighter and drier, little hard yelps like pieces of stone from her throat. Her big pink face and her big pink arms are shaking and straining to catch a mouthful of air" (*FLLR*, 54). Jenny's initiation has ended, and she returns to her previous state, uncomfortable and ungainly in this world. Subsequently, as in "Homemade," the initiation is abysmally useless; the narrator is left alone and unprotected, as he was at the beginning of the story.

The disrupted family, a favorite subject of McEwan's, is again encountered in "Disguises" (first published in *American Review* in September 1973). Young Henry, the protagonist, at the death of his parents is delivered into the hands of his aunt Mina, a woman who is, in turns, very strange and frighteningly abnormal. Henry is taken, then, from a normal life and a mother who is "solid and always sane" (*FLLR*, 105) and placed into the custody of a "surreal mother" (*FLLR*, 100). Henry soon learns that living with his aunt includes partaking in her "hobby"— dressing for dinner in various costumes. Having been an actress and lived the life of the theater, Mina continues her charades and role-playing with her sole companion, providing him with an array of disguises and personas. When she forces him to dress in the garb of a young girl, however, Henry finds himself in dire circumstances.

Through her games, Mina attempts to draw Henry into the tainted world of adulthood, but in doing so she also corrupts his innocence. From the beginning, the relationship between aunt and nephew is anything but normal. Immediately upon his arrival, Mina seems peculiarly, even incestuously attracted to Henry: for instance, when she relates the events of her day, she is "more wife . . . than aunt" (*FLLR*, 102); likewise, in one of their cross-dressing games, she makes a pseudo-pass at him, groping under his dress, pressing his face to her breasts, all the while singing "A soldier needs a girl, a soldier needs a girl" (*FLLR*, 116). For the most part, Henry finds his identity suppressed, even trapped, in Mina's world. At school, away from his aunt, he is different, freer; there he lives an ordinary life, finding joy in the precocious, carefree world of a young boy rather than suffering the pressure of providing companionship to a much older, extremely eccentric woman.

The dressing game, "the motif of this story" (*FLLR*, 101), rapidly develops from one of Mina's idiosyncrasies into something that truly horrifies Henry. At first dressing up is simply a daily chore, something done merely to appease his aunt; Henry obeys the whims of Mina and parades through this new life in an array of costumes: a soldier, an elevator operator, a monk, a shepherd. Although he recognizes the bizarreness of the situation, initially it is also "somehow to Henry ordinary" (*FLLR*,

104). Only when he is forced against his will to don the dress of a girl does he realize that these rituals are "games which are not really games" (*FLLR,* 117). Confronted by the costume, "all flounces and frills, layer on layer with white satin and lace edged with pink, a cute bow falling at the back" (*FLLR,* 104), Henry is at once sickened and horrified; to him "it was wrong to be a girl" (*FLLR,* 105). Nonetheless, he finds himself literally forced by Mina to assume the role, becoming a "sickeningly pretty little girl" (*FLLR,* 106).

Part of his repulsion at dressing as a girl stems from his typical boyhood attitude toward the opposite sex, the seeds of the later, more detrimental patriarchal mind-set: "Like the best of Henry's friends at school he did not care for girls, avoided their huddles and intrigues, their whispers and giggles and holding hands and passing notes and I love I love, they set his teeth on edge to see" (*FLLR,* 105). Soon after suffering the humiliation of cross-dressing, Henry comes face to face with Linda, a new girl in his class who immediately violates his space by being assigned a seat at his desk. Henry, however, finds himself curiously drawn to her, attracted by her young beauty, by her feminine mystique. It is with Linda that he experiences, upon touching hands with her, his first sexual awakenings. Unlike most of McEwan's characters, though, Henry allows these new feelings to remain unexplored; even when the two children lie naked in bed together, their alliance remains innocent, unhampered by sex. His new bond with Linda, in part, helps Henry cope with the tyranny of Mina.

Henry learns to control his fear of his aunt, as well as his repulsion of dressing as this strange blonde girl, by projecting himself into the image of Linda. Dressing in the disguise, he becomes "Henry and Linda at once, closer than in the car, inside her now and she was in him" (*FLLR,* 114). He copes with this bizarre situation by placing it in the context of what he can consider ordinary, identifiable. Ironically, Henry finds himself released from the horror of dressing as a girl by imagining himself *to be* a girl. His association with Linda, a pure and innocent friendship, the sole *normal* relationship in his life, provides him with an escape from the tainted, perverted relationship he endures with Mina.

The relationship that develops between Henry and Linda at first seems to provide a hint of optimism; their friendship is innocent, affirming. In the final scene, however, Henry unwittingly drags Linda into the trap of Mina's unnatural world. At a party in which all the guests are "disguised as ordinary people" (*FLLR,* 122), Linda becomes a bewildered Alice in Wonderland, lost in a world she does not, cannot understand.

Henry watches as she falls prey to one of the guests, and as the story closes, he slowly, drunkenly makes his way toward her; McEwan, however, leaves us with the distinct impression that his intervention will make no difference. Just as the relationship between Jenny and the narrator of "Last Day" was not enough to sustain them in their world, neither is the friendship of Henry and Linda strong enough to protect them from the evils of Mina's adult world. Rather than providing protection, Henry's alliance with Linda ultimately results in an inadvertent betrayal. As in "Homemade" and "Last Day of Summer," the outside adult world closes upon its adolescents, stealing from them the innocence that creates the shadow line between youth and adulthood, between purity and corruption.

Outcasts: Crawling from the Crowd

The vast majority of McEwan's characters long for some sort of a sustaining relationship; they realize that these relationships ease the pains of life. In *First Love, Last Rites* very few of the characters succeed in establishing viable relationships; most of these unions seem to be too meaningless, too insubstantial, to prove enduring. In his presentation of interpersonal relationships, McEwan also creates several characters who stand on the periphery of their societies. They are outcasts: some are pariahs; others are simply rebels, ostracized because they do not follow the dictates of their society. These outcasts also yearn for contact with others, and more often than not, they prove to be incapable of forming any relationship which might offer an escape from their isolation. One of McEwan's most unusual outcasts is the narrator of "Conversation with a Cupboard Man." In this story, which first appeared in the 1972 Spring–Summer issue of *Transatlantic Review,* McEwan presents a man who has been destroyed by his environment. He is forced to live in an intimidating, vicious society, and his attempts to establish supportive relationships—with his mother, with his co-workers, with anyone accessible to him—fail miserably, leaving him a ruin of a person, groveling for security in the darkness and emptiness of a clothes wardrobe.

The story takes the form of a rambling monologue as the Cupboard Man explains his life and peculiar circumstances to a silent, unseen social worker. The character is, by degrees, eccentric and extremely disturbed. McEwan admits that the creation of the narrator was influenced by John Fowles's disturbing character Frederick Clegg: "I very much admired *The Collector*. I still do, I think it's Fowles's best book. And in 'Conversation with a Cupboard Man' I wanted to do the kind of voice of the man in *The Collector*: that kind of wheedling, self-pitying lower middle-class voice" (Hamilton, 18). In portraying the narrator, McEwan develops the story by a means of naturalism, creating a character who is forced toward his fate by and within a cold, unsympathetic society. He is so ravaged by inexorable affectlessness that he is destroyed as a human being.

Since environment is all important in naturalism, it is not surprising that the narrator's mother is a primary factor in his steady disintegration; from the beginning, he announces quite unemphatically, "She was insane" (*FLLR*, 76). His primary problem stems from the fact that his mother attempts "to stop [him] growing up" (*FLLR*, 75). She feeds him baby food, forces him to wear bibs, does not teach him to speak; she so dominates him that he can "hardly move without her" (*FLLR*, 76). The mother's mad fixation with "trying to push [him] back up her womb" (*FLLR*, 77) is the origin of his own desire to regress; throughout his life he harbors a need to return to a fetal state, to rediscover the security of the womb. His mother's control is so complete that when she abandons him in order to remarry (moving away without telling him), he is utterly lost.

If the relationship he has with his mother is disastrous, then the relationships the Cupboard Man forges in the outside world can be considered nothing short of catastrophic. In London, the only job he can obtain is that of a dish washer. There he immediately becomes involved in an antagonistic relationship with the chief cook, who eventually locks him in a huge, cast-iron oven and then turns it on. Severely blistered, the narrator returns the next day to exact revenge by pouring boiling oil into the cook's lap, a blatant, gratuitous shock into literature: "His clothes seemed to dissolve and I could see his balls red and swelling and then turning white. It was all down his legs. He was screaming for twenty-five minutes before the doctor came and gave him morphine. I found out later that Pus-face spent nine months in hospital while they picked out bits of clothing from his flesh. That was how I sorted Pus-face out" (*FLLR*, 82). It is only later that the narrator recognizes his unconscious attraction to the womblike ovens: "I realized that when I went to clean the oven the second time I was secretly wanting to be shut in. . . . I wanted to be frustrated. I wanted to be where I couldn't get out" (*FLLR*, 83).

His desire for the womb stems mainly from his inability to cope with his society. Shortly after arriving in the city, for example, the narrator admits that London "was becoming too much for me" (*FLLR*, 82). Just as the young boy of "Last Day of Summer" thinks of London as a "terrible secret" (*FLLR,* 46), so, too, does the Cupboard Man recognize the horror and inclemency of the city. In McEwan's fiction the city is often portrayed as encroaching and dehumanizing; it is, in all senses, an evil entity. Similarly, other contemporary writers see the city as an intimidating, subversive force. Suddenly, the metropolis is no longer the sustaining entity of Joyce and Woolf, whose Dublin and London, respectively, could nurture and enhance. Instead, the city of the late twentieth century has become a cesspool of modern afflictions. Martin Amis says, "I like cities as a writer. As a citizen and as a human being, I'm not so happy with them. I think they are very deforming, very unnatural, very frightening concentrations."[10] Will Self's Ian Wharton, of *My Idea of Fun,* sees the city in similar terms: "I see the city as mighty ergot fungus, erupting from the very crust of the earth; a groaning, mutating thing" (Self, 303–304).

One can see the contemporary metropolis at its worst in such varied works as Amis's *Money* and *London Fields,* where New York City and London are shown as decaying wastelands filled with alienated, impotent individuals. Angela Carter's *The Passion of New Eve* depicts a near-future New York City rife with rats, racial wars, and marauding bands of angry women who demand equality through violence. In J. G. Ballard's *Concrete Island* and *High-Rise,* the city is seen as an alienating creature that forces its inhabitants to their most spurious, most barbaric states. The novels of the American Brat Pack (those writers like Jay McInerney, Bret Easton Ellis, and Tama Janowitz, whose public lives—the clothes they wear, the nightclubs they frequent, the people they befriend—are as scrutinized as their fiction) portray New York City as a debaucher and discarder of humanity. The city, then, becomes an objective correlative for all that is wrong and confused in today's world; it is not seen as the pantheon of modern civilization but as the core of its depravity and cruelty, an anonymous and impersonal beast.

The Cupboard Man, then, is understandably intimidated by the city, depressed by "the thought of facing thousands of people, thundering traffic, queues and things like that" (*FLLR,* 82). Consequently, he begins to withdraw from society, retreating further into himself. When he is later sent to prison for shoplifting, he experiences his happiest three months since leaving home; he feels safe within the confining walls, he makes friends who accept him, he at last fits into a society. He is so secure in this environment that he requests a longer sentence; unfortunately, he is quickly ejected by a system that cannot and will not understand him.

Exhausting the possibilities of establishing any sort of a meaningful relationship, the Cupboard Man begins again to withdraw from the world. At one point he states, "How did I become an adult? I'll tell you, I never did learn" (*FLLR,* 76). Abandoned and alone in the city, he surrenders his pretenses toward normality and willingly falls into a steady regression. In McEwan's fiction, regression is a common motif; characters, when they are no longer able to withstand the pressures and uncertainties of their lives, the cruelties of their worlds, will often sink into an immature, more innocent state of being. The narrator, for instance, says, "That's why I envy these babies I see in the street being bundled and carried about by their mothers. I want to be one of them" (*FLLR,* 87). He even closes his "conversation" by expressing a yearning to be "one year old again" (*FLLR,* 87). Finally, as a further means of escaping his society, the Cupboard Man also retreats into the secure darkness of a small clothes wardrobe, explaining, "I prefer it in my cupboard" (*FLLR,* 87). No longer able to cope with society, he returns to the womb, safe in his seclusion.

In this study of an extreme reaction to the cruelty of a society, McEwan demonstrates the necessity of relationships. Because he cannot cope in his culture and, most significantly, because he cannot establish a relationship which will nourish him, the Cupboard Man regresses from responsibility and retreats from life. Without these affinities, McEwan argues, individuals are incapable of surviving in a world that offers no hope, a world which also has regressed into an even more savage and primal state.

In "Butterflies" McEwan creates another human monstrosity—someone who, like the Cupboard Man, is incapable of any sort of normal interaction with his society. In an interview with Ian Hamilton, McEwan states that the story "was one of the worst things I could think of. Yet in a nightmarish way I could indulge in it, in the idea of it. I frightened myself with 'Butterflies'" (Hamilton, 20).[11] Such is the emotional intensity of this story, by far McEwan's most patently repulsive tale. This repulsiveness, though, is much in line with a burgeoning trend among contemporary writers. There has been in recent fiction a proliferation of characters who are so repugnant, so vile, so at cruel odds with their encompassing societies that they are virtually subhuman, a sort of netherhero. These creatures are a mutated corollary of the chaos and carnage of the twentieth century.

Certainly Martin Amis's John Self and Will Self's Ian Wharton are netherheroes, both driven to inhuman lengths by their insatiable materialistic needs. Other examples abound. The eponymous protagonist (whose real name is Dennis Cleg—surely an ascertainment that most, if not all, netherheroes are grandsired by Fowles's *Collector*) of Patrick McGrath's *Spider* (1990)—who urinates spiders and smells gas emanating from his body—kills his mother and then disremembers the episode through a cloudy, insane narrative. Scott Bradfield's *The History of Luminous Motion* (1989) relates the story of Phillip, an eight-year-old who partakes liberally of drugs and alcohol, dabbles in devil worship, and contemplates Freud; the boy murders his mother's lover, implementing the various instruments of a nearby toolbox (and later attempts the same ploy with his father). The most notorious netherhero of recent fiction, though, is Patrick Bateman of Bret Easton Ellis's *American Psycho,* whose totally depraved, misogynistic barbarism enraged both publishers (on the grounds of taste, Simon & Schuster dropped the novel after advancing Ellis $300,000) and readers (the National Organization for Women immediately boycotted the eventual publisher Knopf).[12] Unfortunately, the netherhero is not just the figment of a depraved mind. Writers have to look no further than today's headlines: the world is rampant with the insanities of John Wayne Gaceys and Jeffrey Dahmers. Our societies, these authors realize, breed the likes of Ian Wharton and Patrick Bateman every day.

With "Butterflies" McEwan again portrays an individual who is at odds with society. Much of the narrator's estrangement occurs because he suffers from a unique physical deformity: "My chin and my neck are the same thing" (*FLLR,* 63); because of his "chinlessness," he is shunned by society and forced into an isolation that he abhors. Rendered socially incompetent and marked as a freak by his society, the narrator is forced to play the role of the pariah. He despises his loneliness and longs for company, but, at the same time, he is incapable of enjoying any sort of relationship in a city that shuns him. Eventually, his need for acceptance, for any human contact, becomes perverted into his sexual desire for Jane, a nine-year-old neighbor.

In all its sordidness, ugliness, and cruelty, London is a principal component in the narrator's societal exile. Early in the story, the narrator describes the city's bleakness, saying, "There are no parks in this part of London, only car parks. And there is the canal, the brown canal which goes between factories and past a scrap heap, the canal little Jane drowned in" (*FLLR,* 62). The city, then, becomes the embodiment of the hatred and cruelty of its populace. The canal, though, with its brown water, chemical smell, and yellow scum, becomes a reflection of the grosser stagnation of the city; it provides the site for Jane's corruption, and it willingly accepts and conceals her body. The narrator tempts Jane to her fate with the promise of brilliant butterflies, but he secretly knows that they "could never survive near the canal, the stench would dissolve them" (*FLLR*, 69). Similarly, the city itself dissolves many of its own individuals, forcing them into an invisibility.

Because the city has so badgered and bullied him, the narrator is constantly on the defensive; he evolves into the stereotypical paranoid, trusting no one, suspecting everybody. When Jane first approaches him, his paranoia instantly surfaces; when she is behind him, he has "the feeling she was imitating my walk" (*FLLR*, 65). Later he wonders whether she is "making gestures behind my back the way children do" (*FLLR*, 67). Nevertheless, he overcomes his fear, allowing her to tag along. His chance encounter with Jane gives him a momentary sense of purpose. Unfortunately, because he has been so warped by the city, the relationship between the two can end in nothing but calamity.

The narrator has so long been ignored and outcast by his society that any sort of acknowledgment is a triumph. For instance, while walking through the city he meets a group of boys playing football; as he passes them, one throws a small stone at him, and unexpectedly the narrator makes an accidental but graceful move to trap the stone under his foot. The boys are delighted: "They all laughed at this and clapped and cheered me, so that for one elated moment I thought I could go back and join in their game" (*FLLR*, 67). This fleeting moment of acceptance has such a profound effect on him that he returns to it in memory immediately after dropping Jane's body into the murky waters of the canal; the encounter with the boys, amazingly, creates a greater impression on him than does his murder of Jane. The narrator envisions himself taking advantage of the miraculous moment of the stone, returning to the boys to join their group:

> I would be with them, one of them, in a team. I would play with them out there in the street most evenings, learn all their names and they would know mine. I would see them in town during the day and they would call out to me from the other side of the street, cross over and chat. At the end of the game one of them comes over to me and grips my arm.
> "See you tomorrow, then . . ."
> "Yes, tomorrow." We would go out drinking together when they were older, and I would learn to like beer. (*FLLR*, 74)

Reality quickly returns, and he realizes that none of his fantasies will ever come to fruition: "I knew I would not be joining any football games. The opportunities are rare, like butterflies" (*FLLR*, 74).

His brief encounter with Jane also originates because of this terrific desire to interact with someone, with anyone. Jane quickly captures his undivided attention, wedging herself into the narrator's fortressed life, breaking through the walls of isolation as no one has done before. At one point when she grabs onto his arm, he says, "No one had touched me intentionally like that for a long time, not since I was a child. I felt a cold thrill in my stomach and I was unsteady on my legs" (*FLLR*, 67–68). Unable to control his attraction to Jane, his feelings rapidly mutate into sexual desires; suddenly realizing what he plans to do with the child, he at first "sicken[s] at the idea" (*FLLR*, 69) but nonetheless seduces her into following him to the canal. The narrator is incapable of forming an ordinary alliance; his yearnings for company are drowned in the waves of his sexual desire. Completely ostracized by the city, he discovers himself forced to seek a sexual release with his first trusting companion. Luring Jane into the darkness of a tunnel, he forces her to touch his penis, and in his orgasm he experiences a catharsis, a momentary release from his isolation:

> She reached out her hand and her fingers briefly brushed the tip. It was enough, though. I doubled up and came, I came into my cupped hands. . . . [I]t took a long time, pumping it all out into my hand. All the time I spent by myself came pumping out, all the hours walking alone and all the thoughts I had had, it all came out into my hand. . . . [Afterwards] my mind was clear, my body was relaxed and I was thinking of nothing. (*FLLR*, 72–73)

Attempting to escape this monster of monsters, Jane trips and knocks herself unconscious; the narrator then "lift[s] her up gently, as gently as I could so as not to wake her, and ease[s] her quietly into the canal" (*FLLR*, 73). The narrator thus destroys the one person who has reached out to him, offering him at least the hope of a relationship.

In both "Conversation with a Cupboard Man" and "Butterflies" McEwan graphically portrays the destructive power of the city. In the majority of his work, he maintains that this cruelty is the *true*, everyday guise of the city. Those who can accept this harsh normality can survive; those who cannot are lost and abandoned. In expelling individuals, by taking from them the ability to form life-affirming relationships, the city strips these characters of their humanity and remolds them into the shape of the netherhero, cold, heartless. Discarded by their communities, these banished creatures then resort to extreme measures. The Cupboard Man abandons hope, locking himself away from the dangers of his society; the narrator of "Butterflies" becomes the creature the city forces him to be. Both suffer greatly because of their forced exile, and they remain isolated individuals within the overcrowded metropolis; simultaneously, they are rendered incompetent, unable to seek and develop the relationships they so desperately need. The city, McEwan shows, is a merciless creature, the true monster.

In the stories "Solid Geometry" and "Cocker at the Theatre" McEwan introduces outcasts who purposely separate themselves from their respective worlds. Both the narrator of "Solid Geometry" and Cocker refuse to conform to the "acceptable" norms of their surrounding cultures, choosing instead to follow routes that they view as more natural. The former is weary of his familiar marriage and escapes by submerging himself in the past; the latter hilariously heeds instinctual desires, but in doing so he breaks the etiquette of nude acting. As a consequence, both remain isolated, separated from their societies.

In the introduction to *The Imitation Game and Other Plays* McEwan states that "Solid Geometry"

> had very distinct origins. A mathematician friend from Chile had recently told me of a "proof" for a plane without a surface and had outlined for me the consequences of such a proof being valid. Independently of this I had been reading Bertrand Russell's diaries and I wanted to write a story which would somehow illustrate the way diary writing, in its selectivity, closely resembles fiction writing. Thirdly, I wanted to write about the collision of two intellectual worlds. (*IG,* 12)

The story (which, appropriately, first appeared in *Amazing Stories,* a magazine of fantasy and science fiction, in 1973) is the most contrived of those in *First Love, Last Rites.* Looking back on it from a 10-year vantage point, McEwan admits that it is "hardly a profound story. It is a little too neat, and at best simply clever" (*IG,* 13). Still, "Solid Geometry" provides another unique look at relationships in modern culture.

The husband and wife of "Solid Geometry" live in different intellectual worlds (a theme McEwan returns to, more elaborately, in *Black Dogs*). McEwan describes the narrator as "a nasty person, cold, sexless, self-obsessed" (Hamilton, 17). He is an adamant believer in the achingly rational, "the mathematics of the Absolute" (*FLLR,* 37). In addition, his interest in the past borders on obsession. He completely dismisses his wife in order to spend his days poring over the nineteenth-century diaries of his great-grandfather, a true eccentric. The great-grandfather, too, is controlled by an intense appreciation of the logical and the rational: through mathematical deduction he proves, for example, that "the maximum number of [sexual] positions cannot exceed the prime number seventeen" (*FLLR*, 27); he also excitedly plans to write a pamphlet entitled "De Stercore Equorum" ("Concerning Horseshit"), proving that by 1935 London roads will be impassable because of horse manure (*FLLR*, 29). The narrator finds himself irresistibly drawn to his ancestor, even to the point of keeping his own journal. Furthermore, the narrator's prized possession is the penis of a nineteenth-century criminal preserved in a jar, an artifact his great-grandfather bought in an auction in 1875. The narrator allows these interests to consume his life; consequently, he becomes an outcast, expressing no interest in his own, immediate world.

Maisie, the narrator's wife, is representative of a different world and belief, the antirational; she is fascinated with the occult, the fantastical, and, in direct opposition to her husband, the future rather than the past. Her delvings into such things as Buddhism, tarot cards, mysticism, and astrology are important to her because, as she says, "I want to get my head straight" (*FLLR*, 30). Her interests, however, are as fleeting as they are unproductive. She discovers no easy answers to the complexities of life in the antirational; nor does she obtain any sympathy from the narrator, who tells her, "You haven't the originality or passion to intuit anything yourself beyond your own unhappiness" (*FLLR*, 30). Neither husband nor wife can find a venue into the other's world; the result is a rending of their marriage.

Their relationship disintegrates into a series of cruelties and exasperations. What they both fail to realize is that this is normal marriage, something that demands attention. Rather than accepting the ordinary, they resort to childlike, cruel behavior. The narrator describes one such event as "an important stage in the deterioration of our marriage" (*FLLR*, 27). The act occurs when Maisie, in frustration, hits her husband in the head with a shoe. Revealing a cold barbarity, he waits

> quietly and patiently outside the bathroom holding a handkerchief to my bleeding ear. Maisie was in the bathroom about ten minutes and as she came out I caught her neatly and squarely on the top of her head. I did not give her time to move. . . .
> "You worm," she breathed. (*FLLR*, 28)

This incident is the dénouement in the breakdown of their marriage; Maisie is willing, in time, to forgive and continue; the narrator, however, becomes colder, more calculating. When Maisie massages his neck, he thinks, "I would have found it soothing if it had still been the first year of our marriage" (*FLLR*, 33). Now her attention is only a nuisance, interfering with his work on the diaries. When she makes an attempt to talk him into the bedroom, he admits that he feels "no desire for Maisie or any other woman" (*FLLR*, 33); his sole love is his great-grandfather's diary. Soon, the narrator seeks only an escape.

A second childlike altercation becomes their final confrontation. Maisie resents the time and attention that her husband devotes to the diaries; the narrator admits early in the story that a key problem in the marriage is her jealousy "of my great-grandfather's forty-five-volume diary, and of my purpose and energy in editing it" (*FLLR*, 27). After a failed seduction, unable to control her rage and jealousy, Maisie smashes the pickled penis and its jar against the wall, destroying one of the two physical links the narrator has with his ancestor and simultaneously transforming "a treasured curiosity into a horrible obscenity" (*FLLR*, 33). The narrator realizes then that they are irreconcilable, that their two worlds will never mesh.

The narrator discovers the solution to his marital woes in the surface-less plane, an anomaly of rational thought and science. Once he has unraveled the mystery of the "plane without a surface," he lures his wife into their bedroom under the pretense of a reconciliation. There he begins to fold her through the yogalike exercises that open the mysterious plane; Maisie willingly submits because, as the narrator notes, "She liked to be manipulated in this way" (*FLLR*, 39). Suddenly, she disappears into the realm of the antirational: "As I drew her arms and legs through, Maisie appeared to turn in on herself like a sock. 'Oh God,' she sighed, 'what's happening?' and her voice sounded very far away. Then she was gone . . . and not gone. Her voice was quite tiny. 'What's happening?' and all that remained was the echo of her question above the deep-blue sheets" (*FLLR*, 40). The disappearance of Maisie is ironic in that the narrator finally embraces her world of the fantastic, the antirational, in order to rid himself of her. He willingly accepts an entirely new world, a different way of thinking, but he refuses to succumb to a loving wife. His world of the ultrarational, which finally depends on the antirational, provides no room for a sustaining relationship; he remains alone, an outcast of both worlds.

Again McEwan presents a relationship that is not substantial enough to survive. Maisie, a loving, truly giving character, seeks comfort and resolution in her relationship; she alone attempts to revive the faltering marriage. But McEwan pairs her with a character who repudiates the validity of a sustaining relationship; instead, he chooses to "disappear" his problems, escaping the hardships and tribulations of his marriage, ostracizing himself, choosing to remain isolated rather than sharing himself with another.

Like the narrator of "Solid Geometry," the protagonist of "Cocker at the Theatre" is another figure who refuses to conform to the accepted norms of a particular society—here a theatrical troupe rehearsing a nude musical. Although this is a more playful story, McEwan is still obviously interested in examining the role of interpersonal relationships as they are seen and affected by immediate society.

As the story opens and the nude actors prepare to rehearse, they sense the absurdity of their situation; they are uncomfortable, awkward: "There was nowhere to sit so they shuffled about miserably. They had no pockets to put their hands in, and there were no cigarettes" (*FLLR*, 56). Most of the actors are not even professionals but, rather, "friends of friends of the director and needing some cash" (*FLLR*, 56).

Cocker and his partner quickly get caught up in the passion of the sexual simulation, breaching the etiquette of nude acting. As the actors begin their performance, "rock[ing] like children playing at ships" (*FLLR*, 57), the choreographer remarks that Cocker and his partner are "moving well" (*FLLR*, 58); they alone seem to have captured the knack of fake copulation. It soon becomes apparent, however, that the pair is no longer acting. The director is incensed; the other actors are stunned; a member of the troupe brings in a bucket of water to separate the copulating couple.

Despite being the one person who is swept away by natural desire, Cocker becomes the one who is cast out from his immediate society. McEwan shows that even in the most bizarre of circumstances, there are rules of acceptance; and those failing to conform to these mores, those who rebel against their societies, are always the ones made scapegoats and dismissed. Outcasts proliferate in society; they exist in every station and aspect of life, whether willingly or unwillingly separated from their societies. And as McEwan demonstrates, most frequently long for human association, the contact that shows welcome and acceptance.

Survivors: Discovering a Tender Optimism

McEwan has commented that he has "always been trying to assert some kind of tender optimism in my stories, and I don't think I can really do that unless I can do it in a world that seems to me to be fundamentally threatening, so what I really worry about is gratuitous optimism, not gratuitous violence" (Ricks, 526). Throughout the stories of *First Love, Last Rites* characters attempt to attain the security of a supportive relationship; however, almost all fail. In the title story, though, McEwan does offer a ray of hope; a tender optimism is achieved.

In "First Love, Last Rites" the narrator and his live-in girlfriend, Sissel, both 17 or 18, share a healthy and loving relationship. When outside forces begin to invade their idyllic life, however, they discover that their relationship starts to founder; they begin to drift apart. Fortunately, the two lovers realize that survival comes as a result of union; together they are able to become whole, uniting to protect themselves from the afflictions and cruelties of their world.

Their fears and uncertainties about life become manifest in a creature that scrabbles continuously in their bedroom walls. In time, it becomes the couple's "familiar," embodying their doubts and apprehensions. The narrator at first suffers it alone, hearing its faint scratchings and clawings in the calm silences after their lovemaking. Later he equates it more directly with their own lives, imagining that they, too, have the power to "make a creature grow in Sissel's belly" (*FLLR*, 90). In the narrator's fantasies the creature becomes an obsession ruling his every thought:

> It was eggs, sperms, chromosomes, feathers, gills, claws, inches from my cock's end the unstoppable chemistry of a creature growing out of a dark red slime, my fantasy was of being helpless before the age and strength of this process and the thought alone could make me come before I wanted. . . . As we were swept down the long slopes to our orgasms, in those last desperate seconds I struggled to find my way out but I was caught like an eel in my fantasy of the creature in the dark, waiting, hungry, and I fed it great white gobs. (*FLLR*, 90)

He becomes so occupied with his vision of the creature that at times he believes that he and Sissel "were the creatures now in the slime, we were inside fed by gobs of cloud coming through the window, by gases drawn from the mudflats by the sun" (*FLLR*, 90). The creature becomes an amalgamation of his fears, for himself, for Sissel. He agonizes over the

uncertainty of his future: he fears becoming a father; he fears entering an
everyday world, only to become *ordinary*, identical to every other person
and couple; he fears the unknowability of love and relationships. He
believes that the scrabbling nuisance is his own creation, and, subsequently, his problem to solve. When Sissel also hears the tiny scratching,
however, he suddenly realizes that this mysterious creature along with
his fears and uncertainties, are all very real; no longer can they be
excused as dreams and fantasies.

As the story opens, the lovers' relationship is filled with youthful passion: "From the beginning of summer until it seemed pointless, we lift-
ed the thin mattress on to the heavy oak table and made love in front of
the large open window" (*FLLR*, 88). But bliss soon ends, and the two
grow distant; the relationship begins to crumble, falling prey to the
trappings of a mundane environment. McEwan often mirrors the collapse of relations with a growing disorder in the physical surroundings;
thus, the narrator and Sissel's estrangement is reflected in the stagnant
atmosphere and increasing disarray of their room:

> It [the room] was no longer four floors up and detached, there was no
> breeze through the windows, only a mushy heat rising off the quayside
> and dead jellyfish and clouds of flies, fiery grey flies who found our
> armpits and bit fiercely, houseflies who hung in clouds over our food. Our
> hair was too long and dank and hung in our eyes. The food we bought
> melted and tasted like the river. We no longer lifted the mattress on to
> the table, the coolest place now was the floor and the floor was covered
> with greasy sand which would not go away. (*FLLR*, 92)

As the rift between the lovers widens, so, too, does the "dishevelment
and unease" (*FLLR*, 91); eventually they lie silently as "our rubbish
gathered around us, milk bottles we could not bring ourselves to carry
away, grey sweating cheese, butter wrappers, yogurt cartons, over-ripe
salami" (*FLLR*, 93). To make matters even more unsavory, Sissel con-
tracts a case of foot rot, which adds to the growing stench. And in this
ever-growing disarray, the creature persists, becoming "louder" and
"more insistent" (*FLLR*, 93).

One of the dominant factors in the growing alienation between the
two lovers is the horror of descending into the ordinary. Once Sissel
obtains a job, the narrator is shocked to discover that they are no different from any other young, ambitionless couple. Sissel's dreary job forces
him to realize that "we were different from no one, they all had rooms,
houses, jobs, careers, that's what they all did, they had cleaner rooms,

better jobs, we were anywhere's striving couple" (*FLLR*, 93). This shock of the ordinary is further accentuated when the narrator attempts to meet Sissel after work and finds that he cannot pick her out of a crowd of identical co-workers; he feels that they are "lost and our time was worthless" (*FLLR*, 94). This blending into a weary, worthless conformity terrifies the narrator, and he finally realizes that he must break the bonds of this ensnaring society.

Surprisingly, the act that releases the lovers from their entrapment is the killing of the mysterious creature, a rat living in the walls of their room. After they trap the animal, it charges them, and in an act of heroism that startles even himself, the narrator stands his ground and swats it with a poker, splitting the rat "from end to end like a ripe fruit" (*FLLR*, 98). This monstrous creature, however, is soon revealed as harmless, an innocent just as the lovers themselves are:

> It [the rat] rolled on its side, and from the mighty gash which ran its belly's length there obtruded and slid partially free from the lower abdomen a translucent purple bag, and inside five pale crouching shapes, their knees drawn up around their chins. As the bag touched the floor I saw a movement, the leg of one unborn rat quivered as if in hope, but the mother was hopelessly dead and there was no more for it. (*FLLR*, 98)

The creature suddenly becomes not fearsome but pathetic; Sissel, obeying a maternal instinct, pushes the sack back into the rat and then gently disposes of it. Suddenly the fears and uncertainties are destroyed. Sissel and the narrator realize that they can tangibly control their own lives; they can break free of imaginary and social restraints: they rid themselves of the creature, Sissel quits her job, and they agree to clean the room and go for a long walk.

In the closing line of the story, the narrator "press[es] the flat of my palm against her warm belly and [says], Yes" (*FLLR*, 99). No longer is the being within Sissel a "creature in the dark"; it is now a life they both willingly accept. Throughout *First Love, Last Rites* McEwan writes about characters who strive to establish viable relationships; however, most fail miserably. With "First Love, Last Rites" McEwan allows a hopefulness, an optimism, to rule. In an interview with John Haffenden, McEwan says, "I think the story is about pregnancy. The narrator has a sure sense of the girl's power as she kneels by the dead rat. I've always thought of it as an affirmative and tender story" (Haffenden, 30). With the "affirmative and tender" success of the young couple, McEwan demonstrates the positive power of relationships. With love and determination, these characters *can* escape the destructive and debilitating forces of those around them. Society can be outwitted; love can prevail.

With his first published work McEwan introduces many of his primary concerns, especially those themes circumscribing the attempts to establish and to maintain personal relationships. In this first collection most of the relations McEwan presents are bizarre, unusual, shocking. The more perceptive readers, however, see beyond the inherent shock, the morbid and forbidding images, to discover that McEwan possesses a shrewd understanding of today's world. He clearly sees and articulately portrays the ordinary, day-to-day struggles of everyday people; he captures the fears, the uncertainties, the frustrations that are so terribly prevalent in modern society. More importantly, with *First Love, Last Rites* McEwan acquaints us with a variety of interpersonal relationships, preparing for maturer explorations of similar alliances in his later works.

Chapter Three

The Momentum of Childhood Fantasy: *The Cement Garden*

In his first novel, McEwan's literature of shock is prevalent, even overwhelming at times, with the author treating us to such sensational tidbits as incest, regression, and a corpse in the cellar.[1] With this work, however, McEwan also begins to achieve an obvious maturity; the novel certainly echoes the macabre subjects of his earlier stories, but in *The Cement Garden* he also delves deeper into the psyches of his characters, progressing beyond the simple desire to shock and repulse.

Though *The Cement Garden* marks a progression away from *First Love, Last Rites,* many of the themes and motifs of the collection are echoed in the novel. For instance, the brother-sister incest in "Homemade" becomes the climactic event in *The Cement Garden*; likewise, Jack's fascination and preoccupation with masturbation are carried over from the same story. Most obviously, McEwan more fully develops the concept of the parentless commune introduced in "Last Day of Summer." Similarly, in both "Last Day" and *The Cement Garden* there is the young girl who must assume the role of mother. The idea of Tom's regression into infancy stems from the Cupboard Man's desire to return to babyhood. The ideas of the depleted wasteland of modern society and the encroaching city introduced in the story "First Love, Last Rites" are elaborated on in the novel. Henry's forced cross-dressing in "Disguises" is evident in Tom's desire to dress as a girl. Of these recurrences, McEwan says, "It seemed as though the novel was being, in a very condensed way, recapitulative of certain themes that were emerging in my fiction, and that I'd found different ways of expressing them—possibly more economical—ways of treating a messy range of themes and anxieties and putting them into a self-contained little box."[2] They can be seen, then, as reiterations, not repetitions.

When *The Cement Garden* was published by Jonathan Cape in September of 1978 (it was released in the United States by Simon & Schuster in October of the same year), McEwan was immediately confronted with accusations of plagiarism. Several reviewers noted a remarkable similarity between McEwan's first novel and Julian Gloag's *Our Mother's House* (1963); even Gloag himself jumped into the fracas, claiming that McEwan had stolen his ideas.[3] The circumstances that begin the two novels *are* similar (Gloag's story involves seven children who bury their mother in a backyard garden in order to fend off the threat of being sent to an orphanage); however, from this point in plot, the two authors diverge onto entirely separate paths. McEwan has been called upon to defend himself many times, and he does so with intensity:

> The plots did resemble each other, but then plots often do. . . . This was slightly closer than usual, and in retrospect I suppose that people were right to point it out. But they're very different books. I hadn't read Gloag's. I was annoyed at the time of publication because you work hard on a novel and suddenly the only issue is the extent to which it's like another novel. Gloag's concerns were more the supernatural and religious. I came at the subject from an entirely different route, which was partly through a wish to examine power relationships in the family and also an interest in the sexuality of young children. (Smith, 69)

With *The Cement Garden* McEwan has, in fact, relied upon what can be considered a popular story line, the familiar plot of children suddenly abandoned and isolated; this plot device occurs in such diverse works as R. M. Ballantyne's *The Coral Island* (1857), Richard Arthur Warren Hughes's *High Wind in Jamaica* (1929), Arthur Ransome's children's adventure *Swallows and Amazons* (1930), and, of course, Sir William Golding's dark and fascinating *Lord of the Flies* (1954). The concern with the savagery that lurks beneath the veneer of civilization has also been adopted by more recent writers, such as Marianne Wiggins and J. G. Ballard. Wiggins, for example, composes what many reviewers see as a feminist *Lord of the Flies* with her novel *John Dollar* (1989). In this work eight young English girls are stranded on a small island off the coast of Burma around 1920. As in *Lord of the Flies* all ideas that the girls have received from education, religion, and society are broken down, even perverted. Without guidance, they quickly revert to savagery, painting their faces, covering their bodies in feces, eventually partaking in murder and cannibalism; Monkey, one of the girls, at one point thinks, "All of them had learned to do things that they'd never done before, things that marked them out as creatures, beings in the wild."[4]

Ballard, in both *Concrete Island* and *High-Rise*, also explores the primitive inner being of modern humanity, emphasizing the violence of the urban populace. Rather than placing the action on deserted islands,

Ballard situates his novels in the heart of the city. In *Concrete Island* Robert Maitland finds himself stranded on a postmodern deserted island: a small traffic island in the middle of London, encompassed by three converging superhighways. He is forced to assume the role of a contemporary Robinson Crusoe (the archetypal survivor), scrounging for food, water, and shelter. By novel's end, Maitland has decided to remain on his island, the ruler of his own small world. In *High-Rise* the inhabitants of a high-rise apartment complex cut themselves off from the surrounding city and become embroiled in small-scale warfare between floors. Civilization collapses completely with residents dividing into primitive tribal clans and regressing into savage states (characters mark territory by urination, paint their faces with blood and lipstick, lose the ability to speak, resort to cannibalism). All these writers take great pleasure in illustrating just how close we all are to barbarism.

Like Ballard, McEwan adopts this familiar plot line, setting his novel in the midst of urban sprawl. Where other writers find savagery and violence beneath the trappings of civilization, however, McEwan discovers a vast and aching *nothingness*. Rather than murdering one another, McEwan's children simply snap rudely at each other and whine about the monotony of their isolation. In essence, McEwan's protagonists have to contend not with the extraordinariness of their situation but with the *ordinariness*. As with the characters of Ballard's novels, the children of *The Cement Garden* are overwhelmed by the sudden bizarreness of the familiar rather than the unfamiliar.

McEwan readily admits the influence of Golding's *Lord of the Flies,* stating that he discovered essences in this foreboding classic which would later serve as a structural basis for his own first novel: "What was so attractively subversive and feasible about Golding was his apparent assumption that in a child-dominated world things went wrong in a most horrible and interesting way. . . . The novel brought realism to my fantasy life . . . and years later, when I came to write a novel myself, I could not resist the momentum of my childhood fantasies nor the power of Golding's model. . . . I had no doubt that my children too would suffer from, rather than exalt in, their freedom" ("Momentum," 15B).

In both McEwan's and Golding's works children find themselves suddenly free from the constraints of a cultured, adult world; however, this newfound freedom soon becomes an unfettered beast, tearing and gnawing at their civilized nature. Golding's characters, stranded on a deserted island, rapidly succumb to being the snarling savages that reside within them. For his story, McEwan excises the exotic and uncivilized

locale, instead choosing to place his children in the midst of the populace. His characters subsequently succumb not to savagery but to the
stagnation of modern society. They become torpid, unconcerned, bored.
Indeed, both authors recognize the trappings of the British civilized society. Early in *Lord of the Flies* Jack proclaims, "We've got to have rules and
obey them. After all, we're not savages. We're English, and the English
are best at everything. So we've got to do the right things."[5] When this
veneer of an overly cultured, too civilized state dissipates so quickly,
Golding and McEwan demonstrate that the results are all the more horrifying. McEwan takes this familiar theme of abandoned and anarchic
children, however, and gives it a contemporary twist, placing his children into the midst of everyday society and forcing them to combat the
terrors of the ordinary.

Before confronting these horrors of the known, the four children—
Jack (who turns 15 during the novel), Julie (17), Sue (13), and Tom
(6)—live the humdrum life of the English lower-middle class. They
reside in a decaying house on the abandoned edge of an unnamed town.
Their relationships with their parents are also stereotypical: the father
frightens and orders them around; the mother attempts to love and nurture but spends more time struggling with her health. Soon after the
novel opens Father dies of a heart attack and is "properly" buried
(though we never see the funeral); several months later Mother dies of a
lingering illness. Suddenly orphaned, the children find themselves residing in a secluded, claustrophobic world, and at first, this self-contain-
ment is a source of joy and freedom. Soon after burying their mother in
the cellar in a block of cement, Jack relates the excitement that he and
his sisters had experienced the first and only time their parents had left
them unattended. It was only for a matter of hours, but the day was joy-
ously filled with pillow fighting, shouting, and childish abandon; to Jack
the time "seemed to occupy a whole stretch of my childhood."[6] Like the
boys in *Lord of the Flies,* McEwan's characters at first see their situation as
an adventure, as a fantasy come wonderfully to life. When Mother tells
Jack that she may have to leave for awhile, he discovers that a "sense of
freedom was tugging at my concern" (*CG,* 58). When she does indeed
die, Jack admits that "beneath my strongest feelings was a sense of
adventure and freedom" (*CG,* 79). Ultimately, Mother's death represents
for the children an embarkment for adventure.

The joy in this unparented freedom quickly dies, however; Jack soon
realizes that there "was no excitement now. The days were too long; it
was too hot; the house seemed to have fallen asleep" (*CG,* 79). Sue reads

because there is "nothing else to do" (*CG,* 107); Jack finds himself, as he says, drifting "through the house, from one room to another, sometimes surprised to find myself in my bedroom, lying on my back, staring at the ceiling, when I had intended to go out into the garden" (*CG,* 82–83). Jack, in fact, reaches such a point of stasis that "any activity I thought of disgusted me in advance" (*CG,* 83). Occasionally, there is the promise of excitement in going to town or in exploring the abandoned prefabs, but every excursion soon reverts to stifling boredom. Jack continuously finds that his "blankness return[s], and significance drain[s] from the event of my day" (*CG,* 84). He and the other children thus discover themselves free from the conventions and dictates of authority only to find nothing, an endless monotony, and they soon wish for a return to the way things were, a return to parents and order.

Because of the lethargy that quietly consumes their lives, their world, in turn, begins to slide into stagnation and deterioration. Shortly after his mother's death, Jack notices that clouds of flies infiltrate the house and that the kitchen floor is "covered with something yellow and sticky" (*CG,* 80). Combining with the filth of the house is the stench of their mother's rotting corpse. When the cement tomb cracks, the odor filters through the house, tainting everything with the smell of corruption. The reek invades their existence, reminding them constantly of what is in the cellar and of what they have done, a symbol of the monotony and lethargy that eats away at their lives. Just as there is no escape from the smell, there is no real escape from the mundaneness that ensnares them.

Their house, too, is subjected to the deterioration and corruption of their new lives. A huge misplaced monolith standing isolated and forsaken in an abandoned section of the city, it is slowly consumed by the surrounding wasteland. As Jack relates, even the architectural style makes it an anomaly: "Our house was old and large. It was built to look a little like a castle, with thick walls, squat windows and crenellations above the front door. Seen from across the road it looked like the face of someone concentrating, trying to remember" (*CG,* 28). The road they live on is "hardly a street at all; it was a road across an almost empty junkyard" (*CG,* 136); further down the road there are abandoned and burned-out prefabs, a place of "no order" (*CG,* 47). This "wasteland next door" (*CG,* 50) is what Jack has discovered his own life to be: an immense emptiness.

This world is made even more lifeless by the empty plains of cement that encompass their lives. After his heart attack, Father decides to "surround the house, front and back, with an even plane of concrete" (*CG,*

21). This self-created void, this inflicted blankness, replicates both the surrounding wasteland and Father's nature: it is a simple solution to tending the garden, and it is an extremely destructive remedy, so much so that Jack refers to it as a "fascinating violation" (*CG*, 21). The "cement garden," too, serves as an apt symbol for the new lives of the four children. They are frozen by a life of monotony and meaninglessness; just as the plane of cement smothers everything beneath it, the parentless life begins to stifle the children. It is also cement in which the children entomb their mother. Like the house, the neighborhood, the city, and the society, the tomb also proves corrupt, splitting open to allow the putrefaction within to permeate the house.

Jack, even in these most outrageous of circumstances, continually insists upon the ordinary; as he witnesses the idiosyncrasies and peculiarities of his family, his attention is constantly drawn to the banal and commonplace rather than the bizarre that abounds about him. For instance, in the confusion during his father's death, Jack notices that the "radio was playing in the kitchen" (*CG*, 24). When he battles incestuous urges while applying tanning lotion to Julie, he notes that "from the radio a piping voice was recounting racing results with malicious monotony" (*CG*, 52). More often than not, Jack's attention is drawn to grosser, baser images: watching his mother sleep, he notes that a "particular arrangement of mucus in her nose caused a faint, high-pitched sound like a sharp blade in the air" (*CG*, 57); riding into town with Derek, he observes that "there were rotting vegetables piled in the gutter" (*CG*, 112); finding Tom crying he does not try to comfort him but rather watches a "large tube of green snot [hanging] out of one nostril" (*CG*, 109). The emphasis upon such crude details assures Jack that his world is as it always was, sane if perhaps a bit strange, a bit grotesque.

This grotesque ordinariness is likewise apparent in Jack's alienation from the rest of his siblings, in Tom's regression into infancy and cross-dressing, in Jack and Julie's incestuous union. Rather than reveling in these sordid events, McEwan chooses to explore the quieter, more elusive changes: Jack's struggle to accept himself, Julie's relationship with Derek, Sue's grief for her mother. The real horrors are there but smoothly covered by a banal, ordinary facade.

This emphasis on facade is evident, too, in the family itself. Long before the children are orphaned, the family unit has begun to disintegrate. Family members wander aimlessly about the house, ignoring one another, vying for love but rarely finding it. Mother is "a quiet sort of person" (*CG*, 30) who is inept in pacifying the silent tyranny of her husband. The patriarch, a "frail, irascible obsessive man with yellowish hands and face" (*CG,* 13), is a subtle ogre who rules by maintaining a constant patter of mental abuse; he succeeds only in proving himself totally ineffectual as a father. He childishly competes with Tom for Mother's attention, and when he loses, he makes sure his son suffers for it. He also sustains a series of cruel running jokes against his family, ridiculing their weaknesses and dreams: "[His jokes were] against Sue for having almost invisible eyebrows and lashes, against Julie for her ambitions to be a famous athlete, against Tom for pissing in his bed sometimes, against Mother for being poor at arithmetic and against me for my pimples" (*CG,* 19). When Jack and Julie turn the tables on him, however, snidely remarking about his garden, Father sulks for two days, refusing to speak to either of them. At another time, he attempts to send Sue to her room during her eighth birthday party because she has apparently disregarded his meticulous and joyless preparations against "noise and chaos" (*CG,* 41). The children live, then, in an unspoken fear of their father, and when he dies (falling, appropriately, into a batch of wet cement after a second heart attack), Jack comments that "his death seemed insignificant compared to what followed" (*CG,* 13). After the body is removed, Jack erases Father from their lives, "carefully smooth[ing] away his impression in the soft, fresh concrete" (*CG,* 24). His effect, then, has been negligible.

Abandoned and alone, Jack and his siblings attempt to rebuild their lives, hoping to maintain familial unity. The situation begins as an adventure and they settle immediately into playing out a grotesque facsimile of the child's game "Mommies and Daddies"; the game, however, soon becomes distorted, even perverted, just as it does in McEwan's earlier story "Homemade." The sense of adventure quickly evaporates. Pål Gerhard Olsen says, "The children let themselves sink into a static, shadowy landscape; they wander around like sleepwalkers, without perception of time, in a different rhythm of life from the surrounding society."[7] Nevertheless, the children endure; they constantly struggle to survive in their extreme circumstances. McEwan structures part 2 of *The Cement Garden* around a psychological and sociological examination of the struggle, exploring the relationships that preexist as well as the relationships that develop among the brothers and sisters as a result of their newfound freedom.

From his opening oedipal intimation, "I did not kill my father, but I sometimes felt I had helped him on his way" (*CG,* 13), Jack portrays himself, inadvertently, as an unlikable, even despicable, character. Jack adjusts to his new life by alienating himself from his siblings; for as long as possible, he staves off the possibility of any kind of a nurturing relationship. In time, he becomes the quintessential bully, looking out for only himself. Early in the novel, as he and his father are moving bags of cement mix, Jack refuses to take more than his share of the weight even though he realizes the exertion may result in a fatal heart attack for his father. Later he avoids working in order to run to the bathroom to masturbate; while he is gone, Father suffers heart failure. Jack is well aware that his ineptitude and laziness and sexual desires are probable factors in his father's death, but he refuses to agonize over this, saying only that except for the "fact that it coincided with a landmark in my own physical growth [Jack's first ejaculation], his death seemed insignificant" (*CG*, 13).

Similarly, at the death of his mother, Jack is more upset over whether Julie will allow him to share the authority as Mother had promised him. When Julie ignores him, he begins "to cry because I felt cheated. My mother had gone without explaining to Julie what she had told me" (*CG*, 61). His cruelty and self-centeredness is also reflected in his relationships with the other siblings: he argues with Julie, antagonizes Sue, manhandles Tom. Becoming a bully is Jack's only defense; it allows him momentary reprieve in this banal existence.

In examining the character of Jack, John Calvin Batchelor, states,

> Jack is not bad. In his sincerity, his acuity, he is dangerous. Jack is quite prepared to adjust happily to a world of ruins, without fathers, without mothers, without schools, without taboos. This isn't the contrived, theatrically violent anarchy exported by the record companies. This is true anarchy. It is nowhere more stark than in the incest scene that closes the story. Jack casually goes beyond rejection of tradition. He won't recognize that any tradition exists. He has no fear whatsoever of the authorities, who, discovering the orphans' secret, come for them in the end. The state, for Jack . . . is a mere annoyance, purposeless and powerless.[8]

At best, however, the rebellion that Jack practices is only a pseudo-anarchy; he is ignorant of the fact that his acts of transgression, his breaking of tabooed barriers, his desires for alienation, are, indeed, anarchic. His assertions of dominance and independence are conducted only because they are convenient. He is never fully cognizant of an outside power, of an omnipresent government; his acts are merely those of adolescent rebellion. Subsequently, his acts of defiance are easily quelled. For instance, when he stands before the hallway mirror contemptuously spitting out curse words, he immediately ceases when Mother corrects him with "weary admonition" (*CG,* 27).

Likewise, his forsaking of personal hygiene is only a half-hearted attempt at anarchy. He abandons washing his face and hair, cutting his nails, taking baths, brushing his teeth. He takes perverse pleasure when his sisters catalog his filth, ridiculing him for his greasy hair, filthy fingernails, smelly feet, and yellow teeth. For Jack, his uncleanliness asserts his isolation, separates him further from Julie, Sue, and Tom; mainly, though, he enjoys the sense of defiance, the nascent sense of anarchy. Later, when Mother's smell begins to saturate the house, Jack thinks that it is coming from him and subsequently abandons his pretense of rebellion, thoroughly cleansing himself. His attempt at anarchy is, consequently, short-lived and purposeless.

A consequence of Jack's self-alienation is his loneliness. Early in the novel he admits, "I had no close friends at school" (*CG,* 26); before and after the death of his parents he lives the life of a loner, effacing himself from the interruptions and annoyances of other people. After Mother's death his isolation becomes exclusion, as Julie and Sue increasingly choose to avoid him, to omit him from their conversations, their activities, their lives. At Mother's death, the sisters seek only to console each other; Jack reaches out to share their sorrow, but "neither of them noticed" (*CG,* 62). Instead, the girls draw closer together, sharing secrets, discussing boys, dressing Tom. Jack's isolation then becomes more of a burden than an act of defiance, and he begins to make conscious efforts to be included; however, with the outsider Derek's arrival, he becomes even more abandoned, saying at one point that he feels "isolated from everyone I knew" (*CG,* 107). He is both pitiful and pitiable.

Also characteristic of Jack's solitariness is his obsession with masturbation. It is yet another meaningless part of his daily ritual, but Jack is so fascinated with the act that he calls his first ejaculation a "landmark in my own physical growth" (*CG,* 13). His mother chastises him for this self-abuse, telling him, "Every time . . . you do that, it takes two pints of blood to replace it" (*CG,* 35). Later Jack even dreams that his mother has returned to scold him about "drubbing" (*CG,* 106). Ultimately, Jack abandons the practice only when it, too, becomes overly banal and mundane, even his sexual desires falling prey to the spiteful monotony of his world.

Jack's only true interaction with the outside world occurs when Derek takes him to the pool hall; however, Jack soon realizes that this is not an invitation to be included but a ploy by Derek to obtain information

about Julie and the strange circumstances of his family. When he introduces Jack to the other patrons, Derek never uses Jack's name; he thus
becomes no one, a nonentity. He achieves the ultimate effacement.
Ironically, it is also during this scene that Jack's true, human emotions
surface; as Derek and the other boys tease him, a single tear of frustration, humiliation, and anger rolls down his face. This is the first time in
the novel that McEwan allows us to feel sympathy for the narrator; with
this single tear, which he angrily snatches away, Jack becomes a sympathetic figure. He is no longer the cruel and antagonistic bully; rather, he
becomes an ordinary 15-year-old boy, struggling to cope with and to
survive in this lonely and suddenly terrifying world.

Jack's difficulty in coping with his world is also evident in his relationship with Julie. Around her he is little more than a hormonal ball of
confusion. Although the two put forth a cool facade, the novel is fraught
with sexual tension. As angry and annoyed as Jack gets with Julie, he is
ever aware of his maddening desire for her. Concerning this sexuality,
McEwan says, "I had an idea that in the nuclear family the kind of forces
that are being suppressed—the oedipal, incestuous forces—are also
paradoxically the very forces which keep the family together. So if you
remove the controls, you have a ripe anarchy in which the oedipal and
the incestuous are the definitive emotions" (Hamilton, 21). Though Julie
is Jack's sister, she also acts as a mother to the family; subsequently, in
the relationship that forms between them, McEwan creates, as he
explains, a "situation in which the oedipal and the incestuous are identical" (Hamilton, 21).

Jack's sexual awareness of Julie is initiated with a "game" that he and
his sisters played when they were younger. To escape the droning arguments of their parents, the three children would lock themselves in
Julie's bedroom and explore Sue's body:

> The game was that Julie and I were scientists examining a specimen from
> outer space. We spoke in clipped Germanic voices as we faced each other
> across [Sue's] naked body. . . . I longed to examine my older sister but the
> game did not allow for that.
>   . . . We stroked [Sue's] back and thighs with our fingernails. We
> looked into her mouth and between her legs with a torch and found the
> little flower made of flesh.
>   "Vot do you think of zis, Herr Doctor?" Julie stroked it with a
> moistened finger and a small tremor ran along Sue's bony spine. I
> watched closely. I moistened my finger and slid it over Julie's.

"Nothing serious," she said at last, and closed the slit with her finger and thumb. "But ve vill votch for further developments, *ja?*" Sue begged us to go on. Julie and I looked at each other knowingly, knowing nothing.

"It's Julie's turn," I said.

"No," she said as always. "It's your turn."

. . . "Out of the question. . . . That's the end of it." (*CG*, 15–16)

Not surprisingly, after the game Jack routinely runs to the bathroom to relieve himself by masturbating, an impotent and unfulfilling task.

Jack, guiltlessly, becomes obsessed with his older sister; he is constantly aware of her growing body, her budding sexuality. At his fifteenth birthday party, Julie's cartwheel, which unashamedly exposes her body, sends Jack into a paroxysm of sexual elation: "In a confused, wild moment I found myself on my feet singing 'Greensleeves' in a trembling, passionate tenor" (*CG*, 45). Later, he again experiences the same uncontrollable excitement when he applies tanning lotion to Julie's barely clothed body: "I rubbed the cream on as quickly as I could, with my eyes half closed. I felt hot and sick in the stomach" (*CG*, 52). Once again, urges become overpowering, and Jack has to run to the bathroom to release himself. He thus finds himself in a perpetual entanglement of sexual desires, a hormonal chaos. He never, however, experiences guilt over his incestuous yearnings; rather, he finds his lust a natural, ordinary urge. To him, there is nothing of which to be ashamed.

Julie, in turn, is at first repulsed by Jack's disregard for hygiene and his hard-headed and bullying demeanor, but she, too, eventually succumbs to the need and desire that grows between them. Slowly, even teasingly, she acknowledges this new awareness: she kisses Jack "lightly on [the] mouth" (*CG*, 90), playfully presses an imaginary knife against his groin, exchanges light but not quite innocent caresses with him in bed. Ultimately, she chooses Jack over Derek, willingly giving herself and her virginity not to her boyfriend but to her brother.

When Jack and Julie engage in intercourse, the oedipal circle is completed: Jack has already admitted to having had an indirect hand in his father's death, and now he beds the family's matriarchal figure. The consummation is, however, never seen by the siblings as unnatural or immoral. Their lovemaking is consummated through gentle and curious caresses, with love and concern, in openness and innocence. Michael J. Adams, in *Postmodern Fiction: A Bio-Bibliographic Guide,* says, "Incest becomes little more than a desperate need to share an experience, any

experience, with someone."[9] The lovemaking, then, is a completely positive experience; not only is the episode gently and lovingly conveyed,
but all the sordidness, all the degradation traditionally associated with
such an act is entirely omitted.[10] Disgust and repulsion are reactions of
the outside world. Jack and Julie, with the secret that binds them and
the nothingness that incessantly surrounds them, have no one else but
each other. Their shared intimacy is seen as "sick" and unnatural only by
Derek, an outsider. McEwan again presents a taboo subject in such a
way that it can be viewed as an act of the ordinary; incest in this novel is
nothing more than a need to share, a need to love.

Though Jack is the most unnerved and unnerving of the children, his
siblings are far from the usual adolescents. Julie, for example, is the
anomaly in her family: she is daring and independent, confident and
beautiful. Early in the novel Jack describes her as having the "deep look
of some rare wild animal" (CG, 15); later he mentions that she is "one of
a handful of daring girls at school who wore starched white petticoats
beneath their skirts to fill out and make them swirl when they turned on
their heel. She wore stockings and black knickers, strictly forbidden"
(CG, 25). Julie's feral nature is obviously an attraction for Jack; whereas
he must strain to create a sense of anarchy, Julie's rebellion is innate and
true. Likewise, her self-confidence is instinctive. Jack says that she "had
the quiet strength and detachment and lived in the separate world of
those who are, and secretly know they are, exceptionally beautiful" (CG,
29). Julie, in many ways, stands alone in her family, and because of this
position she quite naturally falls into the role of authority when her parents die.

This role of motherhood is forced upon Julie, but she willingly, and
naturally, accepts the part. She alone is privy to the seriousness of
Mother's illness; aware of the state of her health, Mother places her
eldest daughter in charge, knowing that she is the most responsible, the
most capable of holding the family together. Julie is comfortable in her
new position; however, for a while, Jack resents her new power, saying
that he "suspected she was exploiting the position, that she enjoyed
ordering me about" (CG, 50). Only reluctantly does he eventually accept
Julie's authority, realizing that she is indeed the new stabilizing force in
their family.

While Julie becomes a matriarchal figure for all her siblings, it is Tom
who forces her to assume completely the role of mother; he makes it
quite clear that without her maternal pampering he could not survive in
this new world. As Michael Adams says, McEwan uses these newly

forged maternal relationships to "satirize the male tendency to make women into mothers to get attention from them. . . . His point seems to be that the family roles people assume are simply that: roles" (Adams, 460). Julie deduces early that all Tom really wants or needs is attention. One evening when Tom is acting "particularly demanding," Julie forces him into a bath, his pajamas, and bed before five o'clock; Tom becomes "utterly subdued," as Julie reveals that "that's what he wanted" (*CG,* 80). Likewise, it is Julie who recognizes and promotes Tom's regression into infancy. Out of necessity, Julie becomes an instant mother; out of love, she manages to hold the family together just a bit longer.

Sue is the most introverted of the family. In describing her, Jack frequently portrays her as an alien: in the sex game she is the "specimen from outer space" (*CG,* 15). Later he says that she "really did look like a girl from another planet" (*CG,* 30). In her role as the "alien," Sue often separates herself from the other members of the family. She is the only one who cries at Father's death; likewise, she is the sole sibling who truly seems anguished over Mother's death, several times crying out her grief behind closed doors. Sue alone spends time beside the tomb. She keeps her mother's memory alive by writing letters to her, telling her of the days' events.[11] Sue also consciously isolates herself, choosing to lock herself in her room with her books and writing tablets. Her response is normal grief; she struggles to accept the loss of her mother and to survive in her new life. In many ways Sue is not the "alien" but the most conventional, the most normal, of the four children.

Tom, the youngest of the four children, is Mother's child from the beginning; he continually whines for her attention, constantly attempts to stay near her, throwing tantrums when he is forced to leave her side. He is the quintessential victim: "Tom was just the kind to be picked on. He was small for a six-year-old, and frail. He was pale, a little jug-eared, had an idiotic grin and black hair which grew in a thick, lopsided fringe. Worse, he was clever in a niggling, argumentative way—the perfect playground victim" (*CG,* 52). Subsequently, when he is beaten up at school, Tom decides that it would be easier to be a girl because "you don't get hit when you're a girl" (*CG,* 54). Julie and Sue are only too happy to comply with Tom's wishes, dressing him in skirt, wig, and ribbons. Jack, of course, is shocked and outraged at this transvestism.

Along with Tom's transformation and Jack's consequent repugnance, a subtle feminism begins to appear in McEwan's work, a theme he continues to explore with greater intensity in later fiction. Jack sees Tom's desire as something "idiotic" and "humiliating," and he thinks that his sisters support Tom only "so [they] can have a laugh" (*CG*, 55). To Jack, this gender transformation is unnatural. Julie's response to her brother's outrage pinpoints one paradox of patriarchal culture: "Girls can wear jeans and cut their hair short and wear shirts and boots because it's okay to be a boy; for girls it's like promotion. But for a boy to look like a girl is degrading, according to you, because secretly you believe that being a girl is degrading" (*CG*, 55–56). The representative of this patriarchal society, Jack, not surprisingly, is shocked when Tom's playmates unhesitatingly accept his new guise; in fact, Jack comments, "They did not even seem to notice" (*CG*, 95). Tom, in turn, enthusiastically adopts his new role, dressing often as a little girl, even crying by putting "his knuckles in his eyes the way little girls do on biscuit tin lids" (*CG*, 109). His cross-dressing is quite different from Henry's experience in "Disguises"; Tom dons his feminine guise willingly, happily, enjoying the new freedom that it gives him. Again, a societal taboo is embraced as ordinary; in time, Tom's transformation is accepted as something quite natural.

Far more disturbing is Tom's slow but sure regression into infancy. With his mother gone, Tom demands the protection and attention of Julie. When Julie does baby him, Tom's "eyes grew larger and farther apart, his mouth slackened and he seemed to sink inside himself" (*CG*, 123). He literally surrenders to an infantile state. At first he simply needs the assurance of a mother figure; soon, however, he slips further into an infantile state, sucking his thumb, wearing a bib, sleeping in his old baby bed, speaking in a new baby voice, wailing and crying for attention, even smearing food over his face. Like Julie's bossiness, Sue's isolation, and Jack's alienation, Tom's regression is a defense mechanism. Through it he achieves a life of little effort and no responsibility; it is the easiest way for him to escape this new and confusing life. Like his cross-dressing, his infantile behavior provides a safe haven.

Jack, too, experiences fleeting desires to regress to a less troublesome age. Near the end of the novel Jack dreams that he is again an infant, wailing for his parents to carry him. In his present state he has discovered that his authority-free life is not the adventure he had once envisioned; he realizes that he wants and *needs* parents (or any authority figure) again to carry and to guide him through his youth. Later, sitting in the baby cot with Tom, he thinks, "I liked it here in Tom's bed. Everything I had just heard did not matter to me. I felt like raising the cot's side and sitting all night. The last time I had slept here everything had been watched over and arranged. . . . I gave up the cot to Sue . . .

when I was two, but lying in it now it was familiar to me—its salty, clammy smell, the arrangement of the bars, an enveloping pleasure in being tenderly imprisoned" (*CG,* 146). Regression is, thus, an escape. Jack realizes that freedom is not fun and adventuresome: relief can come only through the agency of someone who could watch over and arrange his life, destroying his independence and anarchy but freeing him from the banal existence in which he now lives.

Derek, Julie's older and seemingly more cultured boyfriend, wishes to be the watcher and arranger for this unseemly family, to play Daddy to Julie's Mother. When he invades the household, he presents himself as cool sagacity: he nods solemnly, "understanding everything" (*CG,* 102). He is for them the representative of the outside, adult world; however, he turns out to be only a shallow facade of this world, more interested in the flash of his life and in seducing Julie. Jack resents his intrusion because it is an infringement upon his authority-free world. Primarily, however, Jack views Derek as a rival suitor; although he and Julie often have trouble getting along, Jack nonetheless thinks of her as his possession, and he sees Derek's interference as an attempt to "steal" her away. More important than this, however, is that Derek—with his sports car, his fancy clothes, his aloof and suave demeanor—represents a direct contrast to the slovenly, unclean narrator. Jack realizes that he will be forever excluded, forever in shadow, in the presence of this outsider.

Derek's arrival also coincides with the crack in the tomb. He soon discovers the secret in the cellar, but rather than reporting the children, he chooses to repair the fissure. What upsets Derek is not what the children have done with Mother's body, but, as Julie tells Jack, the fact that "we don't let him in on it" (*CG,* 147). In McEwan's world of the grotesque-as-ordinary, the outsider, like the four children, only wishes to be included, to be a part of a sustaining relationship. Julie says, "He wants to be one of the family, you know, big smart daddy" (*CG,* 148). When the children refuse to let him become a part of their world, Derek retaliates by bringing the outside world—in the guise of Authority—crashing down upon them.

Near the end of *The Cement Garden* Jack several times describes his experience as dreamlike, as something imagined: thinking of the tomb he says, "Often what was in the cellar did not seem real enough to keep secret. When we were not actually down there looking at the trunk it was as if we were asleep" (*CG,* 140–41). When Derek leaves the room after discovering Jack and Julie making love, Jack thinks that "it seemed as though we had imagined him" (*CG,* 150); a few minutes later he and

Julie "seemed to wake up" (*CG*, 152). When the outside world invades—in the forms of slamming car doors, hurried footsteps, and a "revolving blue light . . . spinning pattern[s] on the wall" (*CG*, 153)[12]— Julie picks up Tom, whispering to him, "Wasn't that a lovely sleep?" (*CG*, 153). With the entry of Authority, the dream is dispersed; the children are forced to awaken and to rejoin the world of controllers and orphanages—they are forced to join the world of the adult. Referring to the final scene, Sandra Martin says that "McEwan smashes the anarchic metaphor he has so skillfully created and jolts his readers back to the safe territory of policemen and social workers. McEwan has gone soft, a limpness that is both frustrating and surprising for readers accustomed to the frightful progression of his earlier fiction. It's like punk rock sung by Perry Como."[13] Contrary to what Martin asserts, it is McEwan's decision *not* to resort to the literature of shock so evident in *First Love, Last Rites* that displays his maturation as a writer. Shock is overt in *The Cement Garden*; with the conclusion, however, McEwan realizes that there is no need in being lurid. His assessment of the contemporary world has been pointedly and satisfyingly made.

Pål Gerhard Olsen calls *The Cement Garden* a "repulsive novel . . . an unpleasant book" (Olsen, 41). With this first novel McEwan continues his literature of shock, fascinating and repulsing us with incest, dysfunctional families, infantile regression, and decaying corpses. As such, the stifling, self-contained world of *The Cement Garden* mirrors the larger, more suffocating existence of modern society. In this world cities collapse into wastelands, families fall apart, children are abandoned. More often than not, though, the key to survival is discovered in relationships. Tom survives by reverting to infancy, discovering a world wherein his every need and want is satisfied by his siblings. Jack and Julie discover each other, reaching out to share their need, their loneliness, their love. In presenting these inordinate, even taboo, relationships, McEwan offers no moralizing voice of censure; rather, these alliances are presented from the viewpoint of the ordinary. Olsen also states that because of its subject matter, because it *is* repulsive and unpleasant, *The Cement Garden* is "an important and necessary book" (Olsen, 41). In his next works McEwan abandons the disturbing and angst-filled world of the adolescent in love and trouble, focusing instead on the world of the adult, discovering it to be as repulsive, as grotesque.

Chapter Four

Gorillas, Mannequins, and Other Lovers: *In Between the Sheets*

In his second collection of stories, McEwan once again grabs with a stranglehold: we encounter such remarkable characters as an ape in love with his human owner; a woman who orders her date to urinate on himself; a millionaire who falls in love with a mannequin; a man who is shown a ghastly but permanent cure for the clap. McEwan's literature of shock is as obviously prevalent as it was in *First Love, Last Rites* and *The Cement Garden*; however, also just as apparent is the continued maturation in his writing and themes. With *In Between the Sheets* McEwan turns his attention from initiation rites—from the adolescent in angst and anguish—to a closer scrutiny of adult relationships.

Released by Jonathan Cape in January 1978, *In Between the Sheets* was McEwan's second published work (in the United States, the collection was published as McEwan's third work, with Simon & Schuster releasing it in August 1979, almost a year after the publication of the American edition of *The Cement Garden*). This collection of stories serves as a transition between his earlier, more visceral writings and his later, more percipient works. This collection overtly combines a literature of shock with a more ideological study of relationships and society.

As the collection's title suggests, the focus of all seven stories is sex, or, as one reviewer phrased it, the "perplexities of the heart, the grimy desperations of the groin."[1] In his various representations and explorations of the carnal escapades of contemporary society, McEwan discovers not pleasure and fulfillment but—as Dennis Vannatta calls it—a "mundane horror."[2] McEwan sees no genuine reprieve from the doldrums of contemporary existence in sexuality. Unlike, say, D. H. Lawrence, who sees sex and the sensual urge to assimilate and unite with another as an emollient and healer, as, in fact, a virtual life force, McEwan sees sex as a complicator, more a hindrance, at times an annoyance. It is used as a weapon, a power play, an objectifier. Rarely does it provide comfort and solace. A legion of contemporary writers agrees with McEwan. For example, when the narrator of Josephine Hart's

Damage surrenders to his carnal desires, it leads to destruction and dev-
astation and the death of his son. Martin Amis's John Self, of *Money,* is
constantly humiliated, injured, and abandoned by his sexual partners, at
one point awakening to find his back tattooed with high heel pock-
marks, the result of a disgruntled potential partner. The characters of
Steven Berkoff's *Gross Intrusion* seek sex to stave off loneliness but
encounter only horror—one, for instance, discovering that he has been
masturbating his father, another apparently being raped to death in his
first homosexual encounter. This complexity of sexual politicking is most
absurdly (and quiet dark humoredly) presented in Will Self's *Cock and
Bull* (1992), a pair of novellas: *Cock* introduces a woman who sprouts a
penis, while *Bull* presents a man who awakens to discover a vagina
growing in the crook of his knee. Both stories attack the society-based
predetermination of gender-based sex roles; both characters, simultaneously thrilled and horrified by their sexual acquisitions, struggle—and
fail—with their new sexual roles. Sex in the contemporary scene, it
seems, is a goal desperately sought but seldom satisfactorily or *safely* consummated. Like their contemporary counterparts, McEwan's characters
frequently experience failure: what they seek is the rhythmic to and fro
of natural union; what they encounter, however, is rejection, confusion,
battery, even emasculation. Almost never does sex lead to contented fulfillment.

With *In Between the Sheets* McEwan's female characters achieve the
power in relationships; no longer the perpetual victim (as are such characters as Maisie in "Solid Geometry," Jane in "Butterflies," or Connie in
"Homemade"), the female becomes aggressive, self-reliant, domineering.
In these stories, men constantly struggle to come to terms with the
women of their lives, and, frequently, they prove to be far less adept, far
less potent than their female counterparts. These male characters too
often believe that they are the controllers, the manipulators within their
relationships, only to discover that, all along, they have been the controlled, the manipulated ones. In examining these sexual roles, Dennis
Vannatta finds that McEwan's female characters "regularly mutilate the
men physically, emotionally, materially—denying their existence as
meaningful human beings, depriving them of their children. . . .
McEwan's men are unable to cope with adult women and feel their
strongest love—sometimes sexual, sometimes not—for daughters or
daughter figures, young, relatively submissive, unjaded, respectful"
(Vannatta, 143). McEwan allows, then, the fearsome otherness of the

female to emerge; she is no longer the stereotypical submissive creature but, rather, the controller of her own individuality and relationships.

As the male and female characters battle for control and fulfillment, McEwan continues to emphasize the importance of relationships; although the majority of the characters fail to establish any sort of viable alliance, they nonetheless realize that these relationships are essential for worthwhile life. McEwan uses several approaches in presenting these various sexual conquests, entanglements, and oddities. With "Reflections of a Kept Ape" and "Dead as They Come" he enters into a literature of the absurd. In both tales he presents an implausible and parodic example of male-female relations. In "Psychopolis" and "Two Fragments" the city becomes a metaphor for the wasteland of contemporary society, preying on individuals, affecting their relationships. Finally, the remaining stories—"Pornography," "To and Fro," and "In Between the Sheets"—more explicitly examine the complexities (often horrifying, occasionally wondrous and magical) of relationships.

From Abnormality to Absurdity

With "Reflections of a Kept Ape" and "Dead as They Come," McEwan reaches to absurdist extremes (overstepping even the unreal boundaries established in "Solid Geometry"). Both tales are presented as parodic metaphors of the relationships between men and women; both are hilarious glimpses into absurd lives. Like the Latin American magical realists, McEwan does not situate his absurdities and unrealities within experimental form; rather, he examines his subjects from the viewpoint of the ordinary, the commonplace. Consequently, there is no need to explain how an ape has learned to speak and act as a human, there is no need to explain why a seemingly intelligent man has fallen in love with a store-front dummy. In essence, the ordinary becomes absurd, the absurd becomes ordinary.[3]

Originally published in the *New Republic* in November 1976, "Reflections of a Kept Ape" presents a civilized, intelligent, very cultured ape who maudlinly laments the end of his affair with his owner, Sally Klee. In his romantic delusions, the narrator becomes an emblem of man at his most bestial and pretentious.[4] McEwan makes no effort to hide the narrator's monkey-like tendencies; he is, indeed, pure ape, behaving and moving just as one would expect an ape to behave and move. He searches for nits in Sally's hair, scampers up the hat tree to retrieve a scarf, gathers papers with his feet, arranges himself on the chaise lounge in "an attitude of simian preoccupation."[5] Simultaneously, though, he thinks in an extraordinarily intelligent and cultured manner; he is as literate and informed as any liberal arts major. He imitates Uncle Toby's whistling of "Lillibullero," comments on Balzac's coffee-drinking habits, alludes to Browning's "My Last Duchess," compares Sally's shrieks to Edvard Munch's "famous woodcut" (*Sheets*, 36). In fact, the ape's allusiveness knows no bounds: he opens his narrative with a detailed description of the odor of his urine; we discover later that these are, verbatim, the opening lines to Sally Klee's novel. Concerning this "apeness," Julian Moynahan states that "the serious flaw in [the story] is that the narrator's apehood matters scarcely at all. Most of the time he sounds like a timorous and depressed kept *homo sapiens*."[6] Here, though, is McEwan's point: the narrator's apehood should *not* matter because, in essence, he is neither merely ape nor merely man; rather, he is *scorned lover*. The absurdity is peripheral. McEwan's purpose is the exposure of the sexual politics of *human* relations.

As the ape reminisces about his affair with Sally Klee, he paints a portrait of idyllic romance; for him, theirs was the perfect love. When he was not congratulating himself on his "elevation from pet to lover" (*Sheets*, 37), the ape imagines himself in the coveted position of husband: "I would teach myself to hold a pen. I would be man-about-the-house, scaling drainpipes with uxorious ease to investigate the roof gutters, suspending myself from light fittings to decorate the ceiling. Down to the pub in the evening with my husband credentials to make new friends, invent a name for myself in order to bestow it on my wife, take up wearing slippers about the house, and perhaps even socks and shoes outside" (*Sheets*, 38). As the two begin to explore their newfound love, their extreme differences are often noted but easily dismissed: "The long prelude of mutual exploration, she counting my teeth with her ball-point pen, I searching in vain for nits in her copious hair. Her playful observations on the length, color, texture of my member, my fascination with her endearingly useless toes and coyly concealed anus" (*Sheets*, 39).

This is not ape and human, the narrator emphasizes, but male and female, lover and lover. Sex, at first, is also a new pleasure; however, the novelty of the act soon wears thin for Sally, and it subsequently becomes the element that breaks them apart: "it was not long before my tirelessness began to oppress Sally Klee, nor was it long before she complained that the friction of our bodies brought her out in a rash, and that my 'alien seed' . . . was aggravating her thrush. This and my 'bloody gibbering on the bed' precipitated the end of the affair, the happiest eight days of my life" (*Sheets,* 40). At two and a half years old, the narrator is the epitome of innocence; although initiated into the realm of human love and sex, he remains innocent in the rituals involving affairs of the heart.

Reciting the causes of their breakup, the narrator attempts to justify himself, explaining that he had his own reasons for "quitting those sheets" (*Sheets,* 34). He was, he insists, involving himself too deeply in Sally's creative problems. Two and a half years previous, Sally, a writer by profession, had published a novel. Although Sally and the narrator insist on referring to this work as her *first* novel, she has, nonetheless, run into an impenetrable case of writer's block. After ages of agonizing over a blank page, Sally finally begins to type. Unfortunately, desperate to create, desperate to break through her block, she helplessly begins to rewrite, word for word, her first novel. Staring at the uselessly repeated pages, the ape wonders, "Was art then nothing more than a wish to appear busy? Was it nothing more than a fear of silence, of boredom, which the merely reiterative rattle of the typewriter's keys was enough to allay? In short, having crafted one novel, would it suffice to write it again, type it out with care, page by page?" (*Sheets,* 45). For Sally Klee, the writer, repetition is the greatest of sins; she loathes the reiteration, but faced with the admission of creative failure, she returns to her first novel, repeating a formula that she knows will work. For the narrator, the lover, repetition is seen as a renewal, the recurrence—and, hopefully, rejuvenation—of the love they once shared. This repetition, however, ultimately offers neither solace nor salvation; it is as impotent as their now defunct relationship.

As the story closes, the narrator recalls a scene from his youth: "Standing here directly behind Sally Klee I am struck by a vivid memory from my earliest infancy. I am staring at my mother, who squats with her back to me, and then, for the first time in my life, I see past her shoulder as through a mist pale, spectral figures beyond the plate glass, pointing and mouthing silently" (*Sheets,* 48). His memory of the zoo is self-conscious, almost subconscious, and serves more appropriately as a metaphor *not* for his apehood but for his imprisonment—by love, by relationships, by life. Although no longer restrained by bars, the narrator is, nonetheless, just as immobile, a prisoner of a forbidden and unrequited love. Like so many of McEwan's male characters of *In Between the Sheets,* the ape is rejected and abandoned, powerless to obtain the love, the relationship for which he so desperately yearns.

Like "Reflections of a Kept Ape," "Dead as They Come" (originally published in *Bananas* in 1975) is a satirical look at the relations between men and women. This time the narrator is a 45-year-old millionaire who becomes enamored of a store-front mannequin. In loving a nonbeing, he succeeds in finding the perfectly submissive, perfectly coy mistress. As he does in "Kept Ape," McEwan presents the story in the guise of the ordinary; never does the narrator question the absurdity of his actions.[7]

The narrator is an egotistical millionaire, concerned only with the fast-paced business world. Several times describing himself as "a man in a hurry," he emphasizes that he has no time for the trivialities of love and courtships. He, therefore, creates the ideal affair, avoiding the rituals of love.

Even though he names his mannequin Helen, the narrator is captivated not by her beauty but, rather, by her "quiet intensity" (*Sheets*, 80), her rapt gazes, her unfaltering attention. Helen is, thus, the projection of his desires: she has no control outside of what the narrator wishes or commands. She is the perfect *object*, just another piece in his many collections. Consumed with materialism, the narrator can only judge something according to its net worth; it is the acquisition and ownership of any item—no matter how vacuous—that has meaning. When he first discovers Helen in a store window, he says, "I wished to possess her. And to possess her it seemed I would have to buy her" (*Sheets*, 75). He succeeds, then, not only in completely materializing love but also in reducing human interaction to the level of commodity exchange.

In his brief "relationship" with Helen, the narrator is also the complete chauvinist. His view of women is consistently crude, patronizing. For example, he says, "I do not wish to be with women who have an urge to talk when we've finished our coupling. I want to lie still in peace and clarity. Then I want to put my shoes and socks on and comb my hair and go about my business. I prefer silent women who take their pleasure with apparent indifference" (*Sheets*, 75). In his relationship with Helen, then, he finds not only the perfect companion but also the ideal sexual partner: she is both virgin and "demanding lover" (*Sheets*, 80). In turn, the narrator describes himself as a superb lover. Nevertheless, their lovemaking, like the whole of their relationship, is not based on mutuality. In a relationship in which only one is allowed to dominate, McEwan indicates, there can be no sharing, no compromise; whatever is achieved is seen only in relation to the narrator's authority, the narrator's prowess.

Not surprisingly, the narrator, by this point clearly insane, soon surmises deception; he is sure that Helen and Brian, his chauffeur, are involved in an affair. He begins to see Helen's infidelity in every gaze, every gesture. This suspicion soon develops into a raging paranoia; he can hear "between each throb of the electronic tones [of the telephone] Helen in the bedroom gasping with mounting pleasure" (*Sheets,* 90). These mental doubts soon take a physical toll; the narrator begins physically to deteriorate along with the relationship:

> Essentially I was a disintegrating man, I was coming apart. . . . My hair began to loose itself from my scalp. My mouth filled with cankers and my breath had about it the stench of a decaying carcass. . . . I nurtured a vicious boil in my anus. . . . Once I was a man hurrying by a shop window and glancing carelessly in, now I was a man with bad breath, boils and cankers. I was coming apart. (*Sheets,* 90–91)

Unable to cope with this inanimate infidelity, the narrator finds himself driven beyond sanity; to avenge himself (as well as to assert his dominance), he rapes Helen while simultaneously strangling her to death. He notes that he "came as she died" (*Sheets,* 92), and with a last chauvinistic barb, he notes that "her death was a moment of intense pleasure to her" (*Sheets,* 91). Unable to survive in a world not inundated with commodities, the narrator surrounds himself with an array of objects; unable to cope with the true nature of love, he chooses a mannequin, a false woman, as his lover and companion. The narrator soon discovers that even the most perfectly submissive woman is not the ideal woman; consequently, he remains isolated in a world of unlovable objects.

Tom Paulin describes "Dead as They Come" as "a parable which traces all the stages of a non-relationship."[8] Essentially, the alliances portrayed in both "Dead as They Come" and "Reflections of a Kept Ape" can be viewed as nonrelationships; likewise, they both serve as parodic examples for relationships between men and women. The ape represents the male figure at his most pretentious, at his most bestial, deeply concerned about his failure as a lover but incapable of remedying the situation; the narrator of "Dead" is the ultimate male chauvinist, concerned only with his prowess as a lover and as a master. Both figures fail resoundingly in their efforts to establish healthy relationships. The stories present situations that are obviously absurd, obviously unrealistic; through absurdity and parody, however, McEwan demonstrates that the establishing of viable relationships can result only from the efforts of both partners. If this attempt at equality fails or is lacking from the outset, the result is a nonrelationship, and the participants remain only alienated *individuals*—a lovesick gorilla, an insane millionaire—desperately searching for love in all the wrong places.

Fragmented Cities, Fragmented Lives

McEwan pictures the city as half Oz, a place filled with wonder and puzzles, and half Sodom, a place of depravation and sexual deviance. Furthermore, his cities are not situated within any particular nation, nor are they limited to any specific time period; rather, they are universal and timeless. Looking out over modern-day Los Angeles, the narrator of "Psychopolis" thinks, "Everywhere on earth is the same" (*Sheets,* 135). Characters strive to survive in these looming metropolises, but frequently they are overwhelmed. The city becomes a tangible entity, encroaching upon and interfering with individual lives and relationships (sometimes slowly and surely, as in "First Love, Last Rites" and *The Cement Garden*; sometimes horribly, vengefully, as in *The Comfort of Strangers*). The city is no longer simply a "terrible secret" (as the narrator in "Last Day of Summer" phrases it) but a teeming, angst-invested reality. It is this ominous variant of the city that is prevalent in both "Psychopolis" and "Two Fragments: March 199–."

Influenced by a brief visit to Los Angeles, McEwan wrote "Psychopolis" (originally published in the November 1977 issue of *New Review*) to capture what he saw as the chaos and endless sprawl of the modern metropolis. Chiefly, McEwan re-creates Los Angeles by exploring the bizarre and eccentric relationships established by characters who are starved for affection and companionship. The city itself is variously described as "a city of narcissists" (*Sheets,* 129), as "psychotic, totally psychotic" (*Sheets,* 132), as a "shithole" filled with "greedy devourers of each other's privacy" (*Sheets,* 134), as a "vast, fragmented city without a center, without citizens, a city that existed only in the mind, a nexus of change or stagnation in individual lives" (*Sheets,* 152). Because of its psychotic and schizophrenic nature, the city too often alienates and abandons its inhabitants; individuals are left helpless, purposeless, lifeless. Likewise, paradoxical to the "insanity of its size" (*Sheets,* 138), the city often isolates its citizens, leaving them alone and bored. Terence, a friend of the narrator, comments, "People here . . . live so far from each other. Your neighbor is someone forty minutes' car ride away, and when you finally get together you're out to wreck each other with the frenzy of having been alone" (*Sheets,* 134). The narrator also comments upon the isolation and extreme boredom that he experiences in the city. Like Jack in *The Cement Garden,* he finds himself wandering purposelessly through his house, combatting the oppressive banality of the city:

> I ate breakfast because I dared not be without the activity. I spent ten minutes cleaning my teeth knowing that when I finished I would have to choose something else. . . . I went from room to room without really intending to, sometimes surprised to find that I was back in the kitchen again fiddling with the cracked plastic handle of the wall can-opener. I went into the living room and spent twenty minutes drumming with my fingers on the back of a book. . . . I sat on the toilet a long time and decided then not to move till I had planned what to do next. I remained there over two hours, staring at my knees till they lost their meaning as limbs. . . . I commenced to prowl from room to room once more, and then, towards the middle of the evening, I fell asleep in an armchair, exhausted with myself. (*Sheets,* 135–37)

In the huge and crowded mass of this megalopolis, people are constantly forced into profound loneliness, desolation;[9] consequently, they so desperately ache for companionship, for intimate contact with other human beings, they often find themselves participants in unusual and extreme relationships.

At the party that closes the story, Terence says, "There will always be problems between men and women and everyone suffers in some way" (*Sheets,* 145). This philosophy is readily evident in all the stories of *In Between the Sheets.* In "Psychopolis" such elements as bondage and humiliation become primary factors in the relationships. The narrator comments that he and Mary, one of the first persons he encounters in Los Angeles, become lovers on the same evening that they meet. Shortly afterwards, Mary asks to be chained to the narrator's bed for an entire weekend. The event is, for the narrator, surprisingly unstimulating; he quickly becomes bored, and, similar to the way in which he staves off the boredom of the city, he wanders purposelessly from room to room. "The idea of asking her if she wished to be set free," he says, "seemed ludicrous, and simply setting her free without her permission was terrifying" (*Sheets,* 127). The incident, then, is pointless; he admits that he does not know whether this was "an ideological or psychosexual matter" (*Sheets,* 127), and Mary never mentions their captive—but not captivating— weekend together. The narrator also relates a bizarre encounter that Terence has had. While eating dinner in a restaurant, Terence declares that he would do anything for his date, Sylvie; without pause, she asks him to urinate in his pants. Before he can give it proper thought, Terence "urinates copiously, soaking his thighs, legs and backside and sending a small, steady trickle to the floor" (*Sheets*, 133). A moment later, Sylvie's parents join them. These situations have virtually become the norm for relationships in the chaos of contemporary society; no matter how bizarre, relationships offer affirmation and acceptance, whereas the city proffers only pain and seclusion.

In writing this story, McEwan says, "I thought it would be better to do it in terms of a series of meetings and then very artificially to bring all the people that your narrator has met into one place to have a conversation and in that way try to represent a city" (Ricks, 526). Los Angeles, then, is re-created in the small party that concludes the story. As the narrator, Mary, and Terence drive to George's for dinner and drinks, the solitariness that the city forces upon each individual soon becomes evident as conversation immediately falters. The three friends promptly annoy one another and halt their dialogues, finishing the drive in silence. At the party, their stubborn silences soon disintegrate, and social interaction recurs as a series of volatile and often pointless arguments. The four loudly and drunkenly express their views on such topics as corporal punishment (George to Terence: "How can you be sure [your problems with women are] not caused by being thrashed by your mother?" [*Sheets*, 145]), religion and feminism (Mary: "women come off pretty badly in Christianity. Through Original Sin they are held responsible for everything in the world since the Garden of Eden. . . . In fact women only exist at all as a kind of divine afterthought, put together out of a spare rib to keep men company and iron their shirts" [*Sheets*, 148]), and guns and violence (the narrator: "driving across the States I saw this sign in Illinois along Interstate 70 which said, 'God, Guts, Guns made America great. Let's keep all three'" [*Sheets*, 149]). The characters care about nothing except voicing their own opinions. At one point the narrator thinks, "For the first time in my life I found myself with urgent views on Christianity, on violence, on America, on everything, and I demanded priority before my thoughts slipped away" (*Sheets*, 149). These characters represent, through their "round[s] of fragmentary dissent" (*Sheets*, 146), the confusion and frustration of living in a violent society. The city, a chaos of personalities and personas, taints all human contact.

The narrator manages to partially alleviate this frenzied nature of the city by escaping into his music; throughout the story he plays his flute, albeit inexpertly, to soothe his tattered nerves, to put at bay the feral qualities of the city. The flute offers solace amid the confusion. "Psychopolis" concludes with the narrator performing a brief solo before his three friends; as imperfect and amateurish as his performance is, the audience is exuberant in its praise. In this brief moment of total acceptance, the narrator finds himself "overwhelmed by nostalgia for a country I had not yet left" (*Sheets*, 153). In this instant, human interactions prevail over the cold and monstrous city, uniting individuals in a bond of mutual interest and caring. McEwan, then, shows that the impersonality of the city can be overcome; occasionally, human emotions not only survive but endure.

With "Two Fragments: March 199–" McEwan shifts continents and timescapes, but still concentrates on the devastating effects of the city. The story presents a bleak portrait of London's immediate future; within a haunting Orwellian cityscape, the population struggles to survive in a ruined and desolate world, a world long touted by doomsayers and now ecologists. The story is divided into two sections (or "fragments"). "Saturday" (originally published as "Without Blood" in *Encounter* in August 1975) is a third-person account of a day in the life of a father and daughter coping in this dismal world; "Sunday" (published as "Sunday March 3 1991" in *Harpers/Queen* in February 1977) switches to a first-person narration and relates the details of the father's afternoon with his lover. Both fragments present scenes of typical happenstance in this collapsed society. The story as a whole examines relationships in the extreme circumstances of a world in ruin.

This future London, this bitter brave new world, is a wasteland of depravation and desolation:

> Human refuse littered the plain. Vegetables, rotten and trodden down, cardboard boxes flattened into beds, the remains of fires and the carcasses of roasted dogs and cats, rusted tin, vomit, worn tires, animal excrement. . . . The air above the fountain was gray with flies. Men and boys came there daily to squat on the wide concrete rim and defecate. In the distance, along one edge of the plain, several hundred men and women still slept. (*Sheets*, 52)

The city is a ruin of civilization, a monument to the luxury and efficiency that used to be: it is a city of no electricity and no automobiles, a world where cooking is done over paraffin stoves and the tap water is "slow poison" (*Sheets*, 58), a society where half-used bars of soap are resold, envelopes are reused, and bananas are rarities. It is a London wherein rainwater must be collected in tarpaulins and where the Thames threatens to dry up completely. Naturally, a city such as this (much like the Los Angeles portrayed in "Psychopolis") isolates and abandons its inhabitants. Although thousands walk beside him, Henry, the father, "rarely recognized a friend [and] if he did they walked together in silence" (*Sheets*, 52). Humans become insignificant in this vast wasteland; Henry and his daughter, Marie, are lost in that "big, miserable place. . . . They were tiny, the only moving figures on the great expanse" (*Sheets*, 52). Similarly, everyday life becomes an exercise in meaninglessness. Like Winston Smith in *Nineteen Eighty-four*, Henry works for the Ministry in a position that is seemingly purposeless, useless. He spends days on end typing insignificant letters, not remembering the beginning of his task when he gets to the end. As epitomized by this job, there is an endless hopelessness that pervades the populace. Their days are a futile cycle: "not of this day alone but of ten thousand previous days and ten thousand days to come. There seemed no way forward" (*Sheets*, 53).

However, in this barren and inhospitable world, the value of relationships is increased a thousandfold. For Henry, the primary concern in his life is the protection of his daughter. The story opens with an affirmation of Marie's innocence; waking her father one morning she unabashedly tells him, "I've got a vagina" (*Sheets*, 49). It is this perfect innocence that Henry strives to shield. Looking in the mirror, he sees himself as "capable of superhuman feats" (*Sheets*, 50). Not surprisingly, the banal, everyday task of surviving in this world, as well as of protecting his daughter's innocence, *is* a superhuman feat that must be reenacted every day. For instance, during the afternoon, Henry and Marie pause to observe a horrific sideshow in which a father promises to thrust a sword through his daughter's belly without drawing blood (a pointed contrast to Henry and his daughter's relationship). Later, when Marie asks what the woman did with the sword, Henry tells her, "She danced. She danced with it in her hands" (*Sheets*, 59). Although he regrets the lie, Henry realizes that Marie's innocence is a necessity of her youth; her unsullied view of the world may well be her key to survival in this world gone mad.

Though far less important than the relationship with his daughter, Henry is also involved with Diane, a lover; their alliance is a remnant from the old world. It is companionship and not sexual satisfaction that cements their alliance: "We failed to please each other, but we did talk. We were sentimentalists" (*Sheets*, 61). Most of their talk centers on reminiscing about the old world; Diane is obsessed with the magical ease and indulgence of the past. For instance, she surrounds herself with "items without function" (*Sheets*, 62), reminders of an easier time: a telephone, a cathode ray tube, vases, ashtrays, glass bowls. For Diane, these items represent security in the present as well as a safe-keeping of the past. When Henry objects to their worthlessness, she explains to him that "not caring for objects is one step away from not caring for people" (*Sheets*, 62).

As Henry leaves Diane and the story closes, he encounters an elderly Chinese man who asks for help in carrying a heavy cupboard to his family's apartment upstairs. Though the man is a complete stranger, Henry offers aid and then finds himself prevented from leaving because of an "obscure sense of politeness" (*Sheets*, 62). Although his wife and daughter object, the old man insists on sharing with Henry their family meal. Henry manages to take a couple of obligatory sips and then bolts for the door; on his way out, "knowing the difficulty of finding paraffin I turned [their lamp] out, then stepped into the black street" (*Sheets*, 72). "Two Fragments" is important for its depiction of the protective and compassionate nature of Henry. The ability to care and share in a world such as this becomes the focus of McEwan's story. Even if civilization crumbles, even if cities disintegrate into barren wastelands, the necessity of relationships will survive. By caring for and sharing with one another, humans are assured of a future. By showing this ray of optimism in a collection dominated by dismal revelations, McEwan demonstrates that love can survive, that relationships can prevail.

The Ancient To and Fro

In McEwan's fiction, relationships work to their best advantage when there is an equal give and take, a natural, rhythmic "to and fro" between the partners. When one partner is too demanding (as with the narrator in "Dead as They Come") or when one is too giving (as with Maisie in "Solid Geometry"), the relationship quickly disintegrates. The stories of *In Between the Sheets* examine the sexual thrusts and parries, the capricious givings and takings that occur between men and women as they struggle through the rituals of establishing and maintaining viable relationships. In "Reflections of a Kept Ape" and "Dead as They Come" the to and fro is emphasized through absurdist means; with "Psychopolis" and "Two Fragments" the city becomes a third party in the relationships, distorting and interrupting the natural rhythm that exists between women and men. In the remaining three stories—"To and Fro," "Pornography," and "In Between the Sheets"—McEwan more intimately and thoughtfully explores the ancient to and fro.

In the experimental prose poem "To and Fro" (originally published in *Bananas*) McEwan contrasts, in alternating paragraphs, the cold anonymity of life in the working world, in the cramping masses of society, to the blissful peace and individuality found in secure relationships. With this story he explores the "ancient, soft to and fro" (*Sheets*, 114) of life and love. These moments of togetherness, these poetic instances of pure love that individuals share are the fortresses against an encroaching world; these moments are the saviors of individuality and personal identity.

The story alternates between two interchanging scenes: one shows the oppression and depression experienced in the working office; the other reveals the happiness and serenity that the narrator discovers while lying beside his lover. McEwan sharply contrasts these two life experiences, showing how separate they truly are. For instance, describing the images that surround his work world, the narrator notes, "The sky a blank yellow-white, the canal odor reduced by distance to the smell of sweet ripe cherries, the melancholy of airlines turning in the stack" (*Sheets*, 113); the images that he associates with the house are entirely different: "In her house it smells sweetly of sleeping children, of cats drying in the warmth, of dust warming in the tubes of an old radio" (*Sheets*, 120). Likewise, with his lover and her children he feels both serenity and excitement, a true sense of belonging, but he finds himself "wedged" into the life of the office where he finds it impossible to fit in smoothly, unobtrusively. Constantly, he combats the monotony of his work, a job that is "not happy, not unhappy" (*Sheets*, 120). At work, he tells a co-worker, "I remember nothing" (*Sheets*, 115), while at home his mind is continually flooded with memories of wondrous discoveries made in the company of his lover. The two worlds are clearly separate, incompatible.

At the office, the narrator is paired with Leech, a co-worker who is every bit the corporate bloodsucker that his name implies. He is the epitome of the office antagonist, greeting the narrator with a "cordial, vicious blow" (*Sheets*, 115), digging into the narrator's arm with fingers that have the "tenacity of a chicken's claw" (*Sheets*, 116), laughing a "deliberate, dirty chuckle" (*Sheets*, 113). Forced into consorting daily with characters such as Leech, the narrator begins to lose his own personal identity, becoming indistinguishable in this anonymous amalgamation of society. The narrator, in fact, becomes virtually indiscernible from Leech: the director calls him Leech, and his colleague replies that "people are always confusing us" (*Sheets*, 121). The narrator even comes to see himself as a twin to Leech, asking, "Are we the same? Leech, are we?" (*Sheets,* 122). Earlier he has noted that "we cannot be told apart from those we fear" (*Sheets,* 118). His greatest fear, then, is embodied in the office; he is terrified of metamorphosing into one of the corporate zombies that populate the work field, being forced into a world where work is life, life is work. The narrator also realizes the antidote, however; he is saved from this anonymous, monotonous life by the ancient to and fro. It is love that is his salvation.

The narrator's companion—to whom he refers only as "friend" (*Sheets,* 118)—provides the essentials for his desire to persevere in this society; she is the life-saving ingredient in his antidote. At peace beside her, he watches the rise and fall of her breathing, listens to the "perilous gap" between breaths, and marvels at "the decision she makes to go on" (*Sheets,* 121). Each breath is an affirmation of life, each effort of breath is a will to survive. This thrill of life is preserved in a memory that the two of them share, a memory of a starfish clinging to a sea-thrashed rock. This starfish, the narrator says, "threatened for being so awake, like a child's shout in the dead of night" (*Sheets,* 122). To be fully alive to life, that eternal ebb and flow, is the secret to surviving in a sometimes cold, often engulfing society; and love, as is found in the narrator's relationship, is the key to being fully alive.

In condensing the story to its bare minimum, McEwan focuses our attention entirely upon the positive qualities of the narrator's relationship; the alliance with his "friend" is the balm that heals the wounds inflicted by society. Likewise, McEwan demonstrates that these moments of togetherness are the stay against a cruel world as well as the assurance of individuality in an anonymous society. With "To and Fro" McEwan once again gives an optimistic assessment of love and relationships.

McEwan opens *In Between the Sheets,* however, with a tale that is far from optimistic. In "Pornography" (originally published in the *New Review* in February 1972) we are introduced to the despicable Michael O'Bryan, a man who works in a pornography shop by day and who beds and juggles two girlfriends by night. It is a coldly delightful tale of revenge, a study of what can happen when one ignores the ancient to and fro of relationships.

The small pornography shop where O'Bryan works as a clerk serves as a microcosm for the surrounding society, a world corrupted and abusive. The men who patronize the shop appear embarrassed, uncomfortable, even guilty about being in such an establishment. When O'Bryan draws attention to them, they all "scattered before him like frightened fowl" (*Sheets,* 12). Nonetheless, they continue to return, unable to resist partaking in the underworld of sexual deviance. The corruption of society is also made evident when O'Bryan discovers that the shop's pornography supplier is warehoused in an unused church where the font now serves as an ashtray. Nothing, it seems, is too sacred to escape the city's debauchery.

Michael O'Bryan himself is the quintessential cad, getting along with no one, abusing and insulting the people with whom he does come in contact. He detests his brother Harold, who owns the pornography shop, and his success; it infuriates him even further having not only to work under Harold but also having to rent a room from him. O'Bryan despises his subjugation but can only feebly appease himself by silently referring to Harold as "Little Runt." Further, when O'Bryan tells his brother that he has the clap, Harold is delighted, telling O'Bryan that he deserves it. O'Bryan is a man who neither gives nor receives sympathy; it simply has no place in his world.

Even more despicable in O'Bryan's character is the fact that he unashamedly and unconcernedly gives the clap to both Pauline and Lucy, the women he is dating. For the most part, the clap is merely a nuisance to him—swollen meatus and green stains in his shorts. He takes the time to bathe before having sex with each woman but more as a means of saving himself from embarrassment—to "purge the faint purulent scent that lately had hung about his fingers" (*Sheets,* 14)—than as a protective or cautionary measure in regard to his partners.

The women O'Bryan beds are quite the opposite; his relationship with each is similar only in the fact that he treats and uses both as objects. Pauline Shepherd, a trainee nurse, is a gentle and loving woman, a "silent girl who once wept at a film about the effects of pesticides on butterflies, who wanted to redeem O'Bryan with her love" (*Sheets,* 13). She is almost motherly in her concern for O'Bryan; she accepts his crass and inconsiderate behavior, hoping to excavate a kinder nature from him. In the portrait of their typical date, O'Bryan ruins the dinner that Pauline has prepared for him by appearing two hours late (and a little drunk at that). Pauline, ever apologetic, never accusative, runs to the store to get something else for dinner. While she is gone, O'Bryan eats the burnt meat pie, grows bored, and decides to leave; meeting her on the steps, he follows her back up, feeling "obscurely cheated" (*Sheets,* 16). Their date is an evening of "senseless minutes" (*Sheets,* 15). Sex, no better than the whole of their relationship, is a passionless exercise, a ritual "without desire" (*Sheets,* 16). Like the narrator of "Dead as They Come," O'Bryan is the typical chauvinist, forcing Pauline into the submissive, culpable role. When they fall asleep (Pauline after a 12-hour shift) without having engaged in sex, O'Bryan wakes in the dark hours to whisper, "Hey, there's something we ain't done yet" (*Sheets,* 17). Because of O'Bryan, the relationship is an alliance without love, without compassion; it is simply a physical union, a meeting of two strangers.

O'Bryan's relationship with Lucy is quite different. Ten years older than Pauline, she is a sister (the equivalent of an American registered nurse) and has much more control of her life and relations. O'Bryan acknowledges her dominance, arriving on time and bearing flowers for their evening together. As with Pauline, the date is only a pretense for sex; however, their sexual activities are entirely different. From the beginning of the relationship, Lucy has insisted that "I'm in charge" (*Sheets,* 22). Their sexual relationship is one of abuse and bullying—with Lucy taking the dominant role (which offers an ominous but pleasing counterpoint to Robert and Caroline's relationship in *The Comfort of Strangers*). The first time that O'Bryan defied her command, Lucy "lashed his face several times with her open palm" (*Sheets,* 22). Other times she abuses him verbally, urinates over his head and chest, or attempts to persuade him to try on her underwear. O'Bryan resists with both "horror and excitement" (*Sheets,* 23), and Lucy "seemed to intuit [his] guilty thrill of pleasure" (*Sheets,* 22). At first O'Bryan is "horrified, sickened, that he could enjoy being overwhelmed, like one of those cripples in his brother's magazines" (*Sheets,* 22), and although he seems secretly to enjoy their sexual bouts, he constantly objects, telling Lucy, "You're a bloody pervert" (*Sheets,* 22). Lucy knowingly replies, "You're scared of what you like" (*Sheets,* 23). As with Pauline, the relationship O'Bryan has with Lucy is one limited to physical pleasures; beyond sex, they share nothing.

Feeling far too superior in his manipulative relations with the two women, O'Bryan—cad, chauvinist, buffoon—falls easily, almost willingly, into the trap that Pauline and Lucy lay for him. When Lucy coyly seduces him, then secures him to the bed with leather straps, O'Bryan feels no panic, only the uneasy excitement he associates with kinky sex. Only when Pauline suddenly appears does an uneasy panic overtake him. With diabolical coolness, the two women exact their revenge on him, telling him, "This is what they should have done for you at the clinic. . . . Stop you spreading round your secret little diseases" (*Sheets,* 29). Bringing out an array of menacing surgical instruments, they promise him, "We'll leave you a pretty little stump to remember us by" (*Sheets,* 30). Even at the height of his panic, O'Bryan finds himself with an erection, experiencing again a "horrified excitement" (*Sheets*, 30). The women avenge themselves by dooming him to a sexless existence.

Throughout most of the stories of *In Between the Sheets* men struggle to maintain control over women; these male characters feel more secure within their worlds if their women remain docile, submissive creatures. As exemplified in the majority of McEwan's works, however, women refuse to remain servants to and victims of a patriarchal society; they fight back, asserting their rights and will, often winning control over their own lives and relationships. Frequently, as in the case of Michael O'Bryan, characters learn the cruel way that women are, indeed, the equals of men. McEwan shows that chauvinism is a trait that cannot, must not persist.

The title story (originally published in the *New Review* in September 1975) is the tale of an ordinary divorcé struggling to confront the difficulties involved in being a part-time father to a maturing 14-year-old daughter. As he copes with the everyday trivialities that pepper his life, he must also do battle with an ex-wife and anguish over the incestuous urges that he suddenly feels for his daughter. In the end he realizes that things will work out, that there is "nothing to be frightened of really" (*Sheets*, 112).

Stephen's divorce serves as an omnipresent element in his life. Throughout the marriage and into their present lives, he and his wife have experienced a deep dissatisfaction with each other, which they attempt to conceal (or at least temporarily restrain) for the sake of their daughter, Miranda. Their divorce is a worst-case scenario: they find themselves in "rare agreement" (*Sheets*, 96), and when forced to convene, Stephen "resigned himself to hostilities" (*Sheets*, 102). Stephen realizes that his wife—who remains nameless throughout the story—hates him "for his fearfulness, his passivity and for all the wasted hours between the sheets" (*Sheets*, 106). He also willingly admits that their union failed because "I never satisfied my wife in marriage, you see. Her orgasms terrified me" (*Sheets*, 104). After the divorce he is soon replaced by a more vigorous lover; consequently, his greatest fear is that he may likewise be replaced as father.

Not surprisingly, Stephen discovers that his disrupted marriage amplifies the problems he has in being a father. For instance, when Miranda asks for £25 for a record player, he at first says no, but then, feeling selfish and unfatherly, overcompensates by sending her £30, "the extra five so clearly spell[ing] out his guilt" (*Sheets*, 98). Later, again to ease the guilt of being an inadequate father, he overindulges in purchasing gifts for her birthday. He ends up, however, throwing everything but a £5 gift certificate into the hall closet. Well aware that his absence hinders his position as a parent, Stephen conscientiously struggles to be the best father possible, his love for Miranda providing the strength to persevere.

Further impeding Stephen's role as father is a haunting wet dream. He recalls that the dream involves a 10-year-old waitress and a coffee machine, and that it "ended in sudden and intense pleasure" (*Sheets,* 97). Though the details are fuzzy, the dream worries him. Thumbing through a book on dreams he reads, "An emission during a dream indicates the sexual nature of the whole dream, however obscure and unlikely the contents are. Dreams culminating in emission may reveal the object of the dreamer's desire as well as his inner conflicts. An orgasm cannot lie" (*Sheets,* 103). Stephen's wet dream is a displacement of his subtle and as-yet-unrealized desires for Miranda; like his impressions of the enigmatic Charmian, Miranda's dwarflike friend, Stephen is uncertain how to handle these mysterious—and unwanted—new feelings. He finds himself both thrilled and terrified.

The object of these subconscious yearnings, Miranda, is at the awkward stage between youth and adolescence, between innocence and maturity. Stephen is uncomfortably aware of both the inner and physical changes that his daughter is going through. He reluctantly realizes that she may be growing away from him. When he hugs her he notices that "she felt different to the touch, stronger perhaps. She smelled unfamiliar, she had a private life at last, accountable to no one" (*Sheets,* 103). More awkward for Stephen, though, are the physical changes. He is aware of her growing breasts and is careful not to touch them as he hugs her. Even so, he cannot ignore or deny his unwanted sexual desire. After holding her, he is both horrified and elated by an erection: "He thought he should be somber, analytical, this was a serious matter. But he wanted to sing, he wanted to play his piano, he wanted to go for a walk. He did none of those things. He sat still, staring ahead, thinking of nothing in particular, and waited for the chill of excitement to leave his belly" (*Sheets,* 110).

Later that night, still confused by these taboo emotions, Stephen hears in Miranda's room the sound that is "the background for all other sounds, the frame of all anxieties" (*Sheets,* 111). It is the "sound of his wife in, or approaching, orgasm" (*Sheets,* 111). Before Stephen can visualize what might be happening between his daughter and her strange friend, Miranda appears at the door, clearly innocent, clearly a little girl.

Without hesitation, Stephen slips naturally into the role of father, a role that fits him comfortably. As he comforts her into sleep, assuring her that there "is nothing to be frightened of really" (*Sheets,* 112), he sees in her a pure and beautiful innocence: "in the pallor of her upturned throat he thought he saw from one bright morning in his childhood a field of dazzling white snow which he, a small boy of eight, had not dared scar with footprints" (*Sheets,* 112). Stephen's fears of fatherhood are thus quelled; he believes that she is safe with him. The reassurance that he provides her applies just as well for him: there really is no reason to be afraid.

With "In Between the Sheets" McEwan avoids the lurid draw of incest; instead he chooses to examine realistically those taboo desires that society would rather ignore, exemplifying the anguish that a father may go through in order to love a daughter purely and naturally. In this story McEwan consciously eschews a literature of shock in favor of a more optimistic outlook. In presenting the positive, love-filled relationship between a father and his daughter, McEwan portrays a maturer, more sentimental vision in his work. Love, that ubiquitous to and fro, he assures, can be innocent and prevailing.

The stories of *In Between the Sheets,* in their unflinching scrutiny of the sexual roles and mores of contemporary society, combine a harmonious fluidity with a terse intensity; they are evidence of a powerful writer. Though McEwan consciously steps beyond the boundaries of reality in several stories, he consistently addresses serious and eminent concerns of his world. *In Between the Sheets* serves as a transitional phase for McEwan; with this collection he begins to hone more maturely his major concerns. Most important, female characters begin to establish more emphatically their power in relationships, asserting their intense displeasure with being treated as subservient creatures. Looking back on his stories, McEwan says,

> I like to think I can come back to writing short stories, but I do have a feeling that I might not be able to write them as well as I did when I was younger. . . . The form itself is a good laboratory. I took the stories very seriously and worked on them very slowly, and I would want to stand by them. I wouldn't want to lose the concentrated exploration of the short stories, not to feel as I grow older that my sole duty is to address the nation on public themes: that would be arid and arrogant. I would always want to keep the excitement and mystery of writing, but I would find it harder to achieve that young man's easy swipe at life. (Haffenden, 35)

After *In Between the Sheets* McEwan turns almost wholly to the craft of novels and film scripts, working in a medium that allows for a deeper, more thorough examination of the elements that plague relationships in modern society. Though the efforts of a young writer, McEwan's stories nonetheless represent a remarkable talent remarkably deployed.

Chapter Five

Danger in a Strange Land:
The Comfort of Strangers

"His new book has the virtue of being morally annoying. . . . McEwan's novel offers a kind of negative stimulus: it is to read a story about people one would run a mile from," groaned Douglas Dunn in *Encounter.*[1] "It is short, it is about sex and it is excellent," elated Lewis Jones in *The Spectator.*[2] Despite such extremely mixed reviews, *The Comfort of Strangers* (published in England by Jonathan Cape in October 1981 and in the United States by Simon & Schuster later that same year) was quickly shortlisted for the Booker Prize, England's most prestigious literary award (so quickly nominated, in fact, that it had yet to be released by the publisher). As a nominee, McEwan joined the company of some of Britain's most innovative and reputable writers; also nominated were Muriel Spark for *Loitering with Intent,* Doris Lessing for *The Sirian Experiments,* Ann Schlee for *Rhine Journey,* Molly Keane for *Good Behaviour,* D. M. Thomas for *The White Hotel,* and the winner, Salman Rushdie, for *Midnight's Children.*

The novel, however, garnered for McEwan more negative reviews than any of his previous work. For example, Eliot Fremont-Smith said that *The Comfort of Strangers* "starts with tingles, promises true shivers and the catharsis of shock, and delivers only gore. . . . It is an unsatisfying suspense-horror, even for an upscale beach read, and therefore quite hateful."[3] Richard Martin called the novel "a sad disappointment";[4] John Leonard labeled it as "definitely diseased."[5] Nonetheless, *The Comfort of Strangers* shows a marked maturation in McEwan's writing; he has, for example, abandoned completely the freaks and human anomalies of his short-story collections and delved more deeply into the dark psyches of genuine adult desires and relationships. More important, he consciously begins to explore the roles of women in a patriarchal culture. He examines both how women view themselves in this male-dominated society as well as how men see themselves in relation to these women. McEwan's novel is, therefore, much more than contemporary Grand Guignol, more than just another view of relationships gone

macabre; rather, it is a thoughtful and powerful assessment of the perversions that often occur as a result of the obsessions that flourish in a
patriarchal world.

Some critics were annoyed that McEwan's latest effort was, like *The
Cement Garden,* only a long story, a novella; others complained that
McEwan had yet to compose an original idea in either of his novels.
Although no critics voiced a concrete accusation of plagiarism (as several
had with *The Cement Garden*), there were more than a few asides that *The
Comfort of Strangers* was remarkably similar to such works as Paul
Bowles's *The Sheltering Sky,* Daphne du Maurier's *Don't Look Now,* and
even Thomas Mann's *Death in Venice.* A simple reading, however, quick-
ly realizes the absurdity of these intimations. Still, in using an unnamed
Venice as the setting, McEwan does consciously bring to his novel a rich
tradition of literature, including not only Mann's and Du Maurier's
novellas but also such sundry works as Ruskin's *The Stones of Venice,*
Dickens's *Pictures from Italy,* Byron's *Childe Harold,* and Mary McCarthy's
Venice Observed. Venice is frequently portrayed as a place of wonder, a
place of mystery, and McEwan's use of the haunting opulence of the
Italian city accentuates the gruesome action of the novel. With the city,
for example, come dark doorways and honeycombed passageways, a
sense of the ominous, the enigmatic. It is the ideal setting in which visi-
tors take missteps and become disoriented, in which tourists and other
strangers make the dearest of mistakes. Ultimately, the unnamed city
becomes a symbolic Everycity, representative of all that is foreign and
strange.

The city, quite naturally, is portrayed as the fifth character of the
novel, and as typical in McEwan's fiction, it serves as hindrance and irri-
tant to the novel's protagonists, Colin and Mary. For instance, the novel
opens as the city encroaches upon their sleep: "Each afternoon, when the
whole city . . . began to stir, Colin and Mary were woken by the method-
ical chipping of steel tools against the iron barges which moored by the
hotel café pontoon."[6] From this point on, the city imposes upon them,
plaguing their vacation, disorienting their lives. At one point Mary says,
"You know this place can be terribly suffocating sometimes. . . . It's
oppressive. . . . It's like a prison here" (*CS,* 49). As the novel progresses,
the city becomes increasingly claustrophobic. Compounding their feelings of unease is the great sense of unfamiliarity they frequently experience. For Colin and Mary the city is not friendly but menacing, not
inviting but intimidating. They also quickly prove to be incompetent
tourists, failing to explore the area with any degree of proficiency.

Always forgetting their maps, they continually become lost in the labyrinthine roadways; so inadequate are they in the city, they are one night forced to sleep in the street because they are unable to find their hotel. Eventually, because of their incompetence, they find themselves forced to rely upon the comfort of strangers.

At their hotel, for example, they find themselves totally dependent upon the maid:

> They became incapable of looking after one another, incapable in this heat, of plumping their own pillows, or of bending down to retrieve a dropped towel. At the same time they had become less tolerant of disorder. One late morning, they returned to their room to find it as they had left it, simply inhabitable, and they had no choice but to go out again and wait until it had been dealt with. (CS, 12)

This dependence on others ultimately leads to their destruction: they inevitably find themselves taking refuge from the city and its confusions through Robert, the archetypal false host, who is more than willing to provide false comfort.

McEwan emphasizes this vulnerability of the traveler in the epigraph he chooses from Cesare Pavese: "Traveling is a brutality. It forces you to trust strangers and to lose sight of all that familiar comfort of home and friends. You are constantly off balance. Nothing is yours except the essential things—air, sleep, dreams, the sun, the sky—all things tending toward the eternal or what we imagine of it" (CS, 7). J. R. Banks in his article "A Gondola Named Desire" echoes this assessment when he states that the novel "looks at how being away from home alters the way we . . . behave towards strangers, trusting ourselves to them unwillingly or, at least as often, willingly, if not always wisely."[7] This unquestioning trust that travelers place in the natives of foreign lands is a motif that spans literary history itself, from Odysseus's encounter with Circe and Theseus's encounter with Procrustes (who would invite travelers into his iron bed, stretching those who were too short and amputating whatever necessary from those who were too long) to Henry James's *Daisy Miller* (1879) and Edith Wharton's "Roman Fever" (1933).

This inherent danger in travel is the heart of McEwan's novel. Thus, by allowing themselves to be seduced by the peculiar and ominous comfort of Robert and Caroline, Colin and Mary lead themselves into horrific straits. Late in the novel Robert, with obvious irony, says, "The thing about a successful holiday is that it makes you want to go home" (CS,

106). In one sense, their trip is a contemporary echo of Henry James's international theme (or what Leon Edel called the "international situation," and what James himself referred to as the "Americano-European legend"), in which foreign innocents wandered abroad and frequently fell prey to conniving and manipulating Europeans. This theme (a literary obsession with James) examined the plight of these (usually) willingly transplanted persons and their inherent, innate vulnerability. James's heroes and heroines, though, often found victory through a transcendent moral spirit, which is the essence exactly that Mary and Colin lack (who are, obviously, more modernized Daisy Millers than they are Isabel Archers). Like the less fortunate of James's characters, these strangers in a strange land wish only to go home again. ✕

Mary and Colin's vacation is an attempt, apparently, to escape the rigors of their everyday lives. After seven years of being together, they have settled into the more leisurely paces that settle over a once passionate relationship. Although they are the focus of virtually every scene, we learn very little about the precise nature of their relationship and even less about their personal backgrounds. They are not married; they do not live together; they have known each other for seven years—this is the extent of what they reveal about their relationship. Of their personal backgrounds we know only that Mary has two children from a previous marriage and that she once acted in an all-female theatrical company; we know that Colin has failed at a singing career and turned to acting. Essentially, they remain as unfamiliar to us as the strangers of the title. By far, there is more concentration upon the idiosyncrasies of their lives, the inconsequential rituals of everyday life. As a result, Colin and Mary appear as shallow and superficial, disinterested passersby of the world around them.

This emptiness is conveyed immediately in the first page: "For reasons they could no longer define clearly, Colin and Mary were not on speaking terms" (*CS*, 9). Much of their relationship is conducted in similar terms; each acts childishly and often does not understand why he/she is unhappy with his/her partner at that specific moment. Early in the story, Mary thinks, "She loved him, though not at this particular moment" (*CS*, 13). There is a tone of discordance that echoes persistently through their affair. For instance, they listen to each other's dreams only because this act allows them the "luxury of recounting their own" (*CS*, 10). Furthermore, sex is no longer "a great passion" but has become an almost somber ritual:

The pleasure was in its unhurried friendliness, the familiarity of its rituals and procedures, the secure, precision-fit of limbs and bodies, comfortable, like a cast returned to its mold. They were generous and
leisurely, making no great demands, and very little noise. Their lovemaking had no clear beginning or end and frequently concluded in, or
was interrupted by, sleep. They would have denied indignantly that they
were bored. (CS, 17)

Their lovemaking is emblematic of the relationship: caring but leisurely,
familiar but unspectacular.

This discordance is magnified by the vacation; their togetherness
becomes a momentary awkwardness, a terse incompatibility: "together
they moved slowly, clumsily, effecting lugubrious compromises, attend-
ing to delicate shifts of mood, repairing breaches. As individuals they did
not easily take offense; but together they managed to offend each other
in surprising, unexpected ways" (CS, 13). Together they are ineffectual.
They are constantly losing their way, wandering helplessly through the
maze of streets and alleyways; at one point they are unable even to
obtain a glass of water from a passing waiter. Seemingly paradoxical to
the ineptitude of their togetherness, however, Colin and Mary also work
best in their relationship not as two individuals but as one unit; essentially, they become a composite person. Early in the novel the narrator
states, "They often said they found it difficult to remember that the
other was a separate person" (CS, 17). Later, Caroline even notes that
they are "almost like twins" (CS, 66). This "oneness" echoes through the
novel. For instance, as they walk through the streets, "their footsteps
resounded noisily on the cobbles, making the sound of only one pair of
shoes" (CS, 24). This intertwining of their personas often provides them
with the strength to combat the ominous city, the weaknesses in their
own relationship, and, later, the vicious strangers.

Unfortunately, though, it is the ineptitude of their union rather than
the precision of the composite person that dominates the relationship; as
a result, a lethargy frequently descends upon them. Like Beckett's Didi
and Gogo, they often propose to go somewhere, to do something, but
then remain motionless. For instance, when Mary suggests that they
leave for the restaurants, "Colin agreed, but neither moved" (CS, 16);
when Colin says they should walk to the hotel, "neither of them stirred"
(CS, 50); when they see Robert, Mary says that they should turn their
faces, but "they continued to watch as he came closer" (CS, 51). This stasis is evident in other facets of their lives as well. Colin shaves twice "for

no particular reason" (*CS*, 11); similarly, Mary addresses and writes three postcards to her children on the first day of the vacation, yet—although she remembers the cards several times (*CS*, 48, 92, 125)—they remain unmailed. This malaise is a plague that haunts and daunts them to a very bitter end.

The odd, curious nature of Mary and Colin is further emphasized in the fact that McEwan offers no physical description of Mary, whereas Colin is described in minute detail. Ironically, it is Colin's beauty that draws both Robert and Caroline. It is, thus, more of a necessity to portray the physical perfection of Colin. The most detailed description of Colin occurs while he and Mary are "visiting" Robert and Caroline the first time. Mary watches her lover, describing him minutely, and, surprisingly, in childlike terms:

> His arms were crossed fetally over his chest: his slender, hairless legs were set a little apart, the feet, abnormally small like a child's, pointing inwards: the fine bones of his spine ran into a deep groove in the small of his back, and along this line . . . grew a fine down. . . . His buttocks were small and firm, like a child's. . . . The nose, like the ears, was long, but in profile it did not protrude; instead it lay flat, along the face, and carved into its base, like commas, were extraordinarily small nostrils. Colin's mouth was straight and firm, parted by just a hint of tooth. His hair was unnaturally fine, like a baby's, and black, and fell in curls onto his slender, womanly neck. (*CS*, 55–56)

Ironically, Colin is several times referred to as a child. For example, Robert, speaking to him, "adopted the tone of one who explains the self-obvious to a child" (*CS*, 71). Later he is portrayed as "nursing" at Mary's breast (*CS*, 90). Like so many of McEwan's female characters, Mary finds herself forced into the role of the mother-figure, the complement to Colin's child self. She, too, however, demands reciprocal attention and care from Colin. The narrator says that the "demand to be looked after was routine between them, and they took it in turns to respond dutifully" (*CS*, 43–44). Colin and Mary, then, find themselves in danger because of their shallowness, their selfishness, their ineptitude. Unable to care adequately for each other, they are eventually forced to seek solace in strangers.

Though Colin and Mary are mutually repulsed and horrified by their first encounter with Robert and Caroline, the only time during the vacation that their relationship comes alive is immediately after this bizarre night with the sadomasochistic couple. This brief yet intense contact

with strangers revitalizes their own dormant desires. Afterwards, Mary
and Colin continually hold hands, caress each other, exchange small kisses; sex becomes immediate, thrilling: "They awoke surprised to find
themselves in each other's arms. Their lovemaking surprised them too,
for the great, enveloping pleasure, the sharp, almost painful, thrills were
sensations . . . they remembered from seven years before, when they had
first met" (CS, 77). Furthermore, they each become more conscious of
their partner, concerned with his or her feelings and thoughts. As
opposed to the conversations earlier in the vacation, "they each let the
other talk for as long as an hour without interrupting" (CS, 79).

The perversity and unbridled cruelty of Robert and Caroline's relationship touches them in ways unimaginable—for them, ways incon-
ceivable. Yet not surprisingly for Colin and Mary, they do not explore the
reasons behind these feelings: "But for all [their] discussion, this analysis
which extended to the very means of discussion itself, they did not talk
about the cause of their renewal. Their conversation, in essence, was no
less celebratory than their lovemaking; in both they lived inside the
moment" (CS, 81). Sex, then, serves merely as an escape, a denial even,
of what they have encountered in Robert and Caroline. Of this sexual
renewal, Michael Adams, in *Postmodern Fiction,* says, "Ironically, the couple can communicate only sexually, and sex becomes the instrument of
their destruction. In McEwan's world, fantasies can turn into night-
mares. Sex can be an escape but also a means of drowning in harsh reality" (Adams, 461). Despite their refusal to discuss Robert and Caroline,
they are, nonetheless, noticeably tainted by the strangers; a masochistic
longing suddenly permeates their desires and colors their fantasies. Mary
tells Colin that she would have his legs amputated, keeping him in a
room, using him "exclusively for sex" (CS, 81); Colin confides that he
would invent a "large, intricate machine" whose sole purpose would be
to "fuck her, not just for hours or weeks, but for years, on and on, for the
rest of her life, till she was dead and on even after that, till Colin, or his
lawyer, turned it off" (CS, 81–82).

The sex, the fantasies, the outbursts of renewed passions then all
quickly dissipate; while at the beach the narrator states that "they were
inhibited by a feeling that these past few days had been nothing more
than a form of parasitism, an unacknowledged conspiracy of silence disguised by so much talk" (CS, 92). The revitalized relationship is indeed a
form of parasitism; Mary and Colin have subconsciously succumbed to
the overt perversities of Robert and Caroline's alliance. Just as they are
powerless against the perverse desires of tainted sexuality, they, too, are

unable to resist the power and machinations of Caroline and Robert, falling helplessly into their hands. When they inadvertently encounter Caroline, they follow her into the house, dropping their hands, severing the bond that has reemerged between them. They are, simultaneously, fascinated and surprised by these strange sexual awakenings and urgings. Likewise, they are drawn to and repelled by the instigators.

Robert, the chauvinistic, sadistic minotaur who preys within the labyrinthine streets, plays the archetypal false host, seductively luring the innocents into his lair and wickedly dispatching them to satiate his own desires. McEwan says that he sees Robert "more as a cipher than as a character. People either buy Robert or they don't. He is part of the premise of the novel rather than an entirely convincing character" (Haffenden, 32). If not entirely a convincing character, he is undoubtedly evil; even before Mary and Colin meet him, he looms continually, ominously in the background. For example, early in the novel there is a passing reference to a man with binoculars—who could well be Robert—who disappears after Colin notices him. When he finally confronts the couple, he literally captures them, tugging and pulling them forcibly down the alleyways. He then quickly insinuates himself into their relationship, coming between Colin and Mary (often physically), eventually separating them, slowly taking possession of Colin. Throughout his manipulations, Robert is constantly touching, caressing Colin, ruffling his hair, steering him by the elbow, massaging him, placing his hand on his shoulder. Once, in a pair of gestures that clearly exposes his sadomasochistic temperament, Robert strikes Colin in the stomach, knocking the wind out of him, then turns and cheerfully winks at him; Robert wishes to befriend and to dominate. This need of Robert to control Colin persists through the novel; on the couple's final visit to his house, Robert "[slides] his arm around Colin's shoulder, as though to help him up the remaining steps, and in so doing [turns] his back conspicuously on Mary" (*CS*, 100); minutes later he "place[s] himself between them" (*CS*, 101). Through all his obvious orchestrations, Robert succeeds in gaining a dominance over Colin. When the two men return to a drugged Mary at the end of the novel, Colin realizes that something is terribly wrong, but rather than insisting on aiding his wife, he quickly (subconsciously? *certainly* powerlessly) retreats to Robert's side when he is called.

Robert begins to spin his web of domination on the night of his first meeting with Mary and Colin, relating to them a bizarre tale of his childhood. The story, a reminiscence concerning Robert and his tyrannical father (and a recollection of McEwan's earlier literature of shock), provides insight into the origins of Robert's destructive patriarchal values as well as into his sadomasochistic nature. The father cruelly dominates his family, controlling them through fear: "Everybody was afraid of him," Robert tells his companions; "When he frowned nobody could speak" (CS, 31). Because Robert is his only son, however, he is his father's favorite, his "passion" (CS, 32). Consequently, the father often uses his son to abuse and to manipulate the other family members. Robert, in turn, sees his father as godhead; he readily and willingly adheres to his father's every command, never "knowing I was being used" (CS, 32). As a result of his father's heartless authority and his condescending attitude toward women—his father tells him, for example, that chocolate "made [boys] weak in character, like girls" (CS, 35)— Robert himself is forever perversely tainted. He, too, harbors the instinctive barbarity of his father, subjecting first his wife to his savage desires and then Colin and Mary.

Not surprisingly, Robert's obsession with his father, his dominance by him, remains with him throughout his life. In his house, for example, he has a museum in which he collects items that once belonged to his father and grandfather. The collection contains such seemingly insignificant articles as murky paintings, opera glasses, novels, smoking and shaving kits.[8] Late in the novel Caroline admits, "He's obsessed with his father and grandfather" (CS, 113). His father's demand to control and dominate becomes further corrupted in Robert; he, too, wishes to dominate those in his life, but his desires are played out in sexual abuse. Consequently, Robert's obsessions become even more perverse, and in order for him to mimic faithfully the domination that his father once achieved, his desires demand that the innocent must suffer.

The person most wickedly affected by Robert's obsessions is his wife, Caroline. She is the unexceptional, shy type, both enigmatic and simplistic: she shuffles stiffly around the house, obviously in tremendous pain but only smiles mysteriously when asked about the reason for her discomfort. On the other hand, she unashamedly admits to Mary that she has watched Mary and Colin as they slept, naked, in her guest bedroom. She unquestioningly, even enthusiastically, acts as both partner to and subject of her husband's demented desires, consequently becoming both a battered wife and an accomplice to murder.

When Caroline first appears, Mary sees her as only "a small pale face . . . a disembodied face" (CS, 59). Similarly, she is never perceived as a whole person by her husband. To Robert she is nothing more than a possession, another object to add to his shrine of obsessions. Like the narrator of "Dead as They Come," Robert's chauvinism prevents him from accepting her as a person; in his eyes she is nothing more than something with which he might satisfy his terrifying longings—and this at any cost. Caroline, however, readily and willingly accepts her husband's domination. She tells Mary that love means that "you'd do anything for the other person. . . . And you'd let them do anything to you. . . . If you are in love with someone, you would even be prepared to let them kill you, if necessary" (*CS*, 62). She also clearly exemplifies the degree to which her husband's patriarchal attitudes have tainted her own thinking when she clarifies her statement, saying, "if I was the man I would [kill the person I'm in love with]" (*CS*, 63). Caroline and Robert's marriage, then, is open to a horrifying range of sexual demands and transgressions.

Unfortunately, but not surprisingly, their initial sexual curiosity has quickly escalated into a horrific sadomasochistic relationship. As a consequence, Caroline lives a life wherein every movement, every position causes agony; she exists in a perpetual haze of pain and terror. When Colin and Mary leave Robert and Caroline's house after their initial visit, they hear a sharp sound that "could as easily have been an object dropped as a face slapped" (*CS*, 76). Before they are initiated into the perverse secrets of the strangers' marriage, Mary and Colin surmise that Caroline needs, even revels in pain:

> After a prolonged silence Colin said, "Perhaps he beats her up." Mary nodded. "And yet . . . and yet she seemed to be quite . . ." He trailed away vaguely.
> "Quite content?" Mary said sourly. "Everyone knows how much women enjoy being beaten up."
> . . . "What I was going to say was that . . . she seemed to be, well, thriving on something."
> "Oh yes," Mary said. "Pain." (*CS*, 91)

Despite her psychological need for brutality, their lifestyle, nonetheless, drains Caroline. When Mary first meets her, Caroline's features are without life, languid: "[Caroline's] small face . . . was featureless in its regularity, innocent of expression, without age. Her eyes, nose, mouth, skin, all might have been designed in committee to meet the barest requirements of feasibility. Her mouth, for example, was no more than the word suggested, a moving, lipped slit beneath her nose" (*CS*, 66). As the trap that she and Robert have designed draws nearer to its close, however, Caroline experiences revitalization. Her features, stirred by the terrifyingly exciting possibilities of the trap, blossom:

> [Her] hair, so tightly drawn back before, was slightly awry, loose strands softened her face which in the intervening days had lost its anonymity. The lips especially, previously so thin and bloodless, were full, almost sensual. The long straight line of her nose, where formerly it had appeared no more than the least acceptable solution to a problem of design, now conferred dignity. The eyes had shed their hard, mad shine and seemed more communicative, sympathetic. (*CS*, 107)

Swept away by the tide of her husband's sadism, Caroline becomes not a victim but a participant, not a brutalized subject but a willing confederate. Obviously, their offering is a comfort only to themselves.

Caroline, as weak and as malleable as she is, succumbs easily, almost too willingly, to the powers of the male, and, consequently, patriarchal dogma dominates the novel. In order to counter the patriarchal attitudes that run rampant through the novel, as well as to provide a foil to the chauvinistic rantings of Robert, McEwan offers a sensitive glance toward feminism. Although McEwan's feminist sensibilities are evident in his earliest writing, they become predominant in many of his later works. For example, McEwan uses both *The Comfort of Strangers* and "The Imitation Game" to demonstrate unflinchingly the destructive nature of the dangerous sexual hierarchies that are allowed, even encouraged, in today's societies.

McEwan's feminist sensibilities are very similar to those of another British novelist, Fay Weldon. Like McEwan, Weldon writes sharp, satiric appraisals of the human condition, concentrating on the experience of women. Her female characters, done in by the wickedness of men (husbands and lovers who are more often than not portrayed as philandering, abusive, unsympathetic), find themselves victims of a patriarchal society. Frequently abandoned by the men in their lives, these women discover life beyond marriage. As Joanna in *The Cloning of Joanna May* says, "I was no longer just a wife; I was a human being" (Weldon, 247). Similar to McEwan's females, Weldon's women—especially characters like Esther in *The Fat Woman's Joke* (1968), the eponymous heroine of *Praxis* (1978), Natalie Harris in *The Heart of the Country* (1987), and Joanna May—discover that though the system and its society heap injustices upon them, in the end it is they who are responsible for their own lives. With this newfound knowledge, these characters do, indeed, survive and prevail.

McEwan immediately introduces his feminist concerns in *The Comfort of Strangers* by quoting an Adrienne Rich poem as one of the novel's epigraphs: "How we dwelt in two worlds / the daughters and the mothers / in the kingdom of the sons." These lines echo the outrage and hopelessness that result when half a society is forced to be subservient, when a partner in a relationship is seen as menial, inferior, objectified. McEwan attempts to oppose these archaic mores with his fiction, showing both the absurdities and the perils of a society under the jurisdiction of a destructive patriarchy.

The microcosmic world inhabited by Mary, Colin, Robert, and Caroline has long since been consumed by the negative capabilities of patriarchy. Mary acts as the representative of the feminist movement, but she can in no way alone stem the angry and brutal flow of male chauvinism (whose endless source is Robert) that floods *The Comfort of Strangers*. This world, this society has long since been imbued by the prevailing patriarchy. For instance, when Mary tells Caroline that she is a part of an all-female theatrical group, Caroline has no understanding of the concept until she sees it in terms of men. When Mary explains to her that this troupe could perform a play "about two women who have only just met sitting on a balcony talking," Caroline replies, "Oh yes. But they're probably waiting for a man" (*CS*, 67). Likewise, earlier in the novel, when Mary comments on the feminist posters that demand castration for rapists, both Colin and Robert attack the idea. Robert typically oversimplifies, saying, "These are women who cannot find a man. They want to destroy everything that is good between men and women. . . . They are too ugly" (*CS*, 27). Even the police, interviewing her after Colin's murder, "compliment" Caroline on the "precision and logical consistency" of her statement, saying that it is "not like a woman's statement at all" (*CS*, 124). Mary thus finds herself in a world grown demented because of male privilege, a world possessed by the patriarchy. She alone is unable to turn the tide. As McEwan implies, the deleterious hierarchicalization that results from male domination cannot be thwarted by a single effort, a lone voice; rather, the defeat must ensue from the making of a new communal if not universal consciousness concerning difference and desire.

One reason Mary alone cannot defeat the demeaning views of Robert is that his beliefs are beyond that of an everyday male chauvinist. He is a militant patriarch, perverted and demented by years of warped conviction. His obsessions with his father and grandfather are a primary factor in the shaping and sustaining of his beliefs. Of these men he says, "My

father and his father understood themselves clearly. They were men, and
they were proud of their sex. Women understood them, too. . . . There
was no confusion" (CS, 71). From these convictions, Robert formulates a
theory—one that becomes an adamant law of his life—concerning the
rules that should govern the relationships between men and women.
Explaining this dogma to Colin, he says,

> [Today] men doubt themselves, they hate themselves, even more than
> they hate each other. Women treat men like children, because they can't
> take them seriously. . . . But they love men. Whatever they might say
> they believe, women love aggression and strength and power in men. It's
> deep in their minds. Look at all the women a successful man attracts. If
> what I'm saying wasn't true, women would protest at every war. Instead,
> they love to send their men to fight. The pacifists, the objectors, are
> mostly men. And even though they hate themselves for it, women long
> to be ruled by men. It's deep in their minds. They lie to themselves. They
> talk of freedom, and dream of captivity. . . . It is the world that shapes
> people's minds. It is men who have shaped the world. So women's minds
> are shaped by men. . . . Now the women lie to themselves and there is
> confusion and unhappiness everywhere. (CS, 71–72)

Using a series of gross overgeneralizations and false deductions,
Robert rationalizes his brutal nature, his cruelty to Caroline. Essentially,
he justifies his barbaric sadism. As J. R. Banks notes, the entire novel is
a "working-out of [Robert's] ideas and a demonstration of how dangerous attitudes like Robert's can be" (Banks, 29). Likewise, the novel
protests these crucial assumptions that so many in society naturally
make—that the male should be the dominant subject and the female
should be the subservient object. Caroline, then, is representative of the
ideal, cowering woman in Robert's master plan. She willingly, even joy-
ously, succumbs to the ruthless demands of her husband, all the while
simultaneously horrified and elated by the brutality. Theirs is a relationship filled with sexual violence, the epitome of a sadomasochistic
alliance.
   Caroline explains to Mary that she, in fact, enjoys the physical and
mental pain that Robert demands in their lovemaking. She clarifies, however, that "it's not the pain itself, it's the fact of the pain, of being helpless
before it, and being reduced to nothing by it. . . . I was ashamed of
myself, and before I knew it, my shame too was a source of pleasure. . . . I
wanted it more and more. I needed it" (CS, 110). Despite the need,
despite the pleasure, the relationship virtually destroys Caroline, wreck-

ing her body, ravaging her spirit. She confides everything to Mary, relating every horrifying detail:

> [Robert] used a whip. He beat me with his fists as he made love to me. I was terrified, but the terror and the pleasure were all one. Instead of saying loving things into my ear, he whispered pure hatred, and though I was sick with humiliation, I thrilled to the point of passing out. I didn't doubt Robert's hatred for me. It wasn't theater. He made love to me out of deep loathing, and I couldn't resist. I loved being punished.
>
> . . . My body was covered with bruises, cuts, weals. Three of my ribs were cracked. Robert knocked out one of my teeth. I had a broken finger. . . . Neither of us could resist it. Quite often I was the one to initiate it, and that was never difficult. Robert was longing to pound my body to a pulp. We had arrived at the point we had been heading towards all the time. Robert confessed one night that there was only one thing he really wanted. He wanted to kill me, as we made love. He was absolutely serious. (*CS*, 110–11)

Plummeting ever downward, Robert and Caroline soon, inevitably, reach the nadir of their relationship, the unavoidable conclusion of their sado-masochistic alliance: Caroline is not killed, but her back is broken. Robert destroys her spirit, leaving her spineless. Caroline's injury is a direct consequence of her masochistic desires, an indirect consequence of her society's patriarchal demands.

Despite the savage repercussions of their desires, Robert and Caroline quickly discover that they are incapable of satiating their sadomasochistic longings with only the two of them; the only solution, they determine, is to shift their perverse desires onto an unsuspecting third. Surprisingly, the focus of their united attention is Colin—one would think that Robert's blatant machismo would dictate that the third party be a woman. Robert's need to dominate, however, simply knows no bounds. It is not the gender of the third that matters but the thrill of the murder that promises ecstasy; it is not the sexual desire that controls but the need to dominate. The novel then rushes toward its inevitable conclusion. The climactic scene is every bit as violent, every bit as sinister as those in McEwan's stories. Caroline and Robert experience the ultimate in their sadomasochistic fancies, manipulating, as Caroline notes, their fantasies into reality. As the strangers play out their "obscene excesses" (*CS*, 124), Colin and Mary find themselves inescapably ensnared, irrevocably doomed. Before a drugged and stupefied Mary (her drug-induced paralysis eerily reminiscent of her inability to move freely about the city),

Robert easily, almost leisurely, murders Colin: "[Robert] reached for Colin's arm, and turned his palm upward. 'See how easy it is,' he said, perhaps to himself, as he drew the razor lightly, almost playfully, across Colin's wrist, opening wide the artery. His arm jerked forward, and the rope he cast, orange in this light, fell short of Mary's lap by several inches" (CS, 122). Through the night Caroline and Robert continue to live out their fantasy, cavorting in Colin's blood, revelling in the power that results from his slaughter: "[Mary] dreamed of moans and whimpers, and sudden shouts, of figures locked and turning at her feet, churning through the little pond, calling out for joy" (CS, 123). Mary and Colin find themselves the manipulated and expendable pawns in a world ordered only in terms of brutality. Colin's death is senseless, incomprehensible; he is a sacrifice to the creations of a perverted fantasy, a lost and corrupted society.

The murder is made all the more horrifying by the ordinariness that permeates the event. The world, infuriatingly, incomprehensibly to Mary, continues to plod its dreary course. Upon her return to the hotel after the murder, for example, Mary hears that "outside they were banging away as usual on the barges with their steel tools" (CS, 126). Approaching the hospital, she observes the daily rituals of the city beginning as usual: women setting up stalls, a van delivering flowers, a gardener watering the drive. Far more shocking is the fact that Mary discovers that the circumstances of Colin's murder are "wearyingly common, belonging in a well-established category" (CS, 124). As the novel closes and Mary leaves the hospital, the narrator notes, "Ordinariness prevailed for an instant, and she had the briefest intimation of the grief that lay in wait" (CS, 127). Through the horror and the chaos of Mary's experience, McEwan demonstrates that the only constant is the usual, a perversity of the ordinary.

As the novel concludes, Mary formulates a theory that attempts to justify the irrational death of her lover; sitting beside the lifeless body of Colin she thinks of explaining her idea to him: "she was going to explain it all to him, tell him her theory, tentative at this stage, of course, which explained how the imagination, the sexual imagination, men's ancient dreams of hurting, and women's of being hurt, embodied and declared a powerful single organizing principle, which distorted all relations, all truth" (CS, 126). This theory, which echoes exactly that which the chauvinistic Robert has earlier related to Colin, is the warped result of patriarchal ideology. Mary, in despair abandoning her feminist sensibilities, falls prey to the power of the patriarchy, surrendering to the overtly cruel, the overly simplistic mind-set of the dominators. James Campbell, in a review entitled "Dreams of Pain," states, "The weight of the novel seems to me to depend on this [theory]; it may be true but it cannot be the whole truth. . . . Men's ancient dreams of hurting and women's of being hurt may indeed distort the truth, but even if men and women could awaken from these dreams the truth could not be conceived simply. What seals the fate of the wretched Colin and Mary is that they suppose that it can be."[9]

McEwan himself admits that the truth, indeed, is not simple. He says that it was not "enough to talk about men and women in social terms"; rather, he felt he had to address, especially in formulating the concept that serves as the theoretical backbone to the novel, the "nature of the unconscious, and how the unconscious is shaped. It wasn't enough to be rational, since there might be desires—masochism in women, sadism in men—which act out the oppression of women or patriarchal societies but which have actually become related to sources of pleasure" (Haffenden, 32). McEwan is far from alone in recognizing these transcultural sexual politics. Other contemporary writers see, too, the sadistic male/masochistic female as the prototypical sexual interaction in present-day society, the result of corrupted and perverted sexual hierarchies. Kathy Acker, for example, often portrays sex as a brutal and barbaric act, with women usually humiliated and degraded by their male partners. Similarly, the obsessive affair at the center of Josephine Hart's *Damage* has Anna willingly submitting herself to the sexual demands of the narrator (her "lord" as she calls him) in "everything, always." As a result of the warped mentalities and the corrupted hierarchies that produce this theory, sadomasochistic violence is seen as the barbaric aim of every sexual desire. In the end, though, McEwan shows the dire consequences of any relationship controlled by such beliefs. He also unequivocally illustrates the dangers of the majority of a populace basing their ideology upon such distorted assumptions. Quite possibly not satisfied with these end results, McEwan returns to this theory in *The Innocent*. In Leonard's sexual fantasy of raping Maria, McEwan presents a more satisfying conclusion, and, in part, offers solution to this patriarchal dilemma. *The Comfort of Strangers,* though, can be read as a warning, a foreboding for all of contemporary society.

A cursory glance would suggest that *The Comfort of Strangers* contains nothing more than a further exploration of the violent, brutal world of male-female relationships, but there is more than meets the voyeur's eye. Though Colin and Mary are, for the most part, superficial people, they still realize the potential and fulfillment contained within a sustaining relationship; there is a genuine desire to relate.

More important is McEwan's profound concern about the corruptions and perversions that result in a society based on a destructive sexual hierarchy, a patriarchal world that demands the subservience of its female population. Christopher Ricks states that with *The Comfort of Strangers* McEwan has "undertaken a tragedy. Tragedy acknowledges that the injustices of life are sometimes corrigible. *The Comfort of Strangers* is alive with anger at the injustices, for instance, of the politics of sex, and it includes some vivid conversations on these wrongs and rights."[10] With the characterizations of Caroline and Robert, McEwan paints a portrait of the extremes to which a society obsessed with patriarchal desires can be taken. Robert may be a grotesque caricature of male chauvinism, but he nonetheless focuses attention on the abnormalities that can—indeed, *must*—occur in a patriarchal society. Likewise, Caroline embodies the extremities of subservience. Neither, McEwan states, is acceptable. As a result of this belief, in the majority of his subsequent works, McEwan continues to explore the roles of women in society, more and more often showing them as being the positive, cohesive element in relationships.

Chapter Six
Warping Fantasy into Reality: The Film Scripts

As a writer, McEwan has made several forays to the screen. His earliest attempts at film, "Jack Flea's Birthday Celebration" and "Solid Geometry," were closely aligned in both theme and content to his early stories. These works continue to explore the isolated, claustrophobic worlds, the microscopic scrutiny of individuals and their relationships. His later screenplays—"The Imitation Game," *The Ploughman's Lunch,* and *Soursweet*—similarly reflect the more mature, more transcultural concerns that comprise his later fiction. They are, then, a more intense encounter with a world that, as he says, "distresses me and makes me anxious" (Haffenden, 30).

In his first two film scripts for television, "Jack Flea's Birthday Celebration" (an original work) and "Solid Geometry" (an adaptation of the story from *First Love, Last Rites*), McEwan continues to explore some of his favorite themes: the difficulty of establishing viable relationships, regression into an infantile state, the disintegration of family, the ordinariness that persists in the most extreme of circumstances. Although his collection of television plays was published several years after *First Love, Last Rites,* "Jack Flea's Birthday Celebration" and "Solid Geometry," in themes and purpose, are closely aligned to his first collection of fiction.[1] In a sense, they can be considered an extension of that work, and, as with his stories, the plays are sharp, often bitter assessments of life, love, and relationships in modern society.

Both "Jack Flea's Birthday Celebration" and "Solid Geometry" are experimental in nature; both begin as examinations of complacent, ordinary—if sometimes strained—familial relationships in contemporary English society but conclude with these relationships in ruin and with normality turned on its head. In creating the plays McEwan relies heavily on the accepted conventions of television; then, by slow degrees, he warps these clichés to the point that "fantasy [becomes] reality" (*IG,* 11). In "Jack Flea's Birthday Celebration" regression suddenly becomes not a game but an integral part of David and Ruth's relationship; in "Solid

Geometry" the surfaceless plane *does* exist. The clichés of the medium, McEwan says, stem from the naturalism in which current television finds itself embedded:

> Television was, and is, dominated by the powerful, cohesive conventions of its naturalism. . . . Naturalism is the common language of television, not the language we speak, but one we are accustomed to listen to. . . . [This] centrality of television naturalism suggested, or so I thought, that formal experiment could therefore really matter, that by calling into question the rules of the common language the viewer could be disoriented and tempted to regard the world afresh. (*IG,* 9–10)

"Jack Flea" and "Solid Geometry" are, then, attempts to "kick over the traces" (*IG,* 10), to startle audiences from the stupor of mindless television.

"Jack Flea's Birthday Celebration"

"Jack Flea's Birthday Celebration" was written in 1974, soon after McEwan had completed the short stories that would comprise *First Love, Last Rites.* Closely associated to the collection in style and premise, McEwan says that he "[thinks] of this play as really belonging in that volume" (*IG,* 10–11). Produced by Tara Prem and directed by Mike Newell, the play aired as a part of the series "Second City Firsts" on 10 April 1976.

The play begins as a conventional dinner party in which a young man introduces his girlfriend to his parents. It quickly becomes evident, however, that the young man, David, is intentionally orchestrating a confrontation between Ruth, his lover (16 years his senior), and his parents. The purpose, he explains in his autobiographical novel-in-progress, is to establish a scene in which "his real mother and his fantasy mother meet" (*IG,* 38). David forces Ruth to greet his parents alone, which elevates the tension; without him, the three sit uncomfortably in a "threatening silence" (*IG,* 28). This tension develops through the play, creating a sense of claustrophobia in the interaction among the four characters.

Finding himself the willing "fantasy child" of Ruth, David attempts "to get a clearer perspective on it all" (*IG,* 38) by writing a novel that focuses on a character who has also become the fantasy child of an older woman and who has also decided to write a novel so that he might better understand his situation. Through the urging of Ruth and his mother, David reads aloud from a chapter entitled "A Birthday Celebration";

the scene depicts the protagonist, Jack Flea, as having instigated a tense meeting between his parents and his lover in hopes that this chapter of the novel "will write itself" (*IG,* 38). The novel is obviously metafictional, mirroring David's own life. More to the point, when Mrs. Lee angrily snatches away the page from which David reads, she and the others discover that it is blank; simultaneously, the audience realizes that the story of Jack Flea is not fiction but fact, not fantasy but reality.

In his novel David writes that Jack Flea runs away from his home in order to "escape his miserably ineffectual father and the stifling, sinister attentions of his mother" (*IG,* 38). These descriptions prove to be thinly disguised portraits of his own parents. Mr. Lee proves to be as ineffective a father as he is a husband; he is the stereotypical henpecked spouse, cowering at his wife's every demand and bark. Mrs. Lee constantly corrects and reprimands him, at one point even demanding that he drink sherry rather than whiskey. Once, during the course of the evening, he momentarily tears free of his wife's reins, breaking into uncontrollable laughter over the grotesque description of her in David's novel. When he finds himself forced by Mrs. Lee to make amends, however, he apologizes in a subservient, doglike manner: he kneels at her feet, resting his head in her lap, while she "strokes his head and smiles" (*IG,* 41). Similarly, Mr. Lee demonstrates his inability at fathering in his "man to man chat" with his son; their talk is nothing more than nonsensical fragments. He is impotent as both father and husband.

Mrs. Lee is, in turn, portrayed as the stereotypical smothering mother. One of her favorite pastimes is correcting her son: she reminds David to say "lavatory" instead of "toilet" (*IG,* 30), she insists that he knows someone he cannot remember, she tells him to "mind [his] language" (*IG,* 37). Mrs. Lee persists in treating David as a child, refusing to acknowledge his right to adulthood. In a sense, the play could be seen as an "uninitiation story" in which the mother attempts to prevent her son from maturing, from leaving his overly protected childhood (much as did the Cupboard Man's mother). In an effort to dominate David, Mrs. Lee overasserts her powers as a mother. For example, she insists that David sit closer to her for his birthday present; later, she embarrassingly relates his ineptitude as a child, recalling that at 12 he was "still getting his shoes on the wrong feet . . . *and* sleeping with the light on when he was fourteen" (*IG,* 33). In Mrs. Lee, McEwan creates a son's worst nightmare; under his mother's domination, David becomes powerless to realize his own life. He depicts his feelings of inadequacy and incompetence, his sense of insignificance, in the name he chooses for his autobiographical protagonist, Jack *Flea.*

Consequently, we can understand his need to create a positive mother figure in Ruth. David's regression in the final scene, then, is not so much a perversity as it is a cry for help and love.

As the play progresses, the dinner party rapidly disintegrates into a battle between the two mothers. In the novel David describes Hermione, Ruth's alter ego, as "a woman nearly twice [Jack Flea's] age, a woman obsessed by the two great failures in her life. The first to have a child, the second to achieve an orgasm. Of the second she has wisely despaired, but of the first . . . she decides to make Jack Flea her child, her fantasy child. It's a role that poor Jack Flea cannot resist" (*IG,* 38). Similarly, Ruth forms her relationship with David to ameliorate the sense of failure in her life; by "adopting" him as a "fantasy child," she is able to attain a sense of accomplishment as well as to bestow motherly love. Likewise, David is attracted to Ruth because he himself seeks a *true* mother. Near the end of the play Mrs. Lee relates a story concerning the time that an 18-month-old David confused a babysitter for his real mother: "He was calling [the babysitter] Mummy and crying when she went off to school in the morning. He wouldn't have anything to do with me. . . . He wouldn't let no one else feed him with his spoon. Only her. . . . There was nothing for it. We had to find another bed and breakfast. What a scene that was. The girl crying. You screaming Mummy. The whole street out watching. I'll never forget that, never" (*IG,* 44–45). Symbolically, David has been seeking a mother ever since, attempting to rid himself of the "stifling, sinister attentions" of Mrs. Lee and trying to find someone who will nurture and love him. He discovers an exaggerated form of this mother in Ruth.

From the outset, it is apparent that Ruth and Mrs. Lee dislike each other. Ruth fills Mrs. Lee's glass "with a certain malice" and watches the interactions between mother and son "with poorly concealed horror" (*IG,* 32). In turn, Mrs. Lee "glares at Ruth with intense hostility" (*IG,* 42) and immediately readjusts the cufflinks Ruth has just clipped onto David's sleeves (*IG,* 33). The two women aggressively assert their mothering domains, laying claim to a son that they both believe is theirs alone. At one point Ruth tells Mrs. Lee that "some women make dangerous mothers" (*IG,* 44). What Ruth and Mrs. Lee both fail to realize is that they are *both* dangerous; they both refuse David his independence, propelling him, instead, into a state of infantile behavior. Mrs. Lee, wishing him to remain forever the child that she reared, constantly brings up stories and memories of David's childhood, persistently reminding the other characters (with an almost paranoid insistence) that she and David "were very close" (*IG,* 44, 45). Ruth, on the other hand, sees him as a compensation for the child she has never had, and she continuously treats him as her own infant, tousling his hair, speaking to him as though he were a small child, reminding everyone that he still wets the bed, brushing his hair "in a motherly way" (*IG,* 45). David refuses to break the strangling bonds of either woman, finding security in their stifling maternal affection; it is, essentially, what he has always sought, always needed.

Although David discovers a perverse satisfaction in these distorted relationships, neither of the women is happy with the situation; they continue to battle for David's full devotion. For instance, after Mrs. Lee's tale of the babysitter fiasco—which is "designed to get at Ruth and succeeds" (*IG,* 45)—Ruth reacts by repossessing David, saying, "Now he's *my* lovely little boy" (*IG,* 45). These words ring ominously true as she and David then proceed to act out the bizarre ritual of his regression:

[RUTH]	*Reaches down for DAVID's napkin and fixes it around his neck like a bib. She takes his spoon out of his hand. While she speaks she feeds DAVID mouthfuls. Her tone is mischievous, paying off a score. All by now should be well and truly boozed.* He doesn't let anyone else feed him with his spoon. It has to be me. He doesn't let anyone else put him to bed. Only me. We're very close.[2] You can see how close we are.
MRS LEE.	He might be living with you but he's still my son.
RUTH.	No, no. He's my little boy now. I'm his Mummy now. . . . Sometimes he comes and curls up in my lap and closes his eyes and I feed him milk (MRS LEE *gasps*) . . . from a baby's bottle . . . yes, my little Jack Flea sucks and remembers he's only a tiny little boy, my little boy. And you know one day I'm going to buy him a big playpen so he can't run away . . . because little boys sometimes run away, and I'll keep him all mine, he'll never leave the house, he'll be mine, all mine. (*IG,* 45–46)

David and Ruth's production is soon exposed as a "joke" that has its desired effect on the Lees: they are shocked. Simultaneously, though, Ruth has made it quite clear that David now belongs to her. This is ultimately realized in the closing scene when fantasy becomes reality as David does regress and Ruth dons the role of his mother:

> *Close-up of* DAVID *in bed, eyes closed.* RUTH *leans forward and they kiss deeply.*

RUTH   *(whispers).* Go to sleep now.

DAVID   *goes to speak.* RUTH *shushes him. We pull away and see that* DAVID *is lying in a large cot.* RUTH *in a nightdress slides the side up, goes to the door, pauses there a moment to look back at* DAVID, *smiles to herself, turns the light out and softly closes the door. A small night-light burns.* (IG, 49)

In a bizarre twist of reality, David has discovered the nurturing mother he has sought, and Ruth has found the child she never had.

"Jack Flea's Birthday Celebration" incorporates two of McEwan's more prevalent themes: that of regression and that of a female who finds herself unexpectedly in the role of surrogate mother. Both of these themes are introduced into the film script as game-playing, as fantasy. In the closing scene, however, they are transformed into the ordinary, the commonplace of David and Ruth's relationship. Just as the blank page of David's self-reflective novel reveals the true essence of the horrors of his life, McEwan twists an everyday family gathering, a popular television cliché, into a scenario of repression and regression. By startling his audience, McEwan attempts to bring a new plateau to television's naturalism, contorting it from banality to originality.

"Solid Geometry"

In 1978 McEwan adapted "Solid Geometry" for television. Commissioned for a series entitled "The Other Side," the play was produced by Stephen Gilbert and directed by Mike Newell. Because of vaguely explained objections, however, the BBC halted production on 22 March 1979.

The film script is a faithful adaptation of the story from *First Love, Last Rites.* The emphasis remains focused on the clashing of two completely separate intellectual worlds: the analytical and rational as represented by Albert (the name McEwan gives the story's unnamed narrator) and the intuitive and spiritual as represented by Albert's wife, Maisie. In the play McEwan goes to further lengths to accentuate their differences. For example, when Albert says they could take a holiday "somewhere cold, clean and treeless," Maisie replies, "Or a hot, dirty jungle" (IG, 88). McEwan also immediately introduces these differences in the stage directions: Maisie is described as "in her late twenties, a product and to some extent a victim of the Sixties—unfocused ambitions, reflective in a self-destructive way. But she has warmth and must be sympathetic" (*IG,* 58), while Albert is described as "thirtyish, self-absorbed, somewhere in his mind he has left his wife far behind" (*IG,* 58). In further explaining the natures of these characters, McEwan says,

> It was . . . important to prevent Albert from becoming too sympathetic. It could easily happen because he is the one with the diaries, and through whom we have access to Great-grandfather, Maxwell and Vienna. Correspondingly, it was necessary to make Maisie as sympathetic as possible in her attempts to rescue the marriage; that way Albert's disposing of her would appear all the more callous. (*IG,* 13)

As in the story, Albert spends all of his time editing his great-grandfather's diaries; for him, his wife has become a nonentity. Maisie, in turn, occupies her time by trying to "get [her] head straight" (*IG,* 72), reading Jung and tarot cards, practicing yoga, studying books on mysticism. Albert discovers, however, that he has to rely on the antirational in order to rid himself of Maisie. On a page in Great-grandfather's diary, Albert finds the cryptic phrase "dimensionality is a function of consciousness" (*IG,* 85). Once Albert *believes* in the existence of the surfaceless plane, it exists; by succumbing to the antirational of his wife's world, Albert is able to "disappear" her. As with "Jack Flea's Birthday Celebration," McEwan again warps the clichés of television drama, startling his viewers and twisting fantasy into reality.

As opposed to the cold and unloving Albert, Maisie represents the nurturing woman that is so prevalent in McEwan's fiction. Similar to such characters as Jenny in "Last Day of Summer," Julie in *The Cement Garden,* and Julie in *The Child in Time,* Maisie attempts to keep the family together, providing the love and care that can strengthen and solidify relationships. These female characters realize that it is love and togetherness that provide the strength necessary for individuals to survive. Unfortunately, Maisie fails, proving herself incapable of withstanding the brutality and cold rationality of Albert and his world.

In the adaptation, McEwan is given the opportunity to strengthen some elements of the story. For example, the bodily contortions that accompany a disappearance into the surfaceless plane are made even more absurd. As David Hunter, the discoverer of the plane, goes through the process, McEwan instructs in his stage directions that "these [contortions] must seem improbable—use tight close-ups and other

people's legs!" (*IG*, 83). Likewise, in the film script the positions are
more closely linked to the antirational world of Maisie; in the story the
narrator discovers a series of sketches that "at first glance *looked like* yoga
positions" (*FLLR,* 36; my italics), whereas in the play, the positions are
unequivocally identified as "a set of numbered yoga positions" (*IG*,
86)—the movements necessary to enter the surfaceless plane are thus
implicitly connected to Maisie's spiritual world. These subtle changes
help to strengthen McEwan's purpose in these early plays; by emphasizing the paradoxical nature of these contortions, he is able to warp fantasy into reality: the surfaceless plane becomes acceptable, even credible,
to both the characters and the audience.

In looking back on his adaptation of "Solid Geometry," McEwan says,
"After a week's rehearsal in March 1979 I began to think that this was,
potentially at least, a far better play than a short story. It had a resonance and life that had not been present previously. . . . What was merely anecdotal in the story now seemed a strong narrative line" (*IG*,
13–14). Unfortunately, the play never aired; the BBC halted production
four days before filming began. Throughout the controversy that followed, the BBC remained ambiguous and enigmatic about its reasons
for banning the production. In a meeting with Shaun Sutton, head of the
BBC's Drama Group, Television, McEwan was told that the play "was
'untransmittable' and that this was not a time for adventurous projects"
(*IG*, 14). Later, the BBC released a press notice that "announced the ban
and referred to 'grotesque and bizarre sexual elements in the play'" (*IG*,
14). McEwan's first impression was that the BBC had been offended by
the preserved penis. In the play the auctioneer describes the "anatomical
curiosity" as measuring "a little under twelve inches and . . . in a beautiful state of preservation" (*IG*, 54). McEwan also calls for three separate
close-ups of the object, and the penis is fully exposed when Maisie
smashes the jar (*IG*, 80). In working around the bottled penis, McEwan
states that the production staff "would have resented a compromise, but
. . . there may have been room for manoeuvre" (*IG*, 14). The BBC, however, refused either comment or compromise.

The film script of "Solid Geometry" was published in the *New
Statesman* in March 1979. In an introduction to the play, McEwan makes
a final comment concerning the censorship of the BBC:

> The cancellation of *Solid Geometry* was not designed to protect viewers
> from radical political ideas, nor from excessive violence; it seems to have
> arisen from smaller notions of respectability. One or two executives in the

> BBC just *know* that a penis in a specimen jar is rude; whatever the dra-
> matic context, it will offend. I was told informally that it was felt that the
> line "My period has started. I need to get something" would be "offensive
> to middle-class ladies.". . . . Television drama is too important to be sub-
> ject to the susceptibilities of one or two administrators. . . . There must be
> more people involved in these decisions, and some of them should be pro-
> gramme makers. At the very least there should be a right of appeal
> against what is considered to be unfair or arbitrary censorship.[3]

Shortly after the banning, the film script became, as McEwan says, "widely celebrated in the press as a play with bizarre sex scenes" (*IG,* 15). As time passed, the BBC remained stubborn, the press lost interest, "the whole thing was forgotten" (15, *IG*), and the chapter closed on one of McEwan's more controversial pieces.

With "Jack Flea's Birthday Celebration" and "Solid Geometry," McEwan effectively broadens his creative scope. Still relying heavily on a literature of shock and Roald Dahl–type endings, McEwan nonethe-less proves himself adept in the art of screenwriting. The two plays suc-cessfully transform the clichéd images and situations of contemporary television, twisting fantasy and fiction into a believable reality. The por-trayals of the worlds of David and Ruth and of Albert and Maisie both begin as the depiction of everyday, contemporary lives. When the sur-face erupts and the ordinary becomes extraordinary, McEwan, as he says, attempts to "disorient" the audiences, tempting them "to regard the world afresh" (*IG,* 10). Although McEwan did not set the television world afire with a desire for intelligent, well-written programs, he did manage to provide himself with valuable experience in the craft of screenwriting, preparing himself for the more complex screenplays he would later create.

With these later, more mature screenplays, McEwan turns to broader realms, examining entire populations and their governments rather than individuals and their claustrophobic lives. In an interview with John Haffenden, McEwan explains this shift, saying,

> [This change] was something I intended. . . . In writing *The Imitation
> Game* I stepped out into the world—consciously to find out about a cer-
> tain time in the past and to recreate it—and at that point I felt I had
> made a very distinct change. . . . I am aware of the danger that in trying
> to write more politically—in the broadest sense—trying to go out more
> into the world, because it is a world that distresses me and makes me
> anxious—I could take up moral positions that might pre-empt or exclude

that rather mysterious and unreflective element that is so important in fiction. (Haffenden, 30)

As a result of these changes, McEwan brings modern English society under a close—and scathing—scrutiny. At the core of each of his major screenplays, some sector of English society plays a devious and unflattering role. In "The Imitation Game" McEwan examines the degrading way in which women were treated by the British government and army during World War II. In *The Ploughman's Lunch* he explores the fickleness of government and how this vast machine manipulates its people, even to the point of altering its history. In *Soursweet* he presents the trials and difficulties of Chinese immigrants attempting to acculturate themselves to British society. Despite the turn toward more politically conscious works, McEwan remains persistent in his exploration of male-female relationships; even in the chaos of manipulative governments and repressive societies, McEwan demonstrates that human relationships remain of the utmost importance.

"The Imitation Game"

As he does in *The Comfort of Strangers,* with "The Imitation Game" (directed by Richard Eyre and aired as a BBC "Play for Today" on 24 April 1980), McEwan takes a critical look at the crimes of a patriarchal society—slipping, Lorna Sage notes, "out of his solipsistic and self-conscious corner [of his fiction] into the (contemporary) breezy climate of sexual politics."[4] In the introduction to *The Imitation Game,* McEwan states,

> I wanted to write a novel which would assume as its background a society not primarily as a set of economic classes but as a patriarchy. . . . The [English] system whose laws, customs, religion and culture consistently sanction the economic ascendancy of one sex over another could be a still richer source; men and women have to do with each other in ways that economic classes do not. Patriarchy corrupts our most intimate relationships with comic and tragic consequences. (*IG,* 16)

The play concerns the injustices and degradations experienced by women as they attempt to subsist in the male-dominated society of World War II England. Although set in 1940, McEwan's portrayal of the sexual exploitation practiced by the British patriarchy is not limited to the past. Richard Johnstone, in his article "Television Drama and the People's War," says,

> What is presented . . . in *The Imitation Game* is a self-conscious, almost self-declaring *illusion* of historical reality, in which certain contemporary preoccupations—with the new feminism, with the function of codes—are dressed up as the past, a past from which, in McEwan's view, they derive. It is not a question, as some perhaps would have it, of falsifying history. Rather *The Imitation Game* . . . consistently reminds us that the relationship between then and now is a shifting one, and that the past cannot be fixed, can only be reinterpreted.[5]

Thus, McEwan's concerns are timeless, reaching into and pointing an accusatory finger at contemporary society.

Likewise, Cathy Raine's plight is transhistorical. McEwan molds the character of Cathy to represent all British women, particularly those mistreated by the British government and army during World War II. Simultaneously, Cathy is also emblematic of women subjugated by *any* patriarchy. In joining the Auxiliary Territorial Service (ATS), a women's branch of the military services, Cathy attempts to deny, and even to break free of, the shackles forced on her by a male-dominated society. As McEwan notes, during the conflict women were allowed to take part only as "housekeepers of the war—cooks, chauffeurs, secretaries" (*IG*, 19). Essentially, the opportunity to do anything meaningful or worthwhile in the war effort was denied women; they were seen as being capable of managing only menial, unskilled tasks. Within the play, exemplifying this belief that women were indeed less capable, less adept than men, the army itself states that "no skilled person is to do what can be done by an unskilled person, and no man is to do what can be done by a woman" (*IG*, 151).

Cathy, however, attempts to break these convictions, insisting that she can and will do something important, something necessary to the war cause. Speaking to Tony, her fiancé, she says, "I just know that something very important is in the air. . . . I want to be *doing* something . . . . I want to learn something difficult" (*IG*, 110–11). Her independent nature is likewise presented in the ordinary events of her everyday life. For example, she shocks her parents when she walks home alone in the dark only because she "felt like walking" (*IG*, 106). As a result of her independent, even rebellious, nature, Cathy joins the ATS because she believes that she can become a necessary component of the war effort.

Richard Johnstone says that "for Cathy, the War seems at first to bring [a] kind of release, a freedom she could not otherwise have expected. Her notions of where such freedom will lead her are vague, but she feels that . . . 'everything is about to change forever'" (Johnstone, 194). In doing something she deems worthwhile, however, she discovers that her society patronizes her action as well as her person.

From the outset of her decision, Cathy feels an immediate disapproval from her family. She comes from the stereotypical patriarchal family: her father rules the family with a firm hand and a perpetual look of disdain. As the play opens she is *"under pressure from her father {to} be 'directed' into war work"* (*IG,* 99), and if she does get work at a munitions factory, she knows that the majority of her pay will be handed over to him. Mr. Raine also views his daughter with condescension, asking, upon hearing that she has been thinking about her part in the war, "And will you be doing any more 'thinking' in the near future?" (*IG,* 106). Not surprisingly, then, Mr. Raine is outraged when he learns that Cathy has joined the ATS. When she leaves for her assignment, he ignores her completely, refusing even to say good-bye. On the other hand, Cathy's mother, a *"comfortable, slightly ineffectual woman"* (*IG,* 105), is more shocked than angered by Cathy's enlistment. When she relates to Cathy how other military personnel react to ATS, she readily reveals that she is far more concerned about her daughter's reputation than safety: "Last week I was at the bus station sitting across from three or four soldiers, nicely turned out boys. Two ATS came by and just smiled right at those young boys, bold as anything. And when they'd gone do you know what the soldiers called them? 'Scum of the earth,' that's what they said. 'There goes the scum of the earth.'. . . The ATS is not a place for respectable young girls" (*IG,* 116).[6] Nonetheless, Cathy bears her family's dissatisfaction and enlists in the ATS.

Like her father, Cathy's fiancé condescends to her. When Tony tells Cathy that intelligence probably will not accept women, he attempts to appease her by saying that she can do her part by teaching him to type and cook, tasks at which all women excel, he stereotypically implies. When it is Cathy and not Tony who is accepted into intelligence operations, Tony is not only shocked and angered at Cathy's enlistment but also humiliated. His only response is that her action "is more or less the end for us" (*IG,* 117). Like Mrs. Raine, Tony sees the ATS as something disreputable, vulgar: "There's something horrible about seeing a whole lot of women in uniform, something sinister. They don't look like women at all" (*IG,* 120). Yet Cathy remains firm in her decision, asking

Tony the question that could be posed to the entire patriarchal society: "Why do you think your war is so much more important than mine?" (*IG,* 119). Cathy enters the ATS as an act of independence, an attempt to escape the patronizing and disdainful way that her family treats her.[7]

Unfortunately, Cathy soon discovers an even more demeaning attitude in the "outside" world. Public opinion toward the ATS, and toward women in general, within the patriarchal society of England is condescending, brutal. For example, Cathy and her friend Mary are ordered by a publican to leave his bar solely because of who they are. He tells them, "This isn't the kind of place you think it is. . . . This is a respectable pub, not a place where you can hang around and wait to be picked up" (*IG,* 143).[8] A dispute ensues, ending when Cathy—undoubtedly relying upon her military training—knees the publican in the groin. Her commanding officer, not surprisingly, supports the man, telling Cathy, "Assaulting a publican. I'm not sure I wouldn't rate that more serious than rape, wouldn't you?" (*IG,* 145). The same sexist attitude is also evident among the men working within Bletchley. When Turner begins to explain the concept of the "imitation game"—a procedure for determining whether machines can "think"—one of his cohorts interrupts him to ask, "Shouldn't you first establish whether the woman can think? It's not something one can take for granted, you know" (*IG,* 154). Cathy continually encounters similar chauvinistic attitudes, but the perspective toward women is never worse, never more petty than that which is exhibited by the army itself.

For instance, the army that Cathy encounters presents an especially despicable attitude toward its female members. Woman is seen by the military as a wholly different, a completely other being from man. This extreme patronage is seen with brutal clarity as an ATS officer addresses a group of army commanders, preparing them for the women who will soon be under their authority. This attitude is incorporated into the film script as a voice-over that occurs during scenes depicting Cathy and other ATS recruits going through basic training. The ATS officer tells his audience that "women are not good at standing" and that "the fatigue engendered by standing has a bad effect upon their capacity to take in instructions and will induce inattention, fidgeting, boredom" (*IG,* 122), that women are "normally lacking in community consciousness" (*IG,* 123), that "their capacity for magnifying and altering any rumour which reaches them is incredible" (*IG,* 125), that "tears are natural with some women, and are frequently perfectly genuine" (*IG,* 125). The army obviously falls easy prey to gross stereotyping, seeing women as caretakers at best, as nuisances in general. In emphasizing such flagrant overgeneralizations, however, McEwan captures precisely the unconscionable attitudes of male patronage and condescension that are so imperative to the machinations of a patriarchy.

These "male" attitudes of the army culminate in the intense secrecy that shrouds much of Ultra (the intelligence operation) in which Cathy plays an incomprehensible role. Cathy refuses to accept a menial job and instead finds a position as a special operative. Her role, though, is a minor one: she listens to indecipherable, nonsensical messages over a wireless, and copies down gibberish. She finds the secrecy infuriating and constantly wishes that she knew more; she even smuggles one of the codes out of the hut in order to "have a crack at breaking the code myself" (*IG*, 141). Later, commenting on this male-ordered secrecy, Cathy says, "All of us girls know nothing, and a few of the men know something" (*IG*, 142). McEwan says that this discrimination against women allowed him to see Ultra as a microcosm for the entire English society.

Cathy soon discovers that this discrimination is multiplied manifold when she is forcibly sent—because of the incident in the pub—to Bletchley, the center of intelligence operations. As McEwan notes in the introduction to *The Imitation Game and Other Plays,* the patriarchal laws that govern all of Cathy's society are especially enforced at this center:

> By the end of the war ten thousand people were working in and around Bletchley. The great majority of them were women doing vital but repetitive jobs. . . . The "need to know" rule meant that women knew as much as was necessary to do their jobs, which was very little. As far as I could discover there were virtually no women in at the centre of the Ultra secret. There was a widely held view at the beginning of the war that women could not keep secrets. (*IG*, 18)

While at Bletchley, Cathy is ordered to do "simple repetitive jobs, backing up the men" (*IG*, 164). She finds herself surrounded by restrictions and mandates: doors with signs ordering "STRICTLY AUTHORIZED PERSONNEL ONLY" (*IG*, 161) are slammed in her face; she is vehemently rebuked and thrown out of secret rooms; Turner tells her that he is unable to talk about his work.

These patronizing attitudes and the intricate levels of secrecy that exclude women are both reflected in the relationship that develops between Cathy and Turner, one of the operatives who is a part of the most secretive sanctums of Ultra. The courtship begins innocently enough, but they eventually find themselves in bed. When Turner confesses that, unlike Cathy, he is not a virgin, she tells him, "You know exactly what to do then. . . . You know all the secrets" (*IG,* 169). Cathy is obviously drawn to Turner because of the Ultra secrets that he does know. McEwan makes it clear, however, that she has no ulterior motive in her involvement with Turner. When Turner fails sexually, he angrily turns on Cathy, telling her, "You wanted to humiliate me and you succeeded. You hate your own job and you're jealous of me for mine. You wanted to even up the score. . . . You vindictive little bitch" (*IG,* 169–70). Once again woman becomes the enemy, the element that poses the real threat to the patriarchal traditions. In the same way McEwan shows that Turner's inadequacies reflect the weaknesses of this same patriarchal society. In an interview with John Haffenden, McEwan says,

> There is among men a fear of women and of their power. What is meant to be clear in the scene is that once Cathy is sexually excited she becomes very demanding, which is very frightening for Turner, and so his anger seemed to be dramatically in order. Once she has made the journey to the centre of official secrets, the other secret—the secret in the private world—creates the same response: she meets the masculine defensiveness that won't admit weakness. I see this defensiveness as a burden for men, and not just as the thing men do to women. I would not like to say who is unhappier in that scene, but it is quite clear who is more powerful. (Haffenden, 31–32)

Though more powerful in this particular scene, Cathy remains the subservient being. She discovers that to be accepted by men she must remain an outsider, existing only on the fringe of male secrets and knowledge.

Immediately after Turner's sexual failure, Cathy is caught looking in a secret file that Turner has inadvertently left behind; consequently, she is quickly trundled off to jail. As she is being sentenced, Cathy steps forward and moralizes on the role of women in war. In doing so, because of McEwan's didacticism, she seems to step momentarily out of the film itself:

> [Turner] thought it was terrible, the idea of women shooting at each other. Shooting each other's pretty little legs off. It is terrifying. It terrifies me because I would hate to lose my legs. But it terrifies men for a different reason . . . you know, on the anti-aircraft units the ATS girls are never allowed to fire the guns. Their job is to work the range-finder. If

> the girls fired the guns as well as the boys . . . if girls fired guns, and
> women generals planned the battles . . . then the men would feel there
> was no . . . morality to war, they would have no one to fight for,
> nowhere to leave their . . . consciences. . . . [W]ar would appear to them
> as savage and as pointless as it really is. The men want the women to
> stay out of the fighting so they can give it meaning. As long as we're on
> the outside and give our support and don't kill, women make the war
> just possible . . . something the men can feel tough about. (*IG*, 173–74)

Women, then, are essential to the conduct of war although they are
excluded from the actual participation. McEwan says that their "moral
and emotional commitment was vital, for they were the living embodiment of what the men fought to protect from the Enemy" (*IG*, 19).
Support by their women allowed the men, momentarily, to suspend willingly their own morality, their own consciences; in essence, the role of
women in this patriarchal society was to enable men to believe themselves the protectors of home, of nation, of culture.

In "The Imitation Game" McEwan shows that even though an occa-
sional individual may see through the facade of a patriarchal society, the
manipulations of this sort of community remain, for the most part,
prevalent and unchallenged. Likewise, the film demonstrates how World
War II, as Richard Johnstone states, was not "a national experience
which seemed . . . to offer new beginnings, new roles, which seemed to
point the way to an exciting and fulfilling future"; rather, it served to
entrench the preexisting patriarchy, "actually consolidat[ing] everything
that had gone before. The rhetoric of common cause had merely
obscured the ways in which the old injustices and inequalities were being
preserved" (Johnstone, 190). Through this play for television McEwan
expresses his concerns for contemporary society's subjugation of women;
essentially, "The Imitation Game" portrays not the way society *was* but
the way society *is*.

The Ploughman's Lunch

With *The Ploughman's Lunch*—his first screenplay for the cinema—
McEwan again collaborated with Richard Eyre, who directed from
McEwan's screenplay. The film was originally released in London (ironically, on the eve of the 1983 general election); it was released later in
1984 in the United States. McEwan's original screenplay was published
by Methuen Publishers in Britain in May 1985; Methuen also released a
paperback edition in the United States that same year.

Having portrayed governmental duplicities in 1940 Britain, McEwan says that he and Eyre wanted to make a film that dealt with current society: "Our film was to be set in the present and to be somehow 'about' the present. We wanted the textures of everyday London—the Underground, Brixton High Street—stylishly done."[9] The play, then, examines contemporary reality, effectively invoking the social and political spirit of Margaret Thatcher's England.

In his portrayal of contemporary British society, McEwan is most interested in presenting the way that nations manipulate and re-create their histories. In the introduction to *The Ploughman's Lunch* he says that he wanted to "encompass the uses we make of the past, and the dangers, to an individual as well as to a nation, of living without a sense of history" (*PL*, v). This reinvention, McEwan demonstrates, is evident in all levels of society. Late in the film Matthew Fox explains to James Penfield the origins of the pub meal called the ploughman's lunch. It is not, he says, "traditional English fare" as most are led to believe, but, rather, "the invention of an advertising campaign they ran in the early sixties to encourage people to eat in pubs. A completely successful fabrication of the past" (*PL*, 29–30). The title, then, becomes "a controlling metaphor for self-serving fabrications of the past" (*PL*, v). The metaphor represents not only the duplicity found in the manipulations of history but also the duplicities that abound in the relationships of the film.

Primarily, McEwan's concern in *The Ploughman's Lunch* is the willful and malicious restructuring of the past in order to maintain a comfortable if bland political present. This historical duplicity is readily evident in the British participation in both the Suez Crisis of 1956 (in which England lost control of the Suez Canal to Egypt) and the Falklands War of 1982 (in which England retook the Falkland Islands from an Argentinean invasion). Although there are clear differences between the two conflicts, McEwan says that he believes they have "their roots in the same illusion: a Churchillian dimension, and also war as serving a certain rallying function for the Right" (Haffenden, 34). Essentially, McEwan finds that the realities of both situations are reinterpreted not as examples of the imperialist intervention of England but as nationalistic endeavors that soundly accrued to British credit.

The film is set during the crisis of the Falklands invasion. This incident never dominates the film—in fact, it only rarely comes to the surface—yet it is perpetually in the background. To emphasize the importance that the invasion has on the characters and actions, McEwan bookends his screenplay with references to the incident: the film opens with a newscast that mentions Argentine movement in the South Atlantic; it concludes with Margaret Thatcher invoking the successful defense of the Falklands as a sign of the renewal of the English spirit. The invasion interests James in writing a book that would reexamine the Suez Crisis (and that would, consequently, add to the proliferation of duplicity that abounds in historical fact). Explaining the connection between the two international conflicts, McEwan says,

> What [James] sees is Britain sending off an invasion fleet, just as it did from Malta in 1956, with some chance of success. And if this is to succeed, and the general climate of opinion is wholly behind it, then this would be a very opportune time to present to Goldbooks the publishers the possibility of writing something which fits. The news that fits. The news on Suez is no longer to be that of national humiliation. James wants us to believe it unfortunate that it failed. A mistake but an honorable attempt, and we should get over all this stuff about deceit.[10]

James sees the Suez Crisis as "*the* key point" in Britain's recent history (*PL,* 5). Presenting the idea to the publisher Gold, James defends Britain's actions, saying, "the British Empire was an ideal. It may have become totally obsolete by the middle of this century, but it wasn't totally dishonorable to try and defend its remains and try and salvage some self-respect, which is what I think the Conservatives were trying to do. . . . If we had not been so scrupulous, we would not have been so ashamed" (*PL,* 6). Essentially, James attempts to view the past conflict in terms of the pragmatism that is so prevalent in a Thatcherite England.

James, however, is far from being the only manipulator of history; McEwan makes it clear that the distortion of history is virtually a national epidemic. For example, the film opens with a newscaster promoting an upcoming segment that examines "how the governments of Eastern Europe distort their recent past in history books to suit their present policies and allegiances" (*PL,* 2). Ann Barrington later emphasizes the danger of this national amnesia when she says, "If we leave the remembering to historians then the struggle is already lost. Everyone must have a memory, everyone needs to be a historian. . . . [W]e're in danger of losing hard-won freedoms by dozing off in a perpetual present" (*PL,* 18).[11] The sense of history that does exist in contemporary society seems to be more that of nonsense than reality, more that of absurdity than actuality. For instance, the lecturer on whom James relies for much of his information for his book continually couches the Suez Crisis in interpersonal terms, calling the incident an "affair of the heart" (*PL,* 12) and referring to the nations as acting "emotionally" (*PL,* 16). The most ironic statement, however, comes from the prime minister herself. At the Brighton conference Thatcher delivers an oratory praising the return of British patriotism, saying at one point, "We will tell the people the truth, and the people will be our judge" (*PL,* 33).[12] Just as the advertisers that sold the ploughman's lunch packaged and promoted a false concept, so, too, do the governments and the people of modern society package the falsified concepts that they *want* to believe.

In order to emphasize this distortion of history that is so manifest in our societies, McEwan uses the deceit and manipulations of relationships to parallel the greater duplicities. In essence, characters like James become emblematic of the treatments of recent English history. James is an opportunistic chameleon: he leans both left and right, depending upon the circumstance. He is also the angry young man of the 1950s and 1960s updated to the greedy and materialistic man of the 1980s. As a person, he is as equally unaffected by the agony of a co-worker who is emotionally distraught over a romantic breakup as he is by the plight of the Women's Peace Camp. McEwan's portrayal of James's family relations, though, is the most revealing glimpse into his character. When he visits home, he feels awkward, out of place; as he greets his father *"the two men fumble awkwardly between a handshake and an embrace. It is James who favors the former"* (*PL,* 7). Later he continues to avoid visiting his dying mother, essentially overlooking his parents—even to the point of denying to both Susan and Ann that he has parents. His mother dies before James finds convenient time in his schedule to see her. The final scene of the film is a freeze-frame of James at his mother's funeral— *"expressionless"* beside his father, whose face is *"immobile with grief"*— glancing at his watch (*PL,* 34). James finds time and sympathy only for what he believes will augment his own life. Not surprisingly, it is this same mind-set that serves as a guideline for his relationships.

James finds himself enamored of Susan Barrington and immediately sets about to win her. From the beginning of their courtship, however, it is evident that Susan is not interested. For instance, Susan calls for a taxi on one date and asks James to leave early. On another date there is the "sense of a long evening of intimate talk, but not much else so far" (*PL,* 14). Susan does not accompany James the first time he goes to interview her mother. In kissing James, Susan *"complies more than responds"* (*PL,* 22). Within all this, James—similar to the British people in their willing acceptance of a misinterpretation of history—maintains a private but self-deluded sense, harboring the belief that Susan is interested.

Though he is infatuated with Susan, James has no qualms about sleeping with her mother, Ann, a left-wing historian who is also an important source of information about the Suez Crisis. At one point Jeremy tells James, "It's obvious what you have to do. Your way into the daughter's pants is through the mother, up the Suez Canal" (*PL*, 11). As Susan has done with him, James "complies" when Ann first kisses him; later he does not protest when she slips into his bed to make love, although his expression is "numb" when she leaves (*PL*, 28). Shortly before their tryst Ann has shown James a picture of her dead brother, a man who bears a striking resemblance to James. This eerie similarity combined with the fact that Ann's husband, Matthew, takes very few precautions to conceal his own love affairs establishes the impression that Ann is reaching out for the solace found in a partner, a lover. Like the alliance between Jack and Julie in *The Cement Garden,* Ann's affair with James is one born of necessity. James once again quickly reveals his true self, however, in giving her the "old heave-ho" (*PL*, 28). James's duplicity in his relationships obviously parallels the duplicity that occurs in the historical interpretation of such incidents as the Suez and Falklands crises, but, just as there is no single source for the distortions, neither is James the only one who practices manipulation within relationships.

Indeed, the film is filled with characters who deceive and manipulate. McEwan says that "most of the characters are unpleasant. . . . They start out bad, and get worse" (*PL*, vi). For the most part, this unpleasantness arises from the characters' duplicity within relationships. Occasionally, there is simply an oddness, as when Susan describes her alliance with her mother, saying, "we were more like lovers, really, or sisters" (*PL*, 10). More often, though, there is unadulterated infidelity; for example, just after James has abandoned Ann, her husband tells him that he approves of the affair, saying, "I'm not telling you how to run your affairs. I'm just saying . . . I don't mind. I'm giving you permission" (*PL*, 30). The relationship that dominates the film in its duplicity, however, is the one that develops between Jeremy and Susan behind James's back. Although the attraction between the two appears obvious to the audience, James is completely oblivious to the intimate developments. For instance, when Susan first approaches the two men, she *"does not take her eyes off Jeremy"* (*PL*, 3). Similarly, when the three travel together to the conference, it is James who is most often left standing alone. Not until he sees them kissing (against the background of Thatcher's English revival speech) does he realize that he has been duped. When Jeremy attempts to tell James what has happened, explaining that he and Susan are "old allies" (*PL*,

34), there is the parallel to the Suez Crisis and its duplicity involving world allies. James has been duped just as the public was duped about Suez and the Falklands. McEwan presents *The Ploughman's Lunch* so that the two worlds—the private one of individual relationships and the public one of historical distortion—are implicitly intertwined. The duplicity of history and the duplicity of love, then, become counterpointed, simultaneously reflecting and accentuating each other.

The Ploughman's Lunch, in one sense, is about numbness. James tells Susan that he has reached a point of numbness in his job: "You do everything right, but you feel nothing either way" (*PL,* 9). His expression is numb when Ann leaves his bed; he is again "numbed" by the discovery of Jeremy and Susan's intimacy (*PL,* 33). McEwan sees a similar numbness in society's attitude toward historical actuality. Governments and societies can reinterpret national histories as easily as an individual can manipulate a relationship—and there is essentially as little distress about either duplicity. In a sense, then, McEwan demonstrates that the wrong knowledge can be as dangerous a thing as a little knowledge.

Soursweet

McEwan's screenplay *Soursweet* is a loyal adaptation of Timothy Mo's 1982 novel *Sour Sweet.* Mo's novel, shortlisted for the Booker Prize, portrays the immigration experience from the viewpoint of a young Chinese family as they attempt to make their home in the Britain of the 1960s. McEwan is faithful to Mo and his novel, making only a handful of necessary changes. For example, McEwan places the screenplay in the present, saying that, as Roger Randall-Cutler, the producer of the film, argued, "it would be difficult enough to get a British audience to identify with Chinese characters; placing them twenty-five years in the past would compound the difficulty."[13] The film premiered at the Cannes Film Festival on 14 May 1988; the screenplay was published in Britain and the United States by Faber and Faber in the same year.

With both humor and poignancy, the screenplay depicts Chen, Lily, and their family struggling to acculturate themselves to the curious ways of a new country.[14] In developing his adaptation, McEwan chose to establish Chen and Lily as the center of his screenplay:

> I proposed that the film's real subject was Lily and Chen, the marriage, their relationship, their adventure in coming to England, the clash of their different personalities. We should play up the affection between

them, and also chart its decline once Fok has located Chen and is black-mailing him. Lily's loss at the end would seem all the more poignant if we were strongly aware of the love that preceded it. (S, x)

Although the film centers on the young couple, it is as much about the sense of family and tradition that unites their small group; in essence, the film is about the strength of familial love.

Lily and Chen travel bravely into a new world, bringing with them strong ties to their homeland, Hong Kong. The young lovers are the quintessential yin and yang, the complements and contrasts that create a unified whole. Chen is the ever-conscious provider and protector of his family—Mui at one point jokingly but accurately calls him the "god of us all!" (S, 38). He has a strong sense of tradition and familial duty. For instance, he becomes indebted to Fok and the Hung Society only when he borrows money from them to assist his parents in Hong Kong. Unlike the rest of his family, Chen adjusts to British life much more slowly. He is, therefore, frequently portrayed as being isolated, as being disconnected from his family and his surrounding society; he is often secluded, a single man against the world. Likewise, he is often alone in his secrets, refusing to share with Lily his father's need for money as well as his brief involvement with the Hung Society.

On the other hand, Lily is the productive counterpart to her husband, the perfect yin to his yang. After five years of living in the strange world of London, she is *as lively and as beautiful as ever* (S, 9). She is also the fighter of the family, the source of strength within their relationship. Trained as a fighter by her father, she in turn trains Man Kee, her son, to fight when he is beaten at school. It is also Lily who wants to establish their own Chinese takeaway, which would simultaneously allow them to venture into the heart of British society and to proclaim their independence. The love that Lily and Chen share is simple yet complete:

LILY.	I've got a present for you. Close your eyes, hold out your hand. *(She presses a pebble into his hand and closes his fingers round it.)*
CHEN.	Thank you. Where did you find such a beautiful thing?
LILY.	My secret.
CHEN.	A precious stone. I am a very lucky man. (S, 57)

After Chen disappears—abducted and murdered by the Hung Society—Lily breaks down and weeps only when she discovers this same tiny pebble in Chen's clothes. Their relationship, their love, then, not only serves as the cohesive element for the film but also strengthens and solidifies their entire family.

Obviously, then, it is the family unit that is most important to each individual. Although they are vulnerable in this new world, often baffled by British society, Chen and his family persevere because they exist as a single unit, a family. They readily accept the challenges placed upon them by London as well as by their own relations. Their greatest strength is their adaptability. In the novel Mo, emphasizing the family's willingness to accept and to improve with almost any situation, describes the unit as an amoeba: "the household (that amoeba), presented with change and challenge, shuddered like a jelly on impact with the obstacle but jelly-like suffered no damage, poured itself around the problem, dissolved what it was able to and absorbed what it could not. And went on its amoeba way."[15]

Chen and Lily welcome first Lily's sister Mui and then Grandpa, Chen's father, into their already-crowded household. They unite to establish a successful takeaway restaurant; they face the surprise of Mui's pregnancy; they bear up to British society, adjusting themselves to a new way of life. The family unit, however, does change, separating and evolving in different directions; just before Chen's disappearance, Lily sits in front of the family shrine, contemplating the changes that have occurred in her family:

> [LILY] *stares at the photographs: her father, Chen's mother, herself and Chen as an engaged couple, shots from the wedding, Man Kee as a baby. . . . Now her attention has settled on a picture of herself and Man Kee taken when he was two. The boy sits contentedly on his mother's lap. Chen stands by her proudly. She studies the photograph, gauging the changes in her life.* (S, 73)

She eventually accepts these changes, understanding the organism's need to evolve in order to survive. At the conclusion Lily is invited to live with Mui and her new husband, but she refuses, preferring instead to remain with her own family unit, understanding that the family amoeba has simply divided in order to create a new organism, a new unit of life.

The serenity of Chen, Lily, and their family is juxtaposed with the harshness of the Hung Society, a criminal band of Chinese immigrants also residing in London. This society, too, is referred to as a "family" (S, 78). Whereas Chen and his family subsist on love and gentleness, the Hung Society feeds on violence and cruelty. For example, as the Chens celebrate the Chinese New Year with friends and a traditional feast, the Hung Society chooses the New Year to brutally attack a neighboring gang. Finding himself indebted to the society and forced to run drugs, Chen manages to escape with his family before he has to commit a crime. Unfortunately, he is soon discovered, and though the society realizes that he is innocent of crimes against them, they decide to murder him because, as one of the members says, "It's a trifling error, but [the murder] could be useful to us . . . an additional factor" (S, 64). Both from Hong Kong, the two families serve to exemplify the vast differences in the immigration experience. Despite the obvious differences, though, the Chens and the Hung Society do share an important similarity: they both adamantly maintain a respect for tradition, the one element that unequivocally connects them to their homeland.

The practice of tradition is not only a connection to their Asian society, but it is also a link to the past, a tie to the entirety of their people. McEwan opens the film with a traditional Chinese wedding—a scene original to the screenplay. Unable to explore thoroughly each character's past as Mo was able to do in his novel, McEwan had to establish immediately for his audience a sense of tradition. A wedding, McEwan says, was the perfect scene: "We would be able to experience an alien culture without needing anything explained to us—everyone understands a wedding" (S, x). Lily, Chen, and their family then continue their practice of tradition, introducing their Chinese heritage to their English home. For instance, they celebrate the Chinese New Year in traditional ceremonies and also set up a small Buddhist shrine in their takeaway. When Grandpa joins the family, he also expresses a desire to remain in touch with Hong Kong, choosing to wear two watches: one with English time, another with Hong Kong time so that he may keep his friends and their activities constantly in mind.

Like the Chens, the Hung Society as well places strong belief in tradition. Red Cudgel, the enforcer of the society, tells initiates that "our ways are rooted in history" (S, 19). Similarly, when the society admits its mistake in killing Chen, they make compensation by sending a regular remittance to the widow Lily, showing that they can take care of their own people. The sense of tradition, then, helps to establish both families in their new countries.

Still, the Chens find themselves in constant clash—sometimes inadvertently, sometimes purposely—with their British neighbors. The Chens, knowing that they are the guests in this nation, attempt to adapt themselves to the British ways. Often, though, they find that their attempts to conform are misunderstood. For instance, when Lily tries to address a young girl in the restaurant, her English comes out *"all wrong"* and her *"tone sounds harsh."* The girl becomes defensive, instinctively deriding Lily, calling her a "Chink!" (*S*, 40). Similarly, when Grandpa tries to express his thanks and concern for his group of elderly British friends by making each one a coffin, they do not understand his gesture of kindness, and are, in fact, insulted. Lily has similar troubles in understanding English society when she is told that the fighting method that she has taught Man Kee—the method that was taught to her by her father—is considered "unfair" by the English. She replies, "Unfair? Unfair? What's fair about fighting? The whole idea is to win. It's an insult to the way of the fist" (*S*, 66).

Not surprisingly, language is also an obstacle. Thus the Chens place a sign in the takeaway reading "TRESPASSER WOULD BE PROSECUTED," and the local Brits transform the takeaway's name from Dah Ling to Darling. Ironically, Lily and Chen find the foreign physiognomies indistinguishable, claiming that the Brits all look alike. Lily says that there are "only a few types of faces, and no expression. It's all pink skin, like pigs, and big clumsy faces. And empty, empty eyes." Chen agrees, saying that he has to remind himself that "they're not really ghosts" (*S*, 44). It is Mui who defends their new neighbors, telling her family, "Take some trouble. Look at them. Some of them have lovely eyes. . . . There are lots of different kinds of faces. . . . They're not pigs. They've got feelings, just like everybody else!" (*S*, 45). Although not always approving of—and certainly not always adapting to—the customs and beliefs of their new country, the Chens do learn to become a part of British society, eventually acculturating themselves, if not into the mainstream, at least into the periphery of a new way of life, a new people.

As the Chens struggle to adapt to the British people and their ways, Lily comes to the forefront, becoming clearly the strength and stabilizer for her entire family. She—like a number of McEwan's female characters—is the force that holds the family and its relationships together. For instance, she has total faith in her husband; even after Chen has mysteriously disappeared, she finds honor in his desertion. When she receives the money from the Hung Society, she believes that Chen has gone away in order to support his family further. The fact that she does not realize the true nature of Chen's disappearance—that he has been murdered by the Hung Society—is not important. She concentrates only on the positive, giving herself the resilience to believe the unbelievable, allowing herself to remain the pillar of her family. Throughout the film she is a fighter; in the last scene, she tells her missing husband, "I love you dearly, more and more each day. . . . I want you to know that I feel strong, like a warrior, and light, so light" (*S*, 83). The film closes as Lily "*adopts the stylized pose of the fighter*" (*S*, 83). Lily is the faith, love, hope of her family, the strength and courage that allow them to survive and to prevail in an alien culture.

Writing about the difficulty involved in adapting a novel to film, McEwan says, "To adapt for the screen a novel you admire, particularly if it is the sort of novel you could never write yourself, can feel like brutal, arrogant work" (*S*, v). Nonetheless, McEwan faithfully captures the hopes and despairs, the victories and defeats of the immigrant family, reinventing, as the title suggests, both the sour and sweet, the positive and negative experiences of the Chens. Though the screenplay is not an original work, *Soursweet* fits nicely into the scope of McEwan's canon. By molding the relationship of Lily and Chen as the centerpiece of the film, he shows how the strength of their alliance helps them to adapt and to survive in their new world.

McEwan's film writing exhibits all the power and social consciousness of his fiction. His later screenplays—"The Imitation Game," *The Ploughman's Lunch,* and *Soursweet*—represent, however, complete departures from his literature of shock, so evident in both "Jack Flea's Birthday Celebration" and "Solid Geometry." No longer relying so heavily on a fiction that startles and stuns, he begins to explore more thoroughly contemporary realities—patriarchal hierarchies, manipulative governments, societies based on prejudice—that morally disturb. At the same time he remains true to his primary concern of presenting and examining relationships, showing how male-female alliances are affected by the societies in which they occur.

Chapter Seven

Vandalizing Time:
The Child in Time

Evading intrusions into the grief of losing his daughter, Stephen Lewis—
the protagonist of McEwan's third novel—tells his friends and family that
he has begun to work on a new book, "something of a departure."[1] The
same sentiment could be said of McEwan's own novel. With *The Child in
Time,* his first novel in six years and his finest achievement, McEwan creates a unique amalgamation of the old and the new: he effectively combines the political and social concerns of his film scripts with the darker,
more visceral edge of his fiction. Commenting on this merger, McEwan
says, "my prose tended to remain private. I always wanted to broaden it,
find the fruitful ground where private and political [could exist] together.
This novel is to some extent a fulfillment of an ambition" (Smith, 69). In
The Child in Time—published in England by Jonathan Cape in September
of 1987 and by Houghton Mifflin in the United States during the same
month—McEwan continues his explorations of duplicitous and inefficient
governments. He complements these political examinations with his
familiar themes: the power of sustaining relationships, regression as a
means of escape, the strength of the female, the detrimental effects of
contemporary society on its individuals.

The novel concerns a child's sudden and mysterious disappearance
and the painful ordeal that the parents must endure in order to accept
their daughterless, and seemingly hopeless, lives. *The Child in Time,* however, is much more than a missing-child novel. With the intricate images
of children and the complexities of time that recur, McEwan portrays the
search for the child that exists in every individual. The search for the
child in time—both Stephen and Julie's daughter, Kate, as well as each
individual's youthful essence—is an often warm and poignant, a sometimes wild and humorous romp through time itself. McEwan creates a
sense of time that is malleable, wondrous, infinitely complex. Time is a
vandal: it is the essence that can make one forget the child, the youthful
joy of life. Simultaneously, time is also vandalized: characters experience
periods that stall in slow motion, that pass in a blur of quickness, that

are even altered, with the past coming round to the present. Time, then, serves as an emblem for the complexities and difficulties that exist in everyday contemporary society.

The Child in Time, in one part, is a political fable, set in the near future of an England controlled by a post-Thatcher conservative extremism. Though set several years in the future, the novel nonetheless serves as a satire of present-day England. McEwan states that the novel takes place "now and not now."[2] Though futurism has traditionally been delegated to the realm of science fiction, several contemporary writers not associated with genre fiction have chosen futuristic settings for their novels. These writers envision a near-future in order to demonstrate the results of our own chaotic present. In many instances, the future is so near that, for all practical purposes, it is *now.* These novels, then, become forewarnings for present society. Many of the settings are postapocalyptic, worlds torn asunder by violence, warfare, chaos. For example, Angela Carter's *Heroes and Villains* (1969) and Russell Hoban's *Riddley Walker* (1980) envision near-future Dark Ages in which humans have returned to an age of barbarism. Carter's *The Passion of New Eve* and Kathy Acker's *Empire of the Senseless* portray worlds rent by civil wars and race riots. J. G. Ballard's *High-Rise* depicts the complete social breakdown of a futuristic apartment complex. Margaret Atwood's *The Handmaid's Tale* (1985) presents a dystopia, a world poisoned by toxic chemicals and nuclear radiation, in which fundamentalist Christians have killed the president and members of Congress, in which women have been reduced to chattel. Other novels, like *The Child in Time,* depict futures that are less violent, more a direct descendant of our own time, but just as detrimental to their populaces. Martin Amis's *London Fields,* for example, is set in a post-Thatcherite London in rapid decline, a world of nuclear madness and environmental deterioration, a world where America and England are slouching toward total destruction.

In McEwan's novel there are numerous references to society ravaged by both time and politics. For example, the novel takes place in a time of miserable weather: it opens in "what was to turn out to be the last decent summer of the twentieth century" (*CT,* 5)—a summer of drought and heat waves. Later the cycle of seasons skips autumn, plunging straight into winter with a 50-day rain. Experts attempt to find reasons, offering theories about "the encroaching ice age, the melting ice caps, the ozone layer depleted by fluorocarbons, the sun in its death throes" (*CT,* 143). As with the problems of society, however, there are seldom any satisfying answers. The weather serves as an appropriate background to the plethora of absurdities that occur in this soon-to-be future. This is a time in which a shoving match between Russian and American sprinters in the Olympic Games quickly escalates into the "sudden threat of global extinction" (*CT*, 34) with the two world powers bringing their "nuclear forces to their most advanced state of readiness" (*CT*, 35). Likewise, this is a society guided by a government that has offered schools for sale to private investors, that has commissioned a child-care book so that the nation can be "regenerated by reformed child-care practice" (*CT*, 191), that has regulated its beggars, forcing them to wear badges, to use regulation begging bowls, and to beg in allotted areas only.

The city, the physical representation of its society, fares no better. Stephen's father is emotionally shocked and physically exhausted by a journey through London. Returning, he says, "It's a new country. More like the Far East at its worst. I haven't got the strength for it, or the stomach" (*CT*, 209). Stephen sums up the desperate state of society when he says, "Everything's getting worse. . . . Isn't anything getting better?" (*CT*, 119). McEwan's emphasis on the absurdity and cruelty of this near-future society not only enables him to echo quietly the darker visions that haunted his earlier fiction, but it also allows him to demonstrate how the unchallenged state continues to make assaults on its individuals, robbing from each person his or her sense of humanity, the essence of childhood. Ultimately, this novel, then, is a cautionary letter for contemporary society.

McEwan also uses the motifs of the child and time to unify *The Child in Time*. These two emblems interweave through the novel, connecting the various episodes as well as accentuating one of McEwan's primary concerns: the delicate relationship between childhood and adulthood, and the search for the child in every being.

Just as the memory of Kate remains alive in her father's mind, so, too, does the child as a symbol remain a constant in the novel itself. For instance, immediately after the experience of seeing his parents "out of time," Stephen relives his mother's decision not to abort him, imagining himself as a fetus:

His eyes grew large and round and lidless with desperate, protesting innocence, his knees rose under him and touched his chin, his fingers were scaly flippers, gills beat time, urgent, hopeless strokes through the salty ocean that engulfed the treetops and surged between their roots; and for all the crying, calling sounds he thought were his own, he formed a single thought: he had nowhere to go, no moment that could embody him, he was not expected, no destination or time could be named. (*CT,* 66)

Later, when Stephen rescues the driver from the wrecked lorry, the man emerges in a parody of birth. Similar to these more complex images are numerous brief references to children and childhood. For example, Julie lives in a house "such as a child might draw" (*CT,* 74); Stephen takes boyish pleasure in railroads; Charles Darke is his wife's "difficult child" (*CT,* 42).

In multiplying these images of the child, McEwan emphasizes the innocence and purity of childhood, something that is quickly and almost completely forgotten in adulthood. Very rarely do adults abandon themselves to childish pleasures, as do Stephen and Julie when they become joyfully captivated in building a sand castle with Kate: "Soon, and without quite realizing it was happening, they became engrossed, filled with the little girl's urgency, working with no awareness of time beyond the imperative of the approaching tide" (*CT,* 121). Unfortunately, the adult must throw off the spell and return to the world of responsibilities and appointments. Stephen later thinks that "if he could do everything with the intensity and abandonment with which he had once helped Kate build her castle, he would be a happy man of extraordinary powers" (*CT,* 122). McEwan, though, suggests that happiness can be achieved in a compromise—but only if the adult is willing to recognize the child within.

Like the image of the child, images of time also serve to unify the novel. Stephen, for example, is constantly slipping into the past of memories through his structured daydreams. Throughout the novel, then, there is a continuous shift from the present to the past and back again. Likewise, there are many references to the seeming instability of time and how it often shifts according to perception; Stephen Lewis is especially susceptible to the shifting qualities of time. For instance, thinking about his aging parents, he feels "the urgency of constricting time" (*CT,* 50); as he is traveling to visit Julie, his sense of time disappears; he feels as if "time had fixed him in his place" (*CT,* 117); when he pursues the girl whom he thinks is Kate, time "had a closed-down, forbidden quality" (*CT,* 166). The constant references to time and childhood help to unify McEwan's work, complementing both theme and structure.

These images of time and childhood are also inexorably linked in Kate, the missing daughter of Stephen and Julie Lewis. Through her mysterious evanescence, she becomes just one of the many children in time who populate the novel. Kate's disappearance is a terrifyingly beautiful passage; McEwan poetically captures the sheer terror of a parent's worst nightmare, describing how Stephen's uneasiness quickly becomes blind panic, how the city's anonymity crumbles and the lost child becomes "everyone's property" (*CT,* 15), how Stephen attempts to distance himself in order to cope with the loss of his daughter. Despite the terror of Kate's disappearance, looking back on the incident, Stephen remembers the day as being perfectly ordinary. He recalls mundane details with clarity: a Coca-Cola can with a straw, a dog relieving itself, a tree. After his daughter vanishes, Stephen (like Mary after the murder of Colin in *The Comfort of Strangers*) finds that he has "to absorb the insult of the world's normality" (*CT,* 18). Cruelly, Stephen's most horrid of days is perfectly ordinary. The world, oblivious to his pain, continues its everyday pace. In one sense, *The Child in Time,* as John Powers notes, begins "where *The Comfort of Strangers* stops, with its survivors trying to live through a horrible event."[3] The novel, then, chronicles ordinary victims attempting to survive extraordinary, even demonic, events.

In a desperate, pathetic attempt to save Kate, to prevent his daughter from forever vanishing from his life, Stephen tries to alter time. He vainly strives to reenter the past but discovers only that time "monomanically forbids second chances" (*CT,* 10). He struggles to see through the veil of time, hoping to discover the person who might have stolen her:

> [He] tried to move his eyes, lift them against the weight of time, to find that shrouded figure at the periphery of vision, the one who was always to the side and slightly behind, who, filled with a strange desire, was calculating odds, or simply waiting. But time held his sight forever on his mundane errands, and all about him shapes without definition drifted and dissolved, lost to categories. (*CT,* 11)

Unable to penetrate the past, Stephen resists the impulse to surrender, remaining adamant in his battle against time, the ultimate kidnapper of his only child. Perceiving himself as "the father of an invisible child" (*CT,* 2), he vehemently maintains the hope that Kate may indeed exist somewhere. To cope, he allows her to continue aging within his mind: "There was a biological clock, dispassionate in its unstoppability, which let his daughter go on growing, extended and complicated her simple vocabulary, made her stronger, her movements surer. The clock, sinewy like a heart, kept faith with an unceasing conditional: she would be drawing, she would be starting to read, she would be losing a milk tooth" (*CT,* 2). This mental child whom Stephen nurtures eventually enables him to accept his pain and, through the course of two events, helps him to continue with his life.

The first such incident occurs two and a half years after Kate's disappearance, during the week that she would have turned six years old. Stephen wants to celebrate her birthday but fears that to "buy a toy would undo two years of adjustment, it would be irrational, indulgent, self-destructive; and weak, above all weak" (*CT,* 145). He soon justifies his need to celebrate for Kate, however, saying to himself that this "would be an act of faith in his daughter's continued existence" (*CT,* 146). Moreover, he sees the action as an act of joy as well as a plea for Kate's return: "To buy a present would demonstrate that he was not yet beaten, that he could do the surprising, lively thing. He would purchase his gift in joy rather than sorrow, in the spirit of loving extravagance, and in bringing it home and wrapping it up he would be making an offering to fate, or a challenge—*Look, I've brought the present, now you bring back the girl*" (*CT,* 146). As he embarks on his shopping spree, Stephen mentally creates through "magical thinking" (*CT,* 146) the image of Kate as a growing, maturing child and buys birthday toys to match her ever-changing needs:

> He needed to test her reactions. She was a reticent girl, in company at least, with a straight back and dark bangs. She was a fantasist, a daydreamer, a lover of strange-sounding words, a keeper of secret diaries, a hoarder of inexplicable objects. . . . She preferred soft toys to dolls, and he dropped into his wire basket a lifelike gray cat. She was a giggler with a taste for practical jokes. He took the cushion and a flower that squirted water. . . . She liked to dress up. He reached for a witch's hat. . . . Beyond all question she was a graceful child, but she was hopeless with a ball and it was time she knew how to throw. He took from the shelves a plastic sock of tennis balls. (*CT,* 148)

Kate's birthday eventually brings more dismay than relief; Stephen ends his celebration—at once one of the most touching and pathetic scenes in the novel—by singing "Happy Birthday" to his missing daughter through a child's walkie-talkie set. Though momentarily upsetting for Stephen, the event is the beginning of a capitulation; for the first time he realizes that Kate is fading and that he has no control over his lost daughter:

He brought to mind the three-year-old, the springy touch of her, how she fit herself so comfortably round his body, the solemn purity of her voice, the wet red and white of tongue and lips and teeth, the unconditional trust. It was getting harder to recall. She was fading, and all the time his useless love was swelling, encumbering and disfiguring him like a goiter. He thought, I want you. I want you back. I want you brought back now. I don't want anything else. All I want to do is to want you to come back. . . . *It hurts.* (*CT,* 151)

This realization sends him back to alcohol; simultaneously, though, his pain reaches a nadir, triggering the second incident, which directs Stephen toward acceptance and recovery.

Stephen's fanatical search for his daughter ultimately ends in finding Kate—unfortunately, it is the wrong Kate. En route to a lunch meeting with the prime minister, Stephen passes a schoolyard filled with children and encounters Kate: "The first girl was closest to him. The thick bangs bobbed against her white forehead, her chin was raised, she had a dreamy appearance. He was looking at his daughter" (*CT,* 165). Confronting the girl, he notices that "what was most strikingly new was a brown mole high on her right cheekbone" (*CT,* 172). The child is obviously not Kate, but Stephen refuses to accept this. His unending search for his daughter and the confrontation with the "false" Kate exhibit the degree of his obsession and desperation. Stephen, in order to survive the madness of his situation, realizes that he must keep Kate alive—even if only in his own mind, for if Kate continues to exist, then he can continue to survive. Eventually, Stephen is convinced by the school principal and by himself that this is not Kate. Once he admits this to himself, the likeness of Kate fades from the girl: "the girl crossing the reception area was taller, more angular, especially about the shoulders, and sharper in her features" (*CT,* 177).[4]

The false recognition concludes in a purging that, in turn, results in Stephen's release from his obsession, his maniacal search:

He was beginning to face the difficult truth that Kate was no longer a living presence, she was not an invisible girl at his side whom he knew intimately; remembering how Ruth Lyle [the false Kate] did and did not resemble his daughter, he understood how there were many paths Kate might have gone down, countless ways in which she might have changed in two and a half years, and that he knew nothing about any of them. He had been mad, now he felt purged. (*CT,* 179)

Stephen never completely abandons the hope that Kate may indeed be alive and that she may someday return. The two confrontations with "Kate" succeed, however, in helping him comprehend the danger of his obsession. Essentially, Stephen realizes that he must continue his own life without Kate; he must remain whole in order to keep Kate as a part of himself.

The Child in Time also presents the search for the lost child that exists within every adult. The appearance of adulthood necessitates, more often than not, the disappearance of innocence and, consequently, the loss of one's childish pleasure in life itself. Commenting on the adult's denial of the child-self, McEwan says,

> It's been a current in my fiction for a long time that we carry about within us our childhood selves. We deny that self at our peril. . . . It was both inevitable and desirable that my own range or preoccupation should change and that my emotional range should increase. Having children has been a major experience in my life in the last few years. It's extended me emotionally, personally, in ways that could never be guessed at. It's inevitable that that change would be reflected in my writing. (Smith, 68)

The search for Kate, then, reintroduces Stephen to his own child-self in time, opening for him a world of freshness and hope.

Charles Darke, one of the few characters in the novel who willingly seeks out the child within himself, tells Stephen that "childhood is timeless" (*CT,* 32). Attempting to persuade Stephen to market his novel *Lemonade* as a children's book, Charles says that the book has "spoken directly to children. . . . [Y]ou've communicated with them across the abyss that separates the child from the adult and you've given them a first, ghostly intimation of their mortality. . . . This is a book for children through the eyes of an adult" (*CT,* 33). As Charles explains, the best of the "so-called children's books" are "those that spoke to both children and adults, to the incipient adult within the child, to the forgotten child within the adult" (*CT,* 30). Stephen reluctantly agrees to this marketing scheme and, inadvertently, then becomes "famous among schoolchildren" (*CT,* 25). Not only does Stephen succeed in communicating with children—including his own inner child—he also becomes metaphorically a child, another of the novel's many children in time.

Throughout the novel, Stephen—like Colin in *The Comfort of Strangers*—is portrayed as a child or in childlike terms. For example, both Charles and the assistant secretary to the prime minister speak to him "as though to a child" (*CT,* 30, 154); he is mothered by Thelma when he goes into a catatonic state shortly after Kate vanishes; at the thought of nuclear war he is "suddenly, childishly, afraid" (*CT*, 193); on his final visit to Julie's, he fulfills a "boyhood dream" by riding in the cab of a train (*CT*, 247). While on the trail of the false Kate, Stephen reverts totally to a childlike state when he enters a classroom and finds himself participating in an art class: when the teacher instructs the children to draw a picture of a medieval village, Stephen earnestly, obediently jumps to the task. Years after leaving school, he finds that he is still eager to impress the teacher with his artistry. In leaving the room, he fulfills yet another boyhood fantasy when he is able to turn his back on the teacher, to ignore her reprimands, and to walk out. Through the novel, Stephen is unashamed, even willing, to express his child-self, succumbing to the youthful innocence, the harmless naïveté that dwells within him. By doing so, McEwan suggests, the adult-self is better able to survive the turmoil and chaos of adult society. Accepting the child within himself helps him to bear the loss of his daughter. And to a large degree, the child within him is an embodiment of Kate, allowing her to live and grow always beside her father.

Like the discovery of the child within him, time, too, plays a major role in Stephen's rejuvenation. Time, in fact, is the key to discovering the child that dwells within each adult. As Roberta Smoodin writes, this lost childhood remains in the mature adult "not only in memory but in a kind of time that spirals in upon itself, seems to be recapturable in some plausible intermingling of Einstein and Proust, quantum physics and magical realism."[5] This magical, whimsical aspect of time is delightfully obvious through Stephen's course of recovery, during which he experiences periods of time that seem to slow, to elongate, or to warp completely out of context.

For example, in journeying to visit Charles and Thelma, Stephen narrowly escapes a serious automobile accident. When a lorry overturns in front of his car and forces him to veer dangerously between the wrecked vehicle and a road sign, Stephen experiences a "slowing of time" (*CT*, 106), one in which time itself seems to stall momentarily, allowing him to record events with unnatural clarity. Dodging the lorry but coming so close to the road sign that it shears away his door handle and side mirror, Stephen is at first elated by the near miss and then stunned by the fact that the entire incident had "lasted no longer than five seconds" (*CT*, 108). Later, after being rescued by Stephen, the lorry driver also expresses having experienced a similar slowing of time. Asking, "How long was I in there? Two hours? Three?" he finds it incredible when Stephen replies, "Ten minutes. Or less" (*CT,* 114). Time, inexplicably, is apparently malleable, a concept that Stephen has difficulty in understanding; nonetheless, it is an idea—like the mysterious child within himself—that he accepts as an ordinary aspect of an extraordinary world.

An even more astonishing distortion of time occurs when Stephen encounters a flaw in time. In an episode of magical realism, Stephen steps into the past and meets his parents.[6] Walking through the countryside, in a place he has never before been, Stephen experiences an overwhelming familiarity, an eerie sense of déjà vu. Coming across an old tavern, he senses that "the day he now inhabited was not the day he had woken into. . . . He was in another time" (*CT,* 63). Seeing a young couple through the tavern window, he experiences "not recognition so much as its shadow, not its familiar sound but a brief resonance" (*CT,* 64). When the young woman looks out and stares intently at Stephen, he suddenly, inexplicably, realizes that she is his mother.

Stephen is baffled by this incident, uncertain about how to accept seeing his parents in a time before he existed. Not until his mother relives the event, through the "timelessness of memory" (*CT,* 195), does Stephen begin to understand the repercussions of his experience with time. Claire tells her son of the courtship between her and his father,[7] and the dilemma that they faced when she became pregnant. It was at the small tavern—where Stephen experienced his contortion of time—that Douglas had indirectly suggested an abortion. Before considering the implications of marriage or abortion, Claire looked out the tavern window and experienced her own distortion of time:

> I can see it now as clearly as I can see you. There was a face at the window, the face of a child, sort of floating there. It was staring into the pub. It had a kind of pleading look, and it was so white, white as an aspirin. It was looking right at me. Thinking about it over the years, I realize it was probably the landlord's boy, or some kid off one of the local farms. But as far as I was concerned then, I was convinced, I just *knew* that I was looking at my own child. If you like, I was looking at you. (*CT,* 207)

From that point in time, she says, the baby was not "an abstraction. . . . It was . . . a complete self, begging her for its existence, and it was inside her, unfolding intricately, living off the pulse of her own blood" (*CT,* 207). Thus, Stephen himself becomes a child in time, magically appearing 44 years later as the face his mother sees just weeks after his conception. In a sense, Stephen confirms his own existence. However, the full significance of his experience is not revealed until the end of the novel;

when he has his interlude with the past, Stephen is just hours away from creating his own child in time.

Stephen continually ponders his seemingly preternatural experiences with time as well as the mysterious nature of time itself. Thelma, a theoretical physicist, offers scientific explanations, speaking to him as she would a classroom full of scientists, revealing that "there's a whole supermarket of theories these days" (*CT,* 135). For example, she lectures, one possibility "has the world dividing every infinitesimal fraction of a second into an infinite number of possible versions, constantly branching and proliferating, with consciousness neatly picking its way through to create the illusion of a stable reality" (*CT,* 135). Another theory states that "time is variable. We know it from Einstein, who is still our bedrock here. In relativity theory, time is dependent on the speed of the observer" (*CT,* 136). Yet another theory suggests that time is a separate entity in and of itself: "In the big-bang theory, time is thought to have been created in the same moment as matter, it's inseparable from it" (*CT,* 136). The only certainty about time, Thelma says, is its uncertainty: "whatever time is, the common-sense, everyday version of it as linear, regular, absolute, marching from left to right, from the past through the present to the future, is either nonsense or a tiny fraction of the truth" (*CT,* 135–36). *The Child in Time* exemplifies how time is not a certainty, not a reality of the world. Rather, as in Stephen's experience, it is a magical essence of life, an inexplicable entity that allows Kate to grow and exist within her father, that allows the ephemeral childhood of each person to continue existing throughout life, that enables Stephen to encounter his mother's decision to let him live. Time, then, is as ambiguous and as difficult as life itself.

Yet another discoverer of the child in time is Charles Darke. Like Tom in *The Cement Garden,* David in "Jack Flea's Birthday Celebration," and the narrator in "Conversation with a Cupboard Man," Charles seeks to escape the confusion and chaos of his world by escaping into the serenity and security of childhood. When he does regress, his wife Thelma (like Julie in *The Cement Garden,* Ruth in "Jack Flea's Birthday Celebration," and Jenny in "Last Day of Summer") is forced into the role of surrogate mother. Thelma finds this role of motherhood comfortable, even natural. For example, after Kate's disappearance, it is Thelma who rushes to mother Stephen, rescuing him from the catatonic state in which he has fallen. She, therefore, readily accepts the regression of her husband as "quite ordinary" (*CT,* 240), happily complying to her new role as mother.

Stephen, however, finds Charles's regression disturbing. When he first encounters Charles in his new state, Stephen thinks that he is, indeed, a little boy, "the kind of boy who used to fascinate and terrify him at school" (*CT,* 122). Stephen is shocked, but nonetheless feigns acceptance and follows the "successful prepubescent" into his world of innocence and tree houses (*CT,* 125). The climb to Charles's tree house accentuates the chasm between their states: Stephen is, momentarily, the terrified adult, the frightened realist, clinging with desperation to the tree; Charles is the carefree, innocent child, scampering from limb to limb, heedless of the danger. Charles's metamorphosis into a child is total. He has built a tree house, made his own lemonade, and stuffed his pockets with all the paraphernalia of childhood, including such items as a magnifying glass, a penknife, a ball bearing, a toy compass, a feather, a fishhook, and pebbles. Stephen views Charles's regression as a calculated move. Examining the contents of Charles's pockets, he is "impressed by what appeared to be very thorough research. It was as if his friend had combed libraries, diligently consulted the appropriate authorities to discover just what it was a certain kind of boy was likely to have in his pockets" (*CT,* 130). Later, cryptically explaining himself, Charles tells Stephen that "it's a matter of letting go" (*CT,* 132). His regression, then, is an escape, a freedom from the pressures of politics, a freedom from the chaos of contemporary society.

Thelma, however, explains her husband's regression differently. After his visit with them, she tells Stephen, "He's completely mad" (*CT,* 140). As a result, the consequences of Charles's fantasy are dire indeed, and they eventually result in his death. Torn between his need "to be famous, and have people tell him that one day he would be prime minister" and his desire "to be a little boy without a care in the world, with no responsibility, no knowledge of the world outside" (*CT,* 238), Charles eventually surrenders, giving up on the world and his life simultaneously. Even in the end, though, his child-self dominates. Like a little boy he commits suicide in a "petulant and childish" way (*CT,* 242), immaturely lashing out at Thelma, his wife/mother, by putting himself out in the snow, stripping off most of his clothing, and dying of hypothermia.

After Charles's death Thelma attempts to explain her husband's torment, calling his regression "an overwhelming fantasy that dominated all his private moments" (*CT,* 238). For Charles, childhood was not only timeless, but it was also a "mystical state" (*CT,* 238). As Thelma explains, he "wanted the security of childhood, the powerlessness, the obedience, and also the freedom that goes with it, freedom from money, decisions, plans, demands" (*CT,* 238). The regression, however, becomes more and more difficult for Charles to maintain; he finds himself torn between his two worlds, the adult and the child. His agony of indecision eventually leads to another breakdown that, in turn, leads to his death. Through Charles's regression into childhood, McEwan suggests that although it is important, even crucial, for the adult to accept the child that resides within himself/herself, it is dangerous, even suicidal, to become wholly that child-self or to surrender entirely to that desire.

Partially responsible for Charles's breakdown is the prime minister. As Thelma states, her husband is "sexually fancied" (*CT,* 239) by the prime minister, and though he is repelled, Charles nonetheless cannot help flirting, attracted by the attention and the power of such a person. After Charles disappears from the political world, the prime minister's constant letters—urging him to return to politics—serve as reminders of his adult duties and responsibilities. The prime minister, in pursuing Charles, visits Stephen at home, bringing an entourage and a battery of telephones, confessing to Stephen that "I became very fond of [Charles]" (*CT,* 222). This national leader had become so attached to Charles—a man "young enough to be my son" (*CT,* 224)—that orders had been given to follow him around the clock. "Having him followed," the prime minister explains, "was a way of being with him all the time. . . . I read [the daily reports on Charles] late at night in bed. . . . I imagined myself at his side. . . . I read back through the pages, as one might a favorite romantic novel" (*CT,* 223). What is so unusual and fascinating about the prime minister's infatuation with Charles is that McEwan gives the political figure no identifiable gender—the attraction, then, cannot be designated as either maternal or paternal, heterosexual or homosexual. Upon meeting the prime minister for the first time, Stephen recalls hearing that "there was a convention in the higher reaches of the civil service never to reveal, by the use of personal pronouns or other means, any opinion as to the gender of the prime minister" (*CT,* 92). In his novel, McEwan, with unique dexterity, plays that political game and leaves the prime minister genderless.[8] This sexual ambiguity and the deceptiveness involved in the courting of Charles serve to emphasize the ambiguity and duplicity of the government itself, especially in its production of *The Authorized Child-Care Handbook.*

Early in the novel the prime minister is described as the "nation's parent" (*CT,* 93). Taking this appellation to heart, the prime minister orders an official committee to create a parenting manual, believing that "the nation is to be regenerated by reformed child-care practice" (*CT,* 191).

Thus, the Official Commission on Child Care is created, and Stephen, because of his fame as a writer of children's books, is given a seat on the Subcommittee on Reading and Writing. For the notion of this child-care book, McEwan states in his acknowledgments that he is indebted to Christina Hardyment's *Dream Babies,* a work that examines three centuries of child-care advice to parents. Commenting on how this work influenced his invention of a parental-advice book, McEwan says,

> What comes out of [Hardyment's] book quite wonderfully is how any age distills itself into its childcare books. The way we look after our children or the way experts advise us to look after our children has a lot to do with how we want to be, the ideal, the dream selves we aspire to. You get late 18th century books that are very much influenced by Rousseau, then mid-Victorian harshness, then Edwardian sentimentality. The '20s and '30s in this century were dominated by the rise of social sciences and therefore generate, too, their own harshness. The postwar era was dominated by Spock and again, libertarian, optimistic ideas of human nature. The thought that crossed my mind was—what next? I imagined, given the collapse of the libertarian consensus as a dominating force in British and American society, that the next childcare book could be authoritarian and that the state would write it. (Smith, 69)

McEwan accentuates the absurdity—and danger—of such a project by showing Stephen's committee reaching such ludicrous conclusions as "boys will be boys" and "children were averse to soap and water, quick to learn, and grew up all too fast" (*CT,* 6). Furthermore, the quotations from *The Authorized Child-Care Handbook* that McEwan uses to headnote each chapter serve to exemplify the extreme authoritarian—even cruel—nature of the work. For example, the book reports, "There is . . . evidence to suggest that the more intimately a father is involved in the day-to-day care of a small child, the less effective he becomes as a figure of authority" (*CT,* 52). And, "It should be remembered that childhood is not a natural occurrence. There was a time when children were treated like small adults. Childhood is an invention, a social construct, made possible by society as it increased in sophistication and resource. Above all, childhood is a privilege" (*CT,* 105). And, "The promise of chocolate in return for, say, good bedtime behavior is, on balance, worth the minor damage to teeth which will in any case soon replace themselves" (*CT,* 142). Stephen, from the beginning, is dubious of the project, aware of the "ever-mutating" and contradictory information given to parents over the centuries by "experts, priests, moralists, social scientists, doctors"

(*CT,* 89–90). Hardyment supports this reservation in her own book: "Telling mothers and fathers how to bring up their children in books is arguably as silly as sending false teeth through the post and hoping that they will fit."[9] Though a fictional creation, McEwan's depiction of the desire for and the acceptance of such a manual is an indictment of our own society. He suggests that this authoritarian—even totalitarian—society is not necessarily years in the future.

When Stephen tells his father of the child-care book, Douglas replies, "This report's already been written in secret and the whole thing's a load of rubbish anyway. These committees are a lot of flannel as far as I can see. . . . It's to make people believe the report when they read it, and most people are such bloody fools, they will believe it" (*CT,* 99). Not surprisingly, weeks before the committee has completed its report, a friend secretly delivers to Stephen a completed copy of the child-care manual. Stephen sends a copy to the newspapers, and controversy soon arises, with politicians howling such things as "'gross and indecent cynicism' and 'a disgusting charade' and 'this vile betrayal of parents, Parliament, and principles'" (*CT,* 211). The prime minister, however, quickly intervenes and—in actions similar to the duplicitous moves of the British government depicted in *The Ploughman's Lunch*—denies any foreknowledge of the book. Ironically, copies of the manual then released to the press are greeted with overwhelmingly favorable reviews.

More surprising is Stephen's discovery of the author behind the manual: Charles Darke. Charles's conflicting desires to be both a child and an adult are reflected in the subject matter as well as its harsh attitude toward child-rearing. Thelma tells Stephen, "It's a perfect illustration of Charles's problem. It was his fantasy life that drew him to the work, and it was his desire to please the boss that made him write it the way he did" (*CT,* 242). The child-care book, then, is emblematic of its society's ambiguity and duplicity: it is composed by a man torn between childhood and adulthood, commissioned and defended by a government that expects total fidelity from a people to whom it blatantly lies, and welcomed by a populace that never questions the authoritarian manner in which they are now expected to rear their children. Such, McEwan implies, could soon be the state of modern society.

Uniting the complex images of time and childhood, the problems of contemporary society, the complicated issues of love and heartache is McEwan's primary concern: the relationship between Stephen and Julie, and the obstacles that these two parents must traverse before learning to cope with the loss of their only child. Before Kate vanishes, Stephen and

Julie share a powerful love: "She loved him fiercely and liked to tell him. He had built his life round their intimacy and come to depend on it" (*CT,* 18). Their daughter's disappearance, however, brutally disrupts their relationship. In the aftermath of their tragedy, Stephen anesthetizes himself with his desperate search for Kate, while Julie collapses into a numbness of inactivity, spending day after day in a listless daze. They become embittered toward each other, their opposing reactions opening a rift in their marriage. Stephen sees his wife's reaction as "a feminine self-destructiveness, a willful defeatism" (*CT,* 22). In turn, she sees his response as "a typically masculine evasion, an attempt to mask feelings behind displays of competence and organization and physical effort" (*CT,* 22). Their sorrow increases, pain multiplies, forcing them further and further apart: "Suddenly their sorrows were separate, insular, incommunicable. They went their different ways, he with lists and daily trudging, she in her armchair, lost to deep, private grief. Now there was no mutual consolation, no touching, no love. Their old intimacy, their habitual assumption that they were on the same side, was dead. They remained huddled over their separate losses, and unspoken resentments began to grow" (*CT,* 22).

Realizing but never openly acknowledging the breach in their relationship, they seek consolation through various means. Julie, like Maisie in "Solid Geometry" and June in *Black Dogs,* momentarily finds solace in mysticism. Stephen escapes by drowning his sorrows in alcohol and television game shows. They soon realize, though, that it is their togetherness that intensifies the pain: "Being together heightened their sense of loss. When they sat down to a meal, Kate's absence was a fact they could neither mention nor ignore. They could not give or receive comfort" (*CT,* 57). Ultimately, even their love falters and, like Kate, disappears: "If there was love it was buried beyond their reach" (*CT,* 58). To save themselves, the two separate, with Julie fleeing to a retreat and Stephen immersing himself in the meaningless, everyday life of television and committee meetings. Surprisingly, it is this separation that saves their marriage and preserves their love. As is the case in so many of McEwan's portraits of relationships, it is again the female who provides the strength that sustains the alliance. By leaving—but not completely abandoning—the marriage, Julie is able to preserve (although at first unwittingly) the love that allows them to reunite. Her time alone is a healing process that enables her to accept Kate's disappearance and to recognize her need and love for Stephen.

The love that Stephen and Julie once shared and, for much of the novel, believe to be buried beyond recovery is, nevertheless, always between them, ready to resurface at the slightest coaxing. For example, when Stephen visits Julie at her retreat, they find it easy to fall momentarily in love again. Reunited, they become "their old, wise selves" (*CT,* 71). As they make love, Stephen connects this immediate experience to the incident in which he broke through time to see his parents: to him there is no "doubt that what was happening now, and what would happen as a consequence of now, was not separate from what he had experienced earlier that day" (*CT,* 70). Not until nine months later does he discover the full fruition of his premonition: his brief tryst with Julie results in a pregnancy that in turn reignites their spirit of love and saves their marriage. Their reunion in the present is short-lived, however, as Kate comes irrevocably, inevitably between them. Stephen and Julie realize that each as an individual must learn to accept Kate's disappearance before they can accept that perpetual emptiness in their lives as a couple, a whole.

Stephen's road to acceptance and recovery is a long and arduous one. At first, thrown into despondency over the loss of both his daughter and his wife, he spends endless hours in nurturing Kate in his mind and in enumerating Julie's weaknesses. Nevertheless, it becomes increasingly evident that he still loves Julie, but his male pride refuses to allow him to seek her out. Instead, he sulks in sorrow and self-pity. Finally, it is the encounter with the false Kate that frees him from his lethargy. Afterwards, yearning to keep his mind busy, he begins to learn classical Arabic, a dead and otherwise useless language except for the fact that it is a distraction from thinking about Kate. Likewise, he also begins physically demanding tennis lessons to keep his body occupied. The advice that his coach gives him is as applicable to his life as it is to his tennis:

> You're passive. You're mentally enfeebled. You wait for things to happen, you stand there hoping they're going to go your way. You take no responsibility for the ball, you're making no active calculations about the next move. You're inert, spineless, you're half asleep, you don't like yourself. Your racket has to be going back sooner, you've got to be moving into the stroke, going in low, enjoying the movement. You're not all here. Even as I'm speaking to you now you're not all here. You think you're too good for this game? Wake up! (*CT,* 185)

As soon as he does awaken, as soon as he begins to take responsibility and to calculate his moves, Stephen also senses—and prepares for—changes in his life: "He sometimes felt himself to be in training for an undisclosed event; he expected change—he had no clear idea of what kind—or perhaps even upheaval, and he was on the lookout for the first signs" (*CT,* 186). These unavoidable yet expected changes occur, leading Stephen to the solution that has been always before him.

Shortly after Charles's death, Thelma tells Stephen that the solution to all of his problems has been in front of him all along: "think back over the last year and all *your* unhappiness, all the floundering about, the catatonia, when right in front of you was . . . Julie. . . . Julie was in front of you" (*CT,* 242–43). As he once more journeys to rejoin his wife, he imagines that the ghosts of his parents accompany him, for just as they were trodding this same path 44 years before, on the verge of crossing the threshold into marriage and family, Stephen, too—though he does not fully comprehend it at this point—is about to be reinitiated into the rites of marriage and love with the news that Julie is pregnant. Suddenly, finally, he is struck with realization. More important, he discovers that all his sorrow, all his wasted and empty days have actually been "enclosed within meaningful time, within the richest unfolding conceivable" (*CT,* 251).

During their reunion, Julie explains to her husband that she "came out here to face up to losing Kate. It was my task, my work, if you like, more important to me than our marriage. . . . It was more important than the new baby. If I didn't face it, I thought I could go under. . . . I had to go on loving her, but I had to stop desiring her" (*CT,* 254–55). With the knowledge that they *will* survive, that their love and need for each other are as strong as ever, they unite in their grief for the first time, mourning "the lost, irreplaceable child who would not grow older for them, whose characteristic look and movement could never be dispelled by time" (*CT,* 256). In their "wild expansiveness" of sorrow "they undertook to heal everyone and everything, the government, the country, the planet, but they would start with themselves; and while they could never redeem the loss of their daughter, they would love her through their new child, and never close their minds to the possibility of her return" (*CT,* 256). Their release of inner grief frees them and cleanses them; once again, they are a couple, a marriage, a whole.

Through the life that they have created, Stephen and Julie are given a second chance. Essentially, they, too, are reborn with this child. Speaking of the seeming inevitableness of the conception, Julie says, "it did seem extraordinary, the ease with which it happened. . . . There had to be a deeper patterning to time, its wrong and right moments can't be that limited." (*CT,* 254)[10] As the baby is born, there is a "shock, a jarring, a slowing down as [Stephen] entered dream time" (*CT,* 261). Again time closes upon Stephen, but this time it slows in joy and wonderment. As the baby—the final child in time of the novel—emerges, it seems to say, *"Had you forgotten me? Did you not realize it was me all along? I am here"* (*CT,* 261). Helping the baby into the world, Stephen is suddenly struck with the simpleness of life. Life itself, he realizes, is the answer to the questions of life. As this family of three huddles together between the sheets reveling in the joy of love, outside their window can be seen the planet Mars, the lone "reminder of a harsh world" (*CT,* 263). For the moment, though, this harsh world is held at bay. The novel closes as Julie slips her hand beneath the covers to determine the sex of the baby. McEwan, however, does not reveal the sex because at this moment for this reborn family, it is not important—for this instant in time, there is only unqualified love, life, and family.

In comparison to McEwan's earlier works, *The Child in Time* appears incredibly sentimental. He has certainly abandoned the shock and degradation that proliferate much of his earlier stories and novels. One must be careful, though, in this assessment, for underlying much of the brutality and chaos of McEwan's canon has been a subtle yet prevailing optimism: the constant struggle and search for comfort in the stories; the tenderness in the union between Jack and Julie; the sweet sincerity of Lily. With *The Child in Time,* however, McEwan for the first time comfortably allows this sentimentality to dominate. Commenting on this seemingly newfound optimism, Roberta Smoodin says, "The ending . . . amazes one with its rightness, but more than this, allows McEwan to transcend the bounds of his style and to leap, with abandon, into new territory. This territory is the possibility of happiness, the continuation of fragile, tenuous life, and even more improbable: love. The gloriousness of this ending, in all its facets . . . is masterful, even more so because it is so deeply felt, so perfectly crafted" (Smoodin, 19). With *The Child in Time,* then, McEwan allows sentimentality and optimism appropriately to prevail. And the novel, aptly, discovers a direction for his future fiction.

Chapter Eight
And the Walls Came Tumbling Down: *The Innocent* and *Black Dogs*

In *The Innocent* and *Black Dogs* McEwan further explores the world of politics and their incorrigible effects on intimate alliances; the relationships within these novels reflect the changes—social, psychological, political—of the latter twentieth century. In conveying these changes in the world consciousness, McEwan uses the Berlin Wall as a central image. In both novels the wall plays a crucial role in a pivotal scene, a scene that emanates hope and *possibility*. The two novels, both intricate and beautifully written, present, too, a more hopeful, optimistic Ian McEwan, a direction that he has been tentatively exploring but that now comes to a sonorous fruition.

The Innocent

The Innocent (published in England by Jonathan Cape in 1990, and simultaneously in the United States by Doubleday) represents yet another departure for McEwan, this time into the mainstream genre of the espionage thriller, an area where such writers as John Le Carré and Tom Clancy currently reign. The accessibility of *The Innocent,* written in a simpler style with more attention to plot, helped make it McEwan's most popular work. It was on the best sellers lists in the United States and in England (where it peaked at number one for several weeks), and it has also given McEwan his biggest commercial success (Cape advanced McEwan £250,000, and Paramount Pictures purchased the film rights before the novel was published). Still, the work tends to be less intriguing than most of his other fiction, and it pales beside the power and intensity of *Black Dogs.*

Despite its classification as genre fiction, the novel is much more than a typical spy-vs.-spy thriller. As ever, McEwan is more interested in the politics of relationships. In his fourth novel, emotional intertwinings are set against the background of postwar Berlin amid the covert actions of Operation Gold, the 1955–56 British-American venture to spy on the

Communists by tunneling into the Russian sector and invading the Soviet communications system. Interestingly, Norman Mailer's 1990 novel *Harlot's Ghost* also dealt, in part, with Operation Gold, though far less effectively (even at 1,300 pages). McEwan has said that "if someone wants to know about Operation Gold, they shouldn't read my book. . . . There's a lot of false information there."[1] This obvious manipulation of history is an admission that signifies that his true interest in Berlin, the tunnel, and the politics of postwar Europe is one of rather overt symbolic repercussions: all serve to represent the squalor and confusion of latter twentieth-century society, illustrating that individuals prove to be little more than pawns mired in the cataclysmic struggles of arrogant and unredeemable powers.

Subsequently, these elements serve, too, as a constant background to Leonard and Maria's relationship. When Leonard Marnham, a telephone technician for the British post office sent to Berlin to assist with the tapping of the Soviet phone lines, arrives in 1955 Berlin—a war-torn and defeated city in the painstaking process of renewal—he quickly discovers that information, on all levels, is scarce, sacred, and reluctantly shared. He learns from Bob Glass, his American supervisor, that the operation is an elaborate and confusing labyrinth of secrecy, of levels upon clandestine levels of clearance and permission: "The point is this," Glass tells him, "everybody thinks his clearance is the highest there is, everyone thinks he has the final story. You only hear of a higher level at the moment you're being told about it."[2] Glass later tells him that secrets are the origins of consciousness, of society; they are the beginnings of individuality, the instigators of language. "Secrecy made us possible," he tells Leonard (*I,* 47), who takes pride in this confidentiality. He is "a sharer in a secret" (*I,* 31), and this pleases him immensely. These deceptions, though, inevitably filter into personal relationships, and Leonard finds himself very quickly consumed and controlled by the secrets of his life: Maria and their relationship, his rape fantasies, the murder and eventual dismemberment.

As always in his fiction, the relationship is the core of McEwan's concerns. With *The Innocent* the focal relationship is between Leonard Marnham, a 25-year-old British naïf, and Maria Louise Eckdorf, a 30-year-old, worldly-wise German. Both are emblematic of their respective countries and cultures. Leonard, an innocent on multiple levels, is constantly amazed by the simplest occurrences of life (a waiter's prompt response, an American's boisterousness, Maria's interest in him). Not surprisingly, he is also a virgin, something that vaguely embarrasses him but that delights Maria. She thrills to this discovery and her eventual conquest. It *frees* her, she says, of the requisite social restraints and expectations: "She would not have to adopt a conventional role and be judged in it, and she would not be measured against other women. Her fear of being physically abused had receded. She would not be obliged to do anything she did not want. She was free, they both were free, to invent their own terms. They could be partners in invention. . . . [S]he had him first, she would have him all to herself" (*I*, 72). She is willing and anxious to guide Leonard into the world of experience, the world of love.

Maria proves to be a thorough instructor, and Leonard is an appreciative and eager pupil: "He learned to love the smells: sweat like mown grass, and the moistness of her arousal with its two elements, sharp but rounded, tangy and blunt: fruit and cheese, the very tastes of desire itself. This synaesthesia was a kind of delirium" (*I*, 97). Soon Leonard is "able to define himself in strictest terms as an initiate, a truly mature adult at last" (*I*, 75). Just as important, Leonard, through Maria's loving and capable hands, also begins to mature as a person, politically and culturally. For example, he begins to see the Germans around him as "no longer ex-Nazis, they were Maria's compatriots" (*I*, 85). Their love, then, is also a symbolic political union, a reuniting of forces torn asunder by the upheavals of the twentieth century. Glass toasts their engagement, saying, "Leonard and Maria belong to countries that ten years ago were at war. By engaging to be married, they are bringing their own peace, in their own way, to their nations. Their marriage, and all others like it, bind countries tighter than any treaty can" (*I*, 167). In *The Innocent*, then, McEwan presents politics as love, individual union as the derivation for transcultural pacification and acceptance.

Quite expectedly for readers of McEwan, this perfect and willing courtship soon takes a sour veer. The freedom from innocence opens for Leonard the untapped, darker side of his id, and, once again, a relationship is fouled by the horror of male sexuality. When Leonard sees Maria for the first time after having met her, he is struck by her seeming vulnerability: "It was the sort of face, the sort of manner, onto which men were likely to project their own requirements. One could read womanly power into her silent abstraction, or find a childlike dependence in her quiet attentiveness" (*I*, 59). Eventually, this initial impression mutates into a fantasy of dominance and submission, a rape fantasy. Soon these thoughts of forcing himself on Maria "grew inseparable from his desire" (*I*, 103). Obviously, McEwan intends Leonard to represent the moral anarchy that entices stronger nations to force their world views on weaker countries; once again *The Innocent* becomes political allegory. Though Leonard realizes that it is horribly against his nature, against *human* nature, these thoughts consume him, tainting every move he makes with Maria. Ultimately, they echo the sadistic desires of Robert in *The Comfort of Strangers*: "[Leonard] wanted his power recognized and Maria to suffer from it, just a bit, in the most pleasurable way" (*I*, 105). With this desire, McEwan returns to the theory that anchors his second novel: the idea which "explained how the imagination, the sexual imagination, men's dreams of hurting, and women's of being hurt, embodied and declared a powerful single organizing principle, which distorted all relations, all truth" (*CS*, 126).

Leonard soon acts upon his desires; but this time the woman refuses to submit, refuses to succumb to the notions and archetypes of the patriarchy. Maria refuses to enable him; she grows stiff, cold, emotionless, all desire and trust abandoning her and, in turn, their relationship. This dissolution, quite naturally, suggests the overt complexities of world politics: there are no easy, all-encompassing solutions. As in individual relationships, politics is a question of equality and moral assiduousness.

Unknowable to Leonard is that Maria has witnessed atrocities during the Russian invasion of Berlin. Just 10 years previous, she had watched a Berliner, a woman who had been shot in both legs, raped by a Russian soldier. Leonard's assault awakens the old memories; just as devastating, it destroys the total trust that she has so willingly placed in him. His actions are all the more heinous, all the more a violation. Leonard quickly realizes his mistake: "As more time passed, the more unbelievable his attack on Maria seemed, and the less forgivable. There had been some logic, some crazed, step-by-step reasoning that he could no longer recall" (*I*, 117). He recognizes the attack as childish, as brutish, as *stupid*. McEwan notes that this instant is the true initiation for Leonard, the real moment of manhood:

> There's a curious myth—which literary fiction promotes—that you lose your innocence when you first have sexual experience. . . . In fact, I think it's the beginning of innocence. It's the beginning, not the end, of the process of learning; it's the emotions that are so difficult to learn how to deal with. So it isn't first sex that transforms Leonard, it's having to explain himself to Maria for the first time. (Muchnick, 102)

In this moment of abuse and denial, of masculine dominance and feminine denial, McEwan makes amends for the theory espoused in *The Comfort of Strangers*. Indeed, men may harbor secret desires to dominate, even to hurt, but women *are* empowered. There is power and respect, then, in the refusal, the denial. This is certainly a much more natural view of relationships and sexuality, and, therefore, along with Stephen and Julie in *The Child in Time* and the Tremaines in *Black Dogs,* one of McEwan's most successful presentations.

In his clumsy attempt to mend the nearly irreparable divide in their relationship and trust, Leonard reminds Maria that he is "the young innocent she had sweetly coaxed and brought on" (*I,* 136). Both are well aware, however, that this is no longer true, that Leonard has progressed beyond innocence and naïveté. Eventually the two do reunite, and only at this point, when Leonard quells his libidinous anarchies and realizes Maria as an equal partner, is he "truly grown-up at last" (*I,* 146).

The climax of both the sexual and political initiations is the dismemberment scene, an episode much touted upon the novel's publication. The scene readily recalls, luridly and lucidly, McEwan's literature of shock—and he seems to revel in snubbing our collective noses in the resultant blood and gore. Suddenly, the word *innocent* takes on new meaning as Leonard attempts to convince others—and himself—that he is, indeed, criminally innocent. After their reconciliation, Leonard and Maria quickly become engaged, and their love begins "its public existence" (*I,* 165). Consequently, Leonard confronts his meanest opponent, Otto, Maria's ex-husband, who shows up occasionally "to demand money and sometimes smack her head" (*I,* 51). Their confrontation is an absurdly grotesque, macabrely absurd tour de force. To prepare the stage (and in a sense, to cleanse our literary palates) for the carnage that follows, McEwan has Maria burst into flames as the result of a discarded cigarette. It is as if McEwan is brazenly suggesting that things could not be more absurd, that the situation could not get worse. They are, they do. The fight that ensues between Leonard and Otto is brutal, animalistic. Otto clamps onto Leonard's testicles: "Burnt ocher blossomed in his vision, and there was a scream. Pain was not a big enough word. It was his whole consciousness in a terrible corkscrewed reverse" (*I,* 195). In turn, Leonard "opened his mouth and bit deep into Otto's face. . . . [H]e let him go and spat out something of the consistency of a half-eaten orange. . . . Through [Otto's] cheek you could see a yellow molar" (*I,* 95). Finally, together Leonard and Maria bring a cobbler's last smashing into Otto's skull, " pierc[ing] the bone toe-first, and [going] deeper still and dropp[ing] him to the floor" (*I,* 196).

With Maria, who has gradually assumed a control in this relationship, leading the deranged and desperate way, the couple do what they must do: to avoid prison and punishments they imagine as worse, they dismember Otto, so as to better conceal the body and erase their crime. Because this is McEwan, the dismemberment goes terribly wrong from the first. Still, perseverers that they have proven to be, they persist, amputating the lower legs below the knee, the arms, and then the head: "[Leonard] was through the bone in seconds, through the cord, neatly guiding the flat of the saw against the base of the skull, snagging only briefly on the sinews of the neck, the gristle of the windpipe, and through . . . with no need for the linoleum knife. . . . Otto's banged-up head clunked to the floor" (*I*, 223). After the upper legs have been removed, Leonard is confronted with yet another horror: the trunk is too big for the case and he must now saw Otto in half:

> Right on the spine was a big mole. He felt squeamish about cutting through it and positioned the blade half an inch lower. . . . He was through the bone easily enough, but an inch or so further in he began to feel he was not cutting through things so much as pushing them to one side. . . . He was keeping his head raised so that he did not have to look into the cut. . . . There was a glutinous sound that brought him the memory of a jelly dessert eased from its mold. It was moving about in there; something had collapsed and rolled onto something else. . . . Both [halves of Otto's trunk] tipped to the floor and disgorged onto the carpet. (*I*, 225–27)

The scene is an appropriately gratuitous fleecing of the remaining vestiges of Leonard's innocence. Having lost his sexual and political innocence, he now loses, most devastatingly, his moral innocence. The gratuitousness of the dismemberment, then, emphasizes Leonard's depravity, his complete forfeiture of innocence, his ultimate perdition.

The disposal of Otto's dismantled body becomes a macabre comedy of errors, an immediate release from the exquisite violence of the dismemberment. The cases are so heavy that Leonard cannot carry them more than 10 or 20 yards at a time; a dog, smelling fresh meat, attempts to scratch and snarl its way into the case; the railway lockers where he had planned to conceal the remains prove to be too small. Finally, Leonard returns to the tunnel, pleads the secrecy of Level 4 clearance, and hides the cases. Having temporarily concealed the body, Leonard then, astonishingly, wanders into the Soviet district and betrays the tunnel. Suddenly, Leonard is far less concerned with killing and butchering a human being and with betraying his friends and country than he is with being caught, with being separated irrevocably from his irretrievable innocence. In the end, relationships, politics, secrecy, and betrayal—dictates of the modern world—all unite to conceal the murder, forever absolving Leonard of his innocence.

The dismemberment proves to be unbearable for Leonard and Maria; their alliance has been irrevocably damaged, sending them in separate directions. Thirty-one years later, in June of 1987, however, Leonard returns to Berlin, carrying with him a letter he has recently received from Maria, now the widow of Bob Glass. In the shadow of the Berlin Wall, the starkest and most corporeal symbol of the division and incommunicability between nations and their beliefs, Leonard rereads the letter and decides to pursue Maria. The coda, too, reveals the final irony: George Blake, a real-life double agent, had long since betrayed the tunnel, allowing the Soviets to divert their most important messages; Operation Gold, then, was meaningless, an impotent gesture. In the end, it had been Blake and not Leonard who had double-crossed the operation. Imagining his and Maria's return to Berlin, Leonard thinks, "They would visit the old places and be amused by the changes, and yes, they would go out to Potsdamerplatz one day and climb the wooden platform and take a good long look at the Wall together, before it was all torn down" (I, 303). With this intimation of the inevitable fall of communism, the novel concludes in hope and promise: the hope of renewal, the promise of reunion.

Set against the evolving complexities and confusions of the twentieth century, disorientations spawned by politics and the radical philosophies of the modern world, McEwan persists in perceiving a hope in humanity, saying, "I think we're a very problematic species. Our capacity for hope and for good acts seems limitless, against the background of a fantastic mess" (J. Smith, 19). *The Innocent* is a macabre comedy of manners about twentieth-century nationality, sexuality, and political mores. Though it does not manifest the originality and intensity of much of McEwan's earlier work, it succeeds on other levels. Most successfully, it can be read as political allegory, an assessment of contemporary tensions and the unequivocal need for international communication and mollification.

Black Dogs

With *Black Dogs* (published by Jonathan Cape in England and by Doubleday in the United States in 1992), McEwan returns to a favorite theme: the incompatible marriage between a rationalist and a spiritualist. McEwan briefly explores this theme in the story "Solid Geometry" and, to a lesser extent, in the marriage of Stephen and Julie in *The Child in Time,* but it comes to a full and satisfying culmination in his fifth novel. In part a novel of ideas, the work addresses monumental themes: the nature of good and evil, the redemptive power of love and the intoxication of violence, the conflict between political reform and religious belief. Also one of McEwan's most human novels, it was enthusiastically received, earning McEwan his second nomination for the Booker Prize.[3]

Presented in the form of a memoir, or a "divagation" as the narrator refers to it,[4] the novel chronicles Jeremy's fascination with his wife's parents, June and Bernard Tremaine. In the opening lines of his preface, Jeremy confesses that "ever since I lost mine in a road accident when I was eight, I have had my eye on other people's parents" (*BD,* xv). He subsequently spends the first part of his life as a six-foot cuckoo, assuming wayward adolescents' parents; only in his mid-thirties, when he marries Jenny Tremaine, in the process "acquir[ing] parents in the form of in-laws," is his search resolved (*BD,* xxv). Jeremy concludes his preface stating that he is an unbeliever; however, he further clarifies by adding, "I would be false to my own experience if I did not declare my belief in the possibility of love transforming and redeeming a life" (*BD,* xxvii). In the end, then, the novel is a redemption, a tender reminiscent, a curious wandering through the lives of two fascinating and marvelous individuals separated by an overbearing metaphysical wall.

June and Bernard Tremaine are an acrimonious union, representatives of diametrically opposing forces and beliefs: they are "rationalist and mystic, commissar and yogi, joiner and abstainer, scientist and intuitionist" (*BD,* xxvi). June is a spiritualist, a believer in the healing power of love and religion and mysticism. She is the author of *Ten Meditations* and *Mystical Grace: Selected Writings of Saint Teresa of Avila*; she visits a healer when she is diagnosed with a rare form of leukemia; she believes in "a luminous countervailing spirit, benign and all-powerful, residing within and accessible to us all" (*BD,* xxvi). Hers is the search for ultimate meaning. Bernard dismisses the whole of June's conviction as "magical thinking" (*BD,* 61). He is an intellect and rationalist, a believer in political ideology, an Establishment man, a Labour party MP, a political pundit for the BBC, a biographer of Nasser. His is the search for immediate solutions. As June explains to Jeremy, the integral difference is that she is a believer in the future and Bernard is grounded in the present.

During their courtship and early marriage, both are enthusiasts for the burgeoning Communist party, the political entity that would allay all world problems, the router of "fascism, class struggle, and the great engine of history" (*BD*, 124). June, though, in a mythological encounter with the black dogs of the title, turns deeply and abruptly religious on their honeymoon, much to the irritation and dismay of Bernard. Still, as June remembers it, her idealism was always tarnished with something other-worldly; she tells Jeremy, "Right from the start, the party and all it stood for . . . was associated in my mind with beechwoods, cornfields, sunlight and barreling down those hills, down those lanes that were tunnels in summer. Communism and my passion for the countryside . . . were all mixed in. . . . [C]ommunism and my love of the countryside were inseparable" (*BD*, 19–20). Early in the honeymoon, this confusion is further revealed in an irrational argument over a dragonfly. Bernard, a budding entomologist, wants to kill it for his collection; June, just pregnant, wants to protect its individual life. For the first time their disparity of beliefs collide. Bernard remembers that during the argument he was, as always, "cold, theoretical, arrogant. I never showed any emotion" (*BD*, 58). The altercation reveals their underlying and overwhelming difference: Bernard is the rational; June, the spiritual. With the appearance of the black dogs, this rift becomes the unhealing wound of their lives.

June abandons the Communist party immediately after her encounter; Bernard, however, clings to his beliefs until the invasion of Hungary in 1956. He later tells Jeremy that "I went in 'fifty-six, I almost went in 'fifty-three, and I should have gone in 'forty-eight" (*BD*, 70). Despite their vast differences, however, the two never abandon each other completely. Though they separate and live the majority of their married lives in different countries (June in France and Bernard in England), they never divorce. Jeremy tells us that, for Bernard, June "felt love and irritation in equal measure" (*BD*, 11). June later admits, "The truth is we love each other, we've never stopped, we're obsessed. And we failed to do a thing with it. We couldn't make a life. We couldn't give up the love, but we wouldn't bend to its power" (*BD*, 32). They exhaust each other, then, not only through their ideological oppositions but also through the love they cannot rein. Their relationship becomes an obvious representation of postwar Europe, a combination of love and hate, politics and sentiment, and their marriage, appropriately, spans the cold war, ending only when June dies in 1987.

Their ideologies, as diverse and adverse as they are, both seem to prove true within the course of the novel. Bernard, for example, sees evil as a result of wrongly implemented social and political policies; it can, therefore, be corrected, even eradicated, by the same social and political means. The construction of the Berlin Wall in 1961 was a testament to the failure of Bernard's early creed. Its fall in 1989, however, bestows credence on his current dogma. Drawn to participate in the bravado of freedom that surrounds the crumbling wall, Bernard and Jeremy encounter a situation that seems to ascertain June's spiritual view of the world. Strolling along the Street of June 17, Bernard tells Jeremy that for months after June's death he looked for her reappearance: "I couldn't stop thinking that if the world by some impossible chance really was as she made it out to be, then she was bound to try and get in touch to tell me that I was wrong and she was right. . . . And that she would do it somehow through a girl who looked like her. And one day one of these girls would come to me with a message" (*BD*, 65). After this confession, they pass a girl with "June's mouth and something of her cheekbones" (*BD*, 65). Later, when Bernard attempts to protect a lone protestor and is set upon by skinheads, the girl reappears to protect him, "whirl[ing] about us, lashing the boys with staccato sentences of piercing rebuke" (*BD*, 80).

Throughout the novel, in defiance of a merely physical existence, June makes other pseudo-appearances after her death: her "presence" protects Jeremy from a scorpion in the *bergerie*; she seems to be present—a "haunting" he calls it (*BD*, 107)—to Jeremy in his protection of an abused child; in Jeremy's thoughts, her voice is alive in a constant bickering with Bernard's voice, in a "self-canceling argument, a multiplication of zeros" (*BD*, 102). Bernard, rationally and off-handedly, dismisses his wife's "appearances" as "quite a coincidence, I suppose" (*BD*, 82). Still, *Black Dogs* is essentially June's story, and McEwan strongly intimates, if a bit smugly at times, that June's reappearances are a stubborn affirmation that there is something greater and more controlling than rationality and logic.

All of June's and Bernard's beliefs, as well as the novel itself, balance upon June's confrontation with the black dogs. A perfectly McEwanesque scene, it is as disturbing and as dark, and as brilliantly written, as the burial of Mother in *The Cement Garden,* the murder of Colin in *The Comfort of Strangers,* the disappearance of Kate in *The Child in Time,* the dismemberment in *The Innocent.* "Black dog" was Churchill's term for the depressions that would temporarily paralyze him. June pluralizes the phrase to represent, as Bernard explains it, a "kind of cultural depression, civilization's worst moods" (*BD*, 86). For June, the encounter is "the defining moment, the experience that redirected, the revealed truth by whose light all previous conclusions had to be rethought" (*BD*,

29), the moment she "met evil and discovered God" (*BD*, 40). For her, the black dogs explained everything: "why she left the [Communist] party, why she and Bernard fell into a lifetime's disharmony, why she reconsidered her rationalism, her materialism, how she came to live the life she did, where she lived it, what she thought" (*BD*, 29–30).[5]

June's tale of the black dogs is "family lore, a story burnished with repetition, no longer remembered so much as incanted, like a prayer got by heart" (*BD*, 29). While hiking through postwar France on their honeymoon, June gets ahead of Bernard, who has stopped to sketch a train of caterpillars, and rounds a bend to see two black mastiffs the size of donkeys; they "resembled mythological beasts" (*BD*, 129). In the instant before the dogs attack, she utters a small prayer—and an immediate transformation occurs:

> She tried to find the space within her for the presence of God and thought she discerned the faintest of outlines, a significant emptiness she had never noticed before, at the back of her skull. It seemed to lift and flow upward and outward, streaming suddenly into an oval penumbra many feet high, an envelope of rippling energy, or, as she tried to explain it later, of "colored invisible light" that surrounded her and contained her. If this was God, it was also, incontestably, herself. . . . Even in this moment of extremity she knew she had discovered something extraordinary. (*BD*, 134–35)

The dogs lunge and, amazingly, miraculously, June defends herself with a small penknife, and the dogs retreat, physically disappearing from her life. Later, in a nearby village where they seek temporary refuge, June and Bernard learn that the dogs had once been Gestapo guard dogs, abandoned during the Allied invasion, rumored to have been trained to rape women.

June ultimately realizes the dogs as revelations of evil, an evil that "lives in us all. It takes hold in an individual. . . . And then, when the conditions are right, in different countries, at different times, a terrible cruelty, a viciousness against life erupts, and everyone is surprised by the depth of hatred within himself" (*BD*, 158). The encounter molds her life's creed, her mantra: that evil is hardly the result of faulty political machinations; rather, it is an individual creation, lurking within each of us and creating, in large part, the pain and chaos of the world. Critics, too, were fascinated by the symbolic constitution of the dogs, variously referring to them as the "incarnations of the savagely irrational eruptions that recur throughout history,"[6] "a terrifying embodiment of the evil and irrationality at loose in the world,"[7] the "intimations of revived fascism and the Hounds of Hell."[8] The black dogs are all of these, and more: they are the obvious manifestations of historical portents, foreboding the evils, from the holocaustic to the everyday, that humans continuously heap upon one another. They are a tangible testament to the pervading darkness, the encompassing violence of the late twentieth century.

Compared with McEwan's previous work, the evil and violence of *Black Dogs* are more mundane, but they are certainly no less ugly. What McEwan so effortlessly demonstrates with this novel is that evil is a continuous, universal entity; it exists everywhere, in all forms, at all times. It exists, for example, in monumental proportions, as in the Nazi death camp of Majdanek, where, even as late as 1981, officials still refused to acknowledge the Jewishness of the victims, becoming, as Jeremy notes, "a disease of the imagination and a living peril, a barely conscious connivance with evil" (*BD*, 92). It exists, too, in more minute, more immediate concentrations: in the skinheads' desecration of liberty and their attack on a 70-year-old man, in the volatile marriage between Jeremy's sister Jean and Harper, in the abuses by parents of their children, even in Jeremy's pummeling of an abusive father, where the beating becomes an "elation" that has "nothing to do with revenge and justice" (*BD*, 115). Evil, then, is a constant, as much a personal as a societal and political creation. As such, McEwan suggests, its antidote can be found, too, in the individual: in the redemption of love and faith and union.

Closing his memoir, Jeremy admits that "it is the black dogs I return to most often" (*BD*, 160). Like June before him and her waking dream of knowing that they will return, Jeremy realizes that the dogs "will return to haunt us, somewhere in Europe, in another time" (*BD*, 160).[9] Much of the novel remains ambiguous: June's appearances, her encounter with the black dogs, the fate of the dogs. Likewise, there is, simultaneously, the suggestion that something grand and wondrous consolidates the world *and* the intimation that the world is entirely in our hands, at our disposal, controlled by the dictates of logic and rationality. Still, what prevails in *Black Dogs,* as it does in *The Innocent,* is McEwan's optimism. In the end, this novel is about love. Though grounded in the rioting confusions and turmoils of the cold war, of the twentieth century, both *The Innocent* and *Black Dogs* offer, again, a tender optimism. What Jeremy and Leonard ultimately discover is that there is hope in love, in its all-accepting, healing, redemptive power.

Chapter Nine
Looking Forward

Commenting on the early frustration he experienced because of his relative obscurity in the world of fiction, McEwan has said,

> You discover that there is only a minority, a small chunk of people who have even heard of you. A few years ago I was staying in a hotel chalet, on a skiing holiday, and each night we sat on different tables, and I was asked what I did. . . . I said I was a writer. And everybody said, "Well, that's incredibly interesting, what's your name?" And there's nothing quite so awful as announcing your name to people whose eyes don't register anything at all, and, this is the next question, although it's totally futile because if they haven't heard of you at this point. . . . "Give me the name of some of your books," they say, and you go through the most humiliating process of naming your books, and even as you do so the very titles sound absurd and you wish you hadn't written the titles. (Danziger, 13)

Although McEwan has been writing and publishing for only a little more than 20 years, one feels certain that today he seldom, if ever, encounters this "humiliating process." With each work he steadfastly becomes further acknowledged and more appreciated as one of today's leading writers.

One element that distinguishes McEwan's fiction is his intense interest in the male-female relations of contemporary society. His study of interpersonal relationships reflects the current condition of our societies and individual lives. He introduces characters who continuously attempt to build alliances, hoping to ward off the encroaching horrors of their societies. The often desperate need with which these individuals seek comfort through another individual (who, more often than not, is just as lost, just as desperate) is a reflection in itself of the collapsing state of contemporary society. These characters believe that relationships—the acceptance by even a single human being—is a means to escape the pain and lovelessness of their all-consuming worlds.

The relationships that McEwan's characters manage to establish, however, are not always life-affirming, are not always situations in which both partners are mutually giving. These alliances are frequently more destructive than instructive. Often, as McEwan illustrates, these discontented relationships are a direct result of the surrounding environment. For example, the city and the government—physical embodiments of the society—are often portrayed as encroaching on individual lives and relations, forcing individuals apart. The city—whether represented as a desolate wasteland (as in *The Cement Garden*) or as an ominous entity (as in *The Comfort of Strangers*)—frequently acts as a destructive force. Likewise, the governments of these societies are every bit as pernicious, especially in their attempts to control and manipulate the populace.

The element McEwan finds most dangerous, however, is the patriarchal hierarchies that are enforced and encouraged by the politics and ideologies of contemporary society. Throughout his fiction, he examines the codes of sexual behavior—and the resultant libidinal manipulations—that exist between the women and men of today. These sexual politics ensue largely because of the beliefs that are initiated and maintained by a male-dominated society. As a result, relationships can range from subtle male dominance (as that between the narrator and his wife in "Solid Geometry") to the brutal and cruel domination of the male over the willingly submissive female (as in the sadomasochistic marriage of Robert and Caroline in *The Comfort of Strangers*) to an aggressive male control of all women (as exemplified in "The Imitation Game"). McEwan, though, remonstrates against these male-dominated alliances, emphasizing that the strongest, most fulfilling relationships are those in which both partners are equally giving, mutually accepting.

To counter the patriarchal ideals that run rampant, McEwan often portrays his female characters as being the intelligence and the strength that ensure the relationship's prosperity. For example, Julie in *The Cement Garden,* Ruth in "Jack Flea's Birthday Celebration," Lily in *Soursweet,* and Julie and Thelma in *The Child in Time* are the characters who are most capable of adapting to their sudden and bizarre circumstances, evolving sufficiently, providing the strength and love that binds and nurtures their relationships. In essence, then, relationships in which women are equal are offered as the barriers against the encroachments of a dehumanizing world.

What is most unique about McEwan's portrayals of contemporary relationships is the disquieting ordinariness that prevails in his fiction. Even in the most bizarre of circumstances—whether it is the incest between a brother and sister, the regression of an adult into childhood, the murder of one person to fulfill another's sexual fantasies, or the love affair between an ape and a human—an essence of the ordinary (occasionally, even of the blasé) persists. This everydayness serves to accentuate the fact that McEwan's stories, novels, and screenplays are, in truth, not creations of imagination but realistic portraits of contemporary society. By emphasizing the ordinary within the extraordinary, the normality within the abnormality, McEwan is able to illustrate the actualities of a bizarre and often demented world. The incidences of his fiction are not fantasy but reality, not fiction but fact.

McEwan's wisdom as a modern prophet—a soothsayer foreboding the horrors of the contemporary world—developed gradually, painstakingly. In his earliest fiction he writes mostly as an entertainer, combining lurid story lines with the blackest of humors. Even in his first stories and film scripts, however, one can detect an interest in the degenerate condition of society. *First Love, Last Rites* and *The Cement Garden,* especially, depict characters who hopelessly struggle against the burdens placed upon them by an unfeeling world. As McEwan progresses, he becomes more conscientious—both politically and socially—as a writer. Works such as *The Comfort of Strangers, The Ploughman's Lunch, The Child in Time,* and *Black Dogs* take on the guise of cautionary letters addressed to an often oblivious public. His writing serves as a warning to the state of contemporary society, cautioning the populace of the horrors and atrocities that result in a blind and pitiless world. Even the optimism that has begun to flourish in his recent works—especially *The Child in Time, The Innocent,* and *Black Dogs*—is a result of a faithful chronicling of society as it is, of verisimilitude rather than whimsy. Commenting on this optimism, McEwan states that it has developed not necessarily because he is feeling better about contemporary society: "Maybe it's because I feel more alarmed about the world that I feel a responsibility to locate what is good. . . . I cling to the idea that people are always better than the systems in which they live" (Muchnick, 102). The optimism is not a reversal in his fiction but a continuation of his investigation of understanding. In exploring the uncertainties and complexities of interpersonal relationships, McEwan, by necessity, presents both the horrors and the pleasures of contemporary society. He is more than a writer of fiction; he is a conscientious historian for our times.

McEwan's future promises even more exposure before the public eye. The film version of *The Comfort of Strangers,* directed by Paul Schrader from a screenplay by Harold Pinter, was released in 1991; *The Cement Garden,* adapted for the screen and directed by Andrew Birkin, was released in 1992. *The Innocent,* released in 1995 with a screenplay by

McEwan and directed by John Schlesinger, promises to be the most commercial of the films based on McEwan's work. McEwan himself has also turned to Hollywood in recent years. His screenplay for *The Good Son*—at first rejected by Fox in 1987 as "too strange," then snapped up by the same production company in 1992—was filmed and released in 1993 (Grimes, 25C). The film became a vehicle for child star Macaulay Culkin and a second screen writer was brought in to revise the script, prompting Jack Kroll, in a review of the movie for *Newsweek,* to comment that "clearly, uncredited rewriting has gutted it of McEwan's usual texture."[1] McEwan admits that he found the rewrite of his psychological thriller "perhaps a little less focused" (Grimes, 25C). Still, he says that screenwriting for Hollywood is an "opportunity to fly first class, be treated like a celebrity, sit around the pool and get betrayed" (Grimes, 25C). He has recently completed another script for a neurological thriller called *The Pleasure Dome* and is currently at work on a new work of fiction.

In the realm of fiction of consequence, Ian McEwan has indisputably proven himself. His revealing glimpses into the politics and machinations of interpersonal relationships have exposed the foibles and lauded the virtues of the modern world. His dark portraits of contemporary society speak to the immediate present, illustrating the necessities and the needs, the dreams and the longings of every individual.

Notes and References

Preface

1. John Leonard, "Books of the Times: *In Between the Sheets*," *New York Times*, 14 August 1979, 12C.
2. Laurie Muchnick, "You Must Dismember This," *Village Voice*, 28 August 1990, 102; hereafter cited in text.

Chapter One

1. "An Only Childhood," *Observer*, 31 January 1982, 41; hereafter cited in text.
2. Ian Hamilton, "Points of Departure," *New Review* 5.2 (1978): 12; hereafter cited in text.
3. Amanda Smith, "PW Interviews," *Publishers Weekly*, 11 September 1987, 68; hereafter cited in text.
4. *Rose Blanche* was originally an Italian children's book created by Roberto Innocenti and Christophe Gallez; the British publishers, not satisfied with the English version of Innocenti's text, asked McEwan to rewrite it. It is, as McEwan explains in a letter to the author, "a very free translation—though I never saw the original Italian. So it is by me, and not by me" (27 November 1990).
5. John Fletcher, "Ian McEwan," *British Novelists since 1960*, part 2, *The Dictionary of Literary Biography*, vol. 14, ed. Jay L. Halio (Detroit: Gale Research, 1983), 495.
6. J. G. Ballard, *Crash* (1973; New York: Vintage Books, 1985), 6.
7. Martin Amis, *Einstein's Monsters* (New York: Harmony Books, 1987), 3.
8. Fay Weldon, *The Cloning of Joanna May* (New York: Penguin Books, 1989), 20; hereafter cited in text.
9. Christopher Ricks, "Adolescence and After—an Interview with Ian McEwan," *Listener*, 12 April 1979, 527; hereafter cited in text.
10. Danny Danziger, "In Search of Two Characters," *Times* (London), 27 June 1987, 13C; hereafter cited in text.
11. Clare Hanson, *Short Stories and Short Fictions, 1880–1980* (London: Macmillan Press, 1985), 161.
12. Jonathan Raban, "Exiles: New Fiction," *Encounter* 44, no. 6 (June 1975): 81.
13. Janet Watts, "When Women Go to War," *Observer*, 20 April 1980, 37.

14. John Haffenden, "Interview: John Haffenden Talks to Ian McEwan," *Literary Review* (Edinburgh) 60 (June 1983): 31; hereafter cited in text.

15. *The Imitation Game and Other Plays* (Boston: Houghton Mifflin, 1982), 16; hereafter cited in text as *IG*.

16. Letter to the author, 4 November 1991.

Chapter Two

1. Julian Barnes, "Tall Truths," *New Statesman,* 2 May 1975, 600.

2. Robert Towers, "In Extremis: *The Cement Garden,*" *New York Review of Books,* 8 March 1979, 8.

3. Angela Carter, *Fireworks: Nine Profane Pieces* (London: Quartet, 1974), 122; hereafter cited in text.

4. Bradford Morrow and Patrick McGrath, eds., *The New Gothic* (New York: Vintage Books, 1992), xiv.

5. Will Self, *My Idea of Fun: A Cautionary Tale* (New York: Atlantic Monthly Press, 1993), 291; hereafter cited in text.

6. Barry Hannah, *Ray* (1980; New York: Penguin Books, 1982), 83; hereafter cited in text.

7. Norman Mailer, "Children of the Pied Piper," *Vanity Fair,* March 1991, 159.

8. *First Love, Last Rites* (1975; New York: Penguin Books, 1989), 12; hereafter cited in text as *FLLR*.

9. "The Unforgettable Momentum of Childhood Fantasy," *Times* (London), 22 September 1986, 15B; hereafter cited in text.

10. Jean W. Ross, "CA Interviews [Martin Amis]," *Contemporary Authors: New Revision Series,* 27, ed. Hal May and James G. Lesniak (Detroit: Gale Research, 1989), 23.

11. McEwan has since admitted that this story and its subject matter would now be beyond his capabilities: "There are things you can do when you are young which you can't do later on. I once wrote a story which I would find impossible to write now. ["Butterflies"] was narrated by a man who sexually assaulted a girl and pushed her into a canal. As a parent now, I find that my responses are so much more complex that it would take a lot more to take me into that situation" (Danziger, 13C).

12. Though *American Psycho* offended just about everyone who read it or heard about it, the novel had its share of impressive supporters. Fay Weldon defended its violence, questioning why it should be censored when there is so much violence already in print and in the world. She says that she found the book a "beautifully controlled, careful, important novel that revolves about its own nasty bits. . . . [Ellis] gets [society] to a 'T.' And we can't stand it" (Fay Weldon, "Now You're Squeamish?" *Washington Post,* 28 April 1991, 4C).

Chapter Three

    1. Shock and the grotesque are so integral to the novel that their presence prompted Stephen King, the contemporary horror writer, to list *The Cement Garden* as one of the more important works of dark fantasy written between 1950 and 1980 (Stephen King, *Danse Macabre* [New York: Everest House, 1981], 389–91).

    2. Ronald Hayman, "Ian McEwan's Moral Anarchy," *Books and Bookmen* 24 (October 1978): 16.

    3. To these accusations McEwan has replied, "I wish Gloag would make straight accusations and produce some textual similarities" (Stephen Pile, "Atticus: Plagued by Plagiarism," *Times* (London), 22 November 1981, 32E). As of yet, Gloag has failed to produce these similarities, but he has persisted in adding salt to McEwan's wounds with his publication of *Lost and Found* (1981), a novel in which a young writer wins the Prix Goncourt for a novel written by someone else.

    4. Marianne Wiggins, *John Dollar* (New York: Perennial Library, 1989), 199.

    5. William Golding, *Lord of the Flies* (1954; New York: Coward-McCann, 1962), 79.

    6. *The Cement Garden* (1978; New York: Penguin Books, 1988), 79; hereafter cited in text as *CG*.

    7. Pål Gerhard Olsen, "The Necessary Unpleasantness of Literature," *Samtiden* 1 (1987): 41; hereafter cited in text.

    8. John Calvin Batchelor, "Killer Instincts on the Family Hour," *Village Voice*, 11 December 1978, 110.

    9. Michael J. Adams, "Ian McEwan," *Postmodern Fiction: A Bio-Bibliographic Guide*, ed. Larry McCaffery (New York: Greenwood Press, 1986), 460; hereafter cited in text.

    10. Incest is far from unusual in contemporary fiction. The incestuous union is more often depicted between parent and child, as in stories by Steven Berkoff (in *Gross Intrusion*) and Clive Sinclair (in *Hearts of Gold* [1979]) or in the novels of Kathy Acker, whose narrators often begin their adult lives by being raped by their fathers (see, for instance, *Great Expectations, Blood and Guts in High School,* and *Empire of the Senseless*). Brother-sister incestuous alliances are more varied, ranging from the genuine but tortuous love of Vladimir Nabokov's *Ada* (1969), to the ignorant but guilt-ridden siblings in Cormac McCarthy's *Outer Dark* (1968), to the consuming desires that haunt the background of Josephine Hart's *Damage* (1991).

    11. Jack, in contrast, often has trouble remembering what his mother looked like: "I tried hard to make a picture of [Mother's] face in my mind. I had the oval outline of a face, but the features inside this shape would not stay still, or they dissolved into each other and the oval turned into a light bulb" (*CG*, 97).

12.   Richard Holmes notes that the police light "has the sudden shocking effect of the trim grey outline of the naval cruiser, which in William Golding's *Lord of the Flies* heralds the return of an ordered, outside, adult world to an island of corrupted innocents" ("Fiction," *Times* [London], 28 September 1978, 8F).

13.   Sandra Martin, "Punk, as Crooned by Perry Como," *Maclean's,* 12 February 1979, 50.

Chapter Four

1.   Barry Yourgrau, "Snot, Sex, and Something New," *Village Voice,* 27 August 1979, 88.

2.   Dennis Vannatta, *The English Short Story, 1945–1980: A Critical History* (Boston: Twayne Publishers, 1985), 143; hereafter cited in text.

3.   These absurd moments are a favorite tendency among other contemporary writers as well. Clive Sinclair often leans toward the amusingly unreal. In *Hearts of Gold* he presents such characters as a vampire, a giraffe that proclaims itself as a member of the lost tribe of Israel, and a man who suffers an invisible creature on his back. In *Bedbugs* (1982) an angel teaches levitation, a witch has Mickey Mouse assassinated, and a skull narrates its marriage to a shrunken head. Will Self, too, occasionally forays into the absurd; in his story collection *The Quantity Theory of Insanity* (1991) a man discovers that his dead mother has returned to live in Crouch End, and a psychologist realizes that there is only a fixed proportion of sanity in any given society. Absurdity, these authors imply, is at times the only way in which to view the reality of society.

4.   "Reflections of a Kept Ape" surely owes something to John Collier's novel *His Monkey Wife; or, Married to a Chimp* (1931) in which Emily, a chimpanzee, falls in love with, endlessly moons over, pursues, and finally tricks into marriage Alfred Fatigay, an English missionary.

5.   *In Between the Sheets* (1978; New York: Penguin Books, 1990), 37; hereafter cited in text as *Sheets*.

6.   Julian Moynahan, "In an Advanced Modern Manner: *In Between the Sheets,*" *New York Times Book Review,* 26 August 1979, 9.

7.   The affair with the imitation woman, too, is a popular contrivance; it is evident, for example, in Tommaso Landolfi's "Gogol's Wife" (in *Gogol's Wife and Other Stories* [1963]) and Steven Berkoff's "False God" (in *Gross Intrusion*). Landolfi's story concerns a biographer of the Russian writer who reveals that Gogol's wife was, in fact, a balloon—a female figure that could be blown up. Similar to the narrator in "Dead as They Come," Gogol accuses his wife of infidelity and, eventually, destroys her. Berkoff's story portrays a man who abandons his search for love, choosing instead to settle down with an inflatable woman.

8.   Tom Paulin, "Books and Writers: Evidence of Neglect," *Encounter* 50 (June 1978): 71.

9. The intense desire to shed the cloak of isolation and loneliness can be seen in the overt friendliness of the narrator's male companions. George is "intimidating in his friendliness" (*Sheets,* 128); Terrence is "intense in his friendships to the point of occasionally lapsing into impenetrable sulks about them" (*Sheets,* 130). These characters realize that intimacy—in any sort of a relationship—is a relief from the ordeals of the city.

Chapter Five

1. Douglas Dunn, "In the Vale of Tears," *Encounter* (January 1982): 51.
2. Lewis Jones, "More Filth," *Spectator,* 24 October 1981, 24.
3. Eliot Fremont-Smith, "Dearth in Venice," *Village Voice,* 15 July 1981, 32.
4. Richard Martin, "The Comfort of Strangers," *American Book Review,* November 1982, 23.
5. John Leonard, "Books of the Times: *The Comfort of Strangers,*" *New York Times,* 15 June 1981, 14C.
6. *The Comfort of Strangers* (1981; New York: Penguin Books, 1989), 9; hereafter cited in text as *CS.*
7. J. R. Banks, "A Gondola Named Desire," *Critical Quarterly* 24, no. 2 (1982): 28; hereafter cited in text.
8. Included in the shaving kit is the razor that Robert uses to murder Colin. The cutthroat razor appears periodically through the novel (*CS,* 59, 71, 107, 122), ominously foreshadowing its final, brutal use.
9. James Campbell, "Dreams of Pain," *New Statesman,* 9 October 1981, 23.
10. Christopher Ricks, "Playing with Terror," *London Review of Books,* 21 January 1982, 14.

Chapter Six

1. In England the collection was published by Jonathan Cape in February 1981 as *The Imitation Game: Three Plays for T.V.*; in 1982 Houghton Mifflin released the compilation in the United States as *The Imitation Game and Other Plays.*
2. With these words Ruth consciously mocks Mrs. Lee, ridiculing the relationship that she has had with David.
3. "Solid Geometry," *New Statesman,* 30 March 1979, 446.
4. Lorna Sage, "Dreams of Being Hurt," *Times Literary Supplement,* 9 October 1981, 1145.
5. Richard Johnstone, "Television Drama and the People's War: David Hare's *Licking Hitler,* Ian McEwan's *The Imitation Game,* and Trevor Griffiths's *Country,*" *Modern Drama* 28, no. 2 (1985): 197; hereafter cited in text.

6. Turner later reveals that his own mother would have the same reaction toward the ATS; he tells Cathy that "if she came in here now and found me drinking tea with a private from the ATS she'd be outraged, outraged beyond belief" (*IG,* 166).

7. In the introduction to *The Imitation Game* McEwan comments that in writing "The Imitation Game" he interviewed several women who had served in World War II and found that "the one word which recurred in their reminiscences was 'independence.' Without the war they would normally have expected to move straight from their father's house to their husband's. Despite the kinds of jobs assigned to them . . . the war presented a unique and guiltless freedom from the strictures of family life, and from economic dependence on a particular man" (*IG,* 19–20).

8. McEwan says that although he reshaped the circumstances, this incident is, in fact, based on a true event: "While I was writing *The Imitation Game* two women were thrown out of a pub in Camden Town for knitting. The publican said knitting was what his customers had come to get away from. The next day, in a way that was silly but right, thirty women turned up at the pub with their knitting, and the publican was well within his legal rights to call the police and have them ejected. That confirmed my view that male behaviour can reach incredibly comic and stereotypical limits. It was farcical and delightful that the power of the State had to be invoked to remove these women" (Haffenden, 31).

9. *The Ploughman's Lunch* (London: Methuen, 1985), v; hereafter cited in text as *PL.*

10. Jill Forbes, "Crossover: McEwan and Eyre," *Sight and Sound* 52 (1983): 233; hereafter cited in text.

11. Ironically, it is Ann's own son who omits the Cromwells in a recitation of the English rulers, saying simply that "they don't count" (*PL,* 17).

12. Filming for *The Ploughman's Lunch* was done at the 1982 Tory party conference with actors and crew filming before actual political speeches. Of these speeches and the ones that he wrote for the screenplay, McEwan says, "I sort of wrote [the ministers'] speeches in advance and they seemed to give them more or less word for word. . . . The script simply gave the Foreign Secretary and the Prime Minister lines about national identity, destiny and the younger generation. . . . Of course, they were talking about the Falklands as well, and it couldn't have been better unless they had actually been making speeches about Suez" (Forbes, 235).

13. *Soursweet* (London: Faber & Faber, 1988), ix; hereafter cited in text as *S.*

14. The exploration of the cultural clash between East and West is also wonderfully portrayed in Kazuo Ishiguro's *A Pale View of the Hills* (1982). As do Mo and McEwan, Ishiguro examines the acculturation of Easterners into English society with both wit and sensitivity. Another contemporary writer, Jay McInerney, reverses this familiar scenario in *Ransom* (1985), which details the

life of a young American in contemporary Japan. McInerney finds similar difficulties in the intermingling of these two diverse societies, these two separate
worlds.
  15. Timothy Mo, *Sour Sweet* (New York: Vintage Books, 1985), 228.

Chapter Seven

  1. *The Child in Time* (1987; New York: Penguin Books, 1988), 152;
hereafter cited in text as *CT*.
  2. Kathy Stephen, "The Bright Young Man Grows Up," *Sunday Times
Magazine* (London), 16 August 1987, 38.
  3. John Powers, "Natural Bonds," *Nation,* 31 October 1987, 492.
  4. Stephen experiences a similar sense of recognition in a young beg-
gar. Early in the novel, handing a begging youth a £5 note, he notices that she
is "pretty, impish and freckled," like Kate (*CT,* 3); encountering her several
months later, he fails to see "how he had seen Kate in this girl" (*CT,* 228).
  5. Roberta Smoodin, "The Theft of a Child and the Gift of Time," *Los
Angeles Times Book Review,* 20 September 1987, 19; hereafter cited in text.
  6. Other contemporary authors have also played with the malleability
of time. Billy Pilgrim, the protagonist of Kurt Vonnegut's *Slaughterhouse-Five*
(1969), becomes "unstuck" in time, visiting and revisiting aspects of his past
and future. The protagonist of Barry Hannah's *Ray* proclaims, "I live in so many
centuries. Everybody is still alive" (Hannah, 41), and he battles in both the
Vietnam and American Civil Wars. The narrator of Martin Amis's *Time's Arrow*
(1991) lives life backwards, from death to birth, a life in which all action, conversation, experience occurs in reverse. Like McEwan, these authors see time, in
its modern unknown and unexplored dimension, as an appropriate analogy for
the chaos and ambiguity of present-day society.
  7. Even the courtship is filled with amusing references to time. For
instance, Claire works in the clock section of a department store, and Douglas,
Stephen's father, meets his future wife when he returns a broken clock.
  8. Nonetheless, some critics have identified the prime minister's
"familiar voice" and hatred of trains as characteristics of Margaret Thatcher.
Gabriele Annan, for example, says, "It's Mrs. Thatcher all right: The familiar
voice, pitched somewhere between a tenor's and an alto's produces a fine flow of
Thatcherspeak. McEwan is good at mimicry" ("Worriers," *New York Review of
Books,* 4 February 1988, 18).
  9. Christina Hardyment, *Dream Babies: Three Centuries of Good Advice on
Child Care* (New York: Harper & Row, 1983), xv.
  10. This ease in conceiving a child is another parallel between Stephen
and Julie's pregnancy and Stephen's parents' pregnancy. When Douglas learns
of his fiancée's pregnancy, he realizes that "other couples . . . tried for months,
years, sometimes without success. It was evidence of their love, of how right it
all was, that they could have a baby with such ease" (*CT,* 206).

Chapter Eight

1. Joan Smith, "Trials of a War Baby," *New Statesman and Society,* 11 May 1990, 19; hereafter cited in text.

2. *The Innocent* (1990; New York: Bantam Books, 1991), 16; hereafter cited in text as *I.*

3. In 1992, for the first time since 1974, the Booker Prize was shared; the winners were Barry Unsworth for *Sacred Hunger* and Michael Ondaatje for *The English Patient.* Others finalists were Christopher Hope for *Serenity House,* Patrick McCabe for *The Butcher Boy,* and Michele Roberts for *Daughters of the House.*

4. *Black Dogs* (1992; New York: Bantam Books, 1994), 16; hereafter cited in text as *BD.*

5. It is interesting that the last section of the novel, the account of June's encounter with the dogs, is presented as *fact,* exactly the contradiction of what Jeremy and the preceding part of his memoir have strongly, if not adamantly, implied. There are no interventions from June and Bernard; it is Jeremy's personal re-creation.

6. Review of *Black Dogs, Publishers Weekly,* 14 September 1992, 103.

7. Michael Glover, "Michael Glover's Pick of Literary Fiction," *Books,* July 1992, 21.

8. Review of *Black Dogs, Observer,* 30 May 1993, 62.

9. McEwan says that within six weeks of completing *Black Dogs* "the catastrophe of Yugoslavia began. . . . If you asked me where the black dogs went, it's exactly there" (William Grimes, "Rustic Calm Inspires McEwan Tale of Evil," *New York Times,* 18 November 1992, 25C; hereafter cited in text).

Chapter Nine

1. Jack Kroll, "The Bad Seed, Part Deux," *Newsweek,* 11 October 1993, 59.

Selected Bibliography

PRIMARY WORKS

Black Dogs. New York: Bantam Books, 1994.
The Cement Garden. New York: Penguin Books, 1988.
The Child in Time. New York: Penguin Books, 1988.
The Comfort of Strangers. New York: Penguin Books, 1989.
First Love, Last Rites. New York: Penguin Books, 1989.
The Imitation Game and Other Plays. Boston: Houghton Mifflin, 1982.
In Between the Sheets. New York: Penguin Books, 1990.
The Innocent. New York: Bantam Books, 1991.
The Ploughman's Lunch. London: Methuen, 1985.
Soursweet. London: Faber & Faber, 1988.

SECONDARY WORKS

Books and Parts of Books

Adams, Michael J. "Ian McEwan." In *Postmodern Fiction: A Bio-Bibliographic Guide.* Edited by Larry McCaffery, 459–62. New York: Greenwood Press, 1986. Unique in its classification of McEwan as a postmodernist. Without ascertaining, however, why McEwan could be considered a post-modern writer, the piece concentrates on the morbid wit and shock of the stories and first two novels; brief but insightful.

Graham, Judith, ed. *Current Biography Yearbook 1993,* 388–91. New York: H. W. Wilson Co., 1993. One of the most thorough and perceptive of the myriad general introductions to McEwan and his work.

Hanson, Clare. *Short Stories and Short Fictions, 1880–1980.* London: Macmillan Press, 1985. States that McEwan's stories are about the codes of (usually sexual) behavior between men and women, but most of the characters are at a loss for the rules. Notes that short fiction lends itself readily to the social commentary that McEwan often incorporates.

Stevenson, Randall. *The British Novel since the Thirties: An Introduction.* Athens: University of Georgia Press, 1986. A brief examination of *The Cement Garden* and *The Comfort of Strangers.* Concentrates on the dark humor and levity of McEwan's fiction, classifying it as contemporary gothic. Also includes sections on Martin Amis and Fay Weldon.

Vannatta, Dennis. *The English Short Story, 1945–1980: A Critical History.*
Boston: Twayne Publishers, 1985. Finds McEwan's stories "unrelentingly
moral," challenging the societal precepts of right and wrong. Sees *In
Between the Sheets,* the stories of a "tired young man," as less original than
First Love, Last Rites. Less thorough than Hanson.

Articles

Banks, J. R. "A Gondola Named Desire." *Critical Quarterly* 24, no. 2 (1982):
27–31. Explores the sexual themes of *The Comfort of Strangers,* tracing
them as they developed in McEwan's earlier fiction. Finds that the real
subject of the novel is the relationship between the sexes and, more dis-
turbingly, the accepted notion concerning men's dominance of women.
Forbes, Jill. "Crossover: McEwan and Eyre." *Sight and Sound* 52 (1983): 232–36.
Interview with McEwan about the writing and filming of *The Ploughman's
Lunch.* McEwan comments on working with Eyre (director of "The
Imitation Game" and *The Ploughman's Lunch*) and on writing for the cine-
ma. More important, McEwan discusses his writing interests in politics
and especially in the capricious role of government in individual lives.
Haffenden, John. "John Haffenden Talks to Ian McEwan." *Literary Review*
(Edinburgh) 60 (June 1983): 29–35. Presents McEwan as a man for all
media, focusing on his middle works and his shift to greater political and
social awareness. Detailed discussions of "The Imitation Game," *The
Comfort of Strangers,* and *The Ploughman's Lunch.*
Hamilton, Ian. "Points of Departure." *New Review* 5, no. 2 (1978): 9–21. The
best of early interviews. McEwan speaks candidly and thoroughly about
his life and the early influences on his writing. Thoroughly discusses the
stories and, briefly, *The Cement Garden.*
Johnstone, Richard. "Television Drama and the People's War: David Hare's
Licking Hitler, Ian McEwan's *The Imitation Game,* and Trevor Griffiths's
Country." *Modern Drama* 28, no. 2 (1985): 188–97. Examines three plays
that present World War II through the eyes of the ordinary citizen and
that posit that instead of introducing the new beginnings and roles of an
improved society, the war actually consolidated the traditional, old ways.
Focuses on McEwan's theme that historical reality is little more than an
illusion, a whim of politics and government.
Muchnick, Laurie. "You Must Dismember This." *Village Voice,* 28 August 1990,
102. Review of *The Innocent* and a general overview of McEwan's fiction.
Briefly discusses McEwan in terms of his contemporaries, finding them
the creators of some of the best and most exciting fiction in recent years.
Ricks, Christopher. "Adolescence and After—an Interview with Ian McEwan."
Listener, 12 April 1979, 526–27. Addresses McEwan's literature of shock
and his fascination with adolescents in his stories and first novel.

McEwan, too, speaks about the maturing morality and social concern in his work.

Smith, Joan. "Trials of a War Baby." *New Statesman and Society,* 11 May 1990, 18–19. Examining the resurgence of dread among critics and readers instigated by the dismemberment scene in *The Innocent,* Smith finds McEwan a much more moral writer than he was during the halcyon days of his literature of shock. States that the novel finds little difference between innocence and violence in today's society. Also briefly examines McEwan's ecological concerns and the persistent, though wary, optimism of his later work.

Watts, Janet. "When Women Go to War." *Observer,* 20 April 1980, 37. Looks at the role of women in war, concentrating on McEwan's "The Imitation Game." Finds that though war is still primarily a man's pursuit, women are, nonetheless, becoming more integral. States that this is especially illustrated in the feminist stance of McEwan's drama and fiction.

Index

The Author

Jack Slay, Jr., is an assistant professor of English at LaGrange College in Georgia. He received his Ph.D. in English literature from the University of Tennessee in 1991 and his B.A. and M.A. in English literature from Mississippi State University in 1983 and 1985, respectively. He has written about Martin Amis, Harry Crews, Katherine Dunn, Bobbie Ann Mason, and Joyce Carol Oates. He lives in LaGrange, Georgia, with his wife, Lori, and their two sons, Kirk and Justin.

ISBN-13: 978-0-8057-4578-8
ISBN-10: 0-8057-4578-5